GROWING UP TOO FAST

ADVANCE PRAISE FOR *GROWING UP TOO FAST*

Dr. Rimm has looked deep inside the lives of middle schoolers. Sometimes her findings are frightening and sometimes encouraging, sometimes surprising and sometimes confirming—but they are always thought-provoking. Dr. Rimm shares her vast experience from 30 years as a psychologist, parent, and grandparent. Her guidance is always clear, direct, and conversational!

—Carol Ann Tomlinson, EdD, professor of educational leadership, foundations, and policy at Curry School of Education, University of Virginia

"Here's to you, Dr. Rimm, for once again guiding us through the all-important job of raising our children. As the mom of a middle school boy, I was heartened to see that we as parents play a large role in guiding our tweens to fulfilling futures. I take to heart all the suggestions found in *Growing Up Too Fast* and thank Dr. Rimm for focusing her intelligence on this often forgotten time of childhood."

—Kathleen Dunn, host of *Conversations with Kathleen Dunn* on Wisconsin Public Radio

Growing Up Too Fast investigates the changing and challenging environment of today's youth. Dr. Rimm fortifies the reader with survival skills for the jungle of modern culture. She brings solid research, wisdom, and practical advice to the subject of how to help students survive and thrive in today's world. I wish I could appoint her United States Parent Laureate. *Growing Up Too Fast* is a must-read for every parent, teacher, and for anyone who cares about future generations.

—Patricia L. Hollingsworth, EdD, director, University School at the University of Tulsa

Growing Up Too Fast is a significant contribution to understanding contemporary middle school students. It is valuable for parents, teachers, academics—everyone concerned about and involved with these kids. Dr. Rimm confirms some of our intuitions and fears, but she offers practical suggestions to counteract them.

—Susan R. Rakow, PhD, assistant professor, Department of Curriculum and Foundations, Cleveland State University

GROWING UP TOO FAST

The Rimm Report on the
Secret World of America's
Middle Schoolers

Sylvia Rimm, PhD,
New York Times best-selling
author of *See Jane Win*

RODALE

© 2005 by Sylvia Rimm

Printed in the United States of America
Rodale Inc. makes every effort to use acid-free ♾, recycled paper ♻.

Book design by Christina Gaugler

Library of Congress Cataloging-in-Publication Data

Rimm, Sylvia B., date.
   Growing up too fast : the Rimm report on the secret world of America's middle schoolers / Sylvia Rimm.
      p.   cm.
   Includes bibliographical references and index.
   ISBN-13 978–1–57954–709–7 hardcover
   ISBN-10 1–57954–709–5 hardcover
      1. Preteens—United States—Social conditions.   2. Preteens—United States—Psychology.   3. Middle school students—United States—Social conditions.   4. Middle school students—United States—Psychology.   5. Child development—United States.
   I. Title.
   HQ777.15.R56   2005
   305.234'0973—dc22   2005014290

Distributed to the trade by Holtzbrinck Publishers

2   4   6   8   10   9   7   5   3   1   hardcover

To our grandchildren, Miriam, Ben, Dan, Rachel, and Hannah, who have navigated or are navigating middle school successfully, and to our younger grandchildren, Sam, Isaac, Avi, and Davida, who will enter the middle school challenge in the future.

CONTENTS

ACKNOWLEDGMENTS

MY FIRST MESSAGE OF APPRECIATION must go to the nearly 6,000 middle school students who completed surveys and met with me in focus groups to give me insights about what they and other tweens were experiencing. They openly shared their perspectives about the pressures and worries they felt. Their understandings of the differences between their generation and what they felt their parents had experienced when they were their ages were perceptive and enlightening. I felt fortunate to have known them through their surveys and their direct voices, and I greatly appreciate their willingness to be vocal and honest. To allow confidentiality, their names aren't included, but hopefully they will know how important I found their contributions to be. I'd also like to thank the school administrators, teachers, and parents who allowed, and even encouraged, their students' participation, in the hopes that all of us would understand these children better.

Thanks so much to my son Eric, who critiqued my survey design and improved it, and to my husband, Buck, for his help with the computer analysis of the data. I thank Marilyn Knackert, Joanne Reidl, and Kari Roth for their assistance in coding the quantities of information, and I appreciate the computer consultation skills of Gary Chase in readying the data for analysis. Thank you to Adrienne Kreger-May for her library research.

My editorial assistant, Erika Steuber, not only aided in providing clear text but contributed many creative and fresh ideas for chapter headings and titles. I not only thank her but miss her now that she has returned to graduate school. I hope her future students will benefit by her experiences with this book. Although Tammy Weisser came late to the task, she also helped with some final parts of the book, and I particularly appreciate her patience in assisting me in learning how to edit on the computer.

To Amy Super, my editor, I extend my grateful appreciation. I was forewarned that she would live up to her name and, indeed, she did. Not only were Amy's suggestions "super," but I appreciated her willingness to hear me out when we had differences so that modifications were arrived at by true collaboration.

Pierre Lehu is primarily my agent, but I appreciate his contribution in many more significant ways. We have worked together for a dozen years, and I believe he truly understands what my approach to parenting is all about. I trust his criticisms and his suggestions, and I know I can count on his support in communicating my most critical messages to my readers. His creativity knows no boundaries. Whether it's tossing around ideas for my research or brainstorming for publicizing my work, he's always fun to work with.

I'd like to extend my appreciation to the administrators and other individuals who helped enlist the participation of schools and students in the survey. Many more schools and individuals who assisted with the survey and study preferred to remain anonymous, and I greatly appreciate their participation as well. If there are any others that slipped my attention and were missed, I thank you all.

Cheré Beavers	Barbara Bennett	Sandi Bisceglia
Mark Bregar	Francine Butzine	Ruth Carlstrom
William Christ	Lisa Christensen	Jeri Cocannouer
Earl Cohen	Anne Marie Cronin	Reno DiOreo
Judy Freeman	Joanne Haddad	Gail P. Hammond
Betsy Hays	Pat Hollingsworth	Susan Jones
Nyle Kardatzke	Howard Kelly	Candice Konicki
Chris Kraay	Roxanne Lopatin	Vivian Lopatin
Joel Orleck	Marianne Richardson	Janet Rimm
Dr. Julia Roberts	Susan Savolainen	Susan Scherer, PhD
Janet Schiller	Brenda Sherman	Frances Sherman
Lynn Sherman	Joan Franklin Smutny	Carol Van Straten
Lori Wehr	Pamela Wells	

Thanks, also, to the following schools and others who preferred privacy for their part in the study.

Atkins Public Schools, Atkins, AR

C.A. Frost K-8 School, Grand Rapids, MI

Center for Gifted, National Lewis University and Quest Academy, Palatine, IL

The Center for Gifted Studies, Western Kentucky University, Bowling Green, KY

Chandler Junior High School, Chandler, OK

Cleveland Sight Center, Cleveland, OH

DeLong Middle School, Eau Claire, WI

Girl Scouts of Genesee Valley, Inc., Rochester, NY

Hathaway Brown School, Shaker Heights, OH

The Heritage School, Newnan, GA

Hopkins Elementary School, Mentor, OH

Lehigh Valley Summerbridge, Bethlehem, PA

The Linsly School, Wheeling, WV

Meigs Magnet Middle School, Nashville, TN

Metrolina Academy, Charlotte, NC

North Middle School, Great Falls, MT

North Star School, Eau Claire, WI

Parkside Intermediate School, Westlake, OH

Plantation Key School, Tavemier, FL

Ridgewood Avenue School, Ridgewood, NJ

St. Henry School, Watertown, WI

St. Mary of the Assumption School, Mentor, OH

School District of Shiocton, Shiocton, WI

Sherwood Park K–8 School, Grand Rapids, MI

South Middle School, Eau Claire, WI

Sycamore School, Indianapolis, IN

University School, Shaker Heights, OH

University School at the University of Tulsa, Tulsa, OK

Vilonia Elementary School, Vilonia, AR

West Elementary School, Great Falls, MT

Other students and adults who participated in the survey, focus groups, or interviews were from the following additional cities.

Allentown, PA	Cleveland Heights,	Macungie, PA
Appleton, WI	OH	Milwaukee, WI
Boiling Springs, PA	Colorado Springs, CO	Ridgewood, NJ
Brandon, MS	Corvallis, MT	Rocky River, OH
Branford, CT	East Brunswick, NJ	St. Paul, MN
Brookline, MA	Eastchester, NJ	San Antonio, TX
Cleveland, OH	Evanston, IL	Wescosville, PA

INTRODUCTION

THE ENVIRONMENTS FOR RAISING middle schoolers today are in many ways dramatically different from those in which their parents were raised. As I began this book, determined to provide parents with a comprehensive guide to leading their middle school children through a very formative stage in their lives, my mind wandered back to the 1960s and 1970s, when my own four children were in junior high school. Benjamin Spock, MD, and Arnold Gesell, MD, PhD, had guided me in parenting my kids through their infancy and preschool years. Dr. Spock solved most of my parenting problems, and Dr. Gesell assured me that my children were normal and were "only going through stages." Neither doctor was too extreme in his advice, and both seemed to encourage confidence in my own parenting. Dr. Spock continued to answer crucial questions about my children's fevers and chicken pox during their elementary school years, but Dr. Gesell's books for elementary-age children weren't popularized at that time, so the only measure I had of my children's development was comparison to their peers and the shared advice of other mothers.

In those days, mothers rarely worked outside the home. Fathers were the sole breadwinners and held few parenting responsibilities. Typically, dads played with their children in the evenings and on weekends. We mothers learned from and supported each other rather well. There surely was some competition during our gatherings as we measured our children's progress against one another and evaluated our competence as mothers by the result, but how else could we have developed our self-esteem? Mothering was all society permitted us to do while our children were growing up. If we did it well, we considered ourselves good people. If our children had problems, we often blamed ourselves.

By the time our children were in third or fourth grade, we were hearing about the horrors of junior high school ahead. Our chats around the coffee table were about bad language, bullying, cliques, lack of discipline, and kids getting academically lost in these larger schools. We heard rumors of cigarettes, alcohol, and drugs. Even back then, those vices loomed as possible dangers. I'm sure all these worries sound familiar to you as well. Our worries then were similar to what parents may be hearing about middle school today, although fewer mothers today have time to chitchat around the coffee table. Two other things are noticeably different: We didn't used to worry about sexual promiscuity in junior high school, and we didn't worry about terror in our country or in our neighborhoods. Concerns about kids experimenting with sex didn't appear on our radar screens until our kids were in high school or college, and our streets and backyards seemed safe for our kids to play in while wars took place somewhere else.

When our children actually reached junior high school, we found that guiding them was more challenging than it had been in their younger years. There wasn't much parental advice available for the tween or teen years. Even so, our worries about junior high of that time seem minimal compared with the challenges facing parents of middle schoolers today.

So much has changed so rapidly. The children of our generation had no computers, cell phones, or video games. Though television was available, there was usually only one for the whole family to watch—and programming was almost always appropriate for the entire family to enjoy together. There were no cable or satellite TV channels, so families were limited to a few network stations. Movies weren't rated—they didn't require ratings because they had mostly simple, harmless themes. TV and theaters showed plenty of family musicals that kids could sing along with, like *Mary Poppins* and *The Sound of Music*. Despite the vast differences between then and now, I don't think junior high school was particularly easy for the children of our generation.

As a mom, I did my share of worrying while my kids were in junior high. There were weird behaviors and popularity issues among girls at that age; they would isolate the girls they didn't like and would talk about each other. I was never sure whether the loneliness and hurt my daughters occasionally felt was part of a developmental stage or if it was theirs alone.

I found that junior high classes didn't challenge some kids, although others struggled. I was concerned that all kids were being taught the same material in the same way. My kids' educators told me that students at this age weren't "developmentally ready" for challenge, but I persevered. After being elected to the school board, I helped make things happen for kids who wanted to learn more and for those who had disabilities.

There were other differences between grade school and junior high. In junior high, extracurricular activities like cheerleading, school-elected offices, forensics, music, and sports (only for boys at that time) provided competition and the new experiences of winning and losing. Not making a sports team or not being selected for a drama production was a big disappointment that kids (and their parents) had to cope with for the first time in junior high school. Grading also became competitive. Kids started grouping each other as winners and losers, as popular, weirdos, brains, and dirts. I remember our daughter asking why so many kids said bad things about their parents, a sure indication that rebellion had begun among some of her classmates by eighth or ninth grade.

While junior high school wasn't easy for those children, I can assure you that it was easier than middle school is today, and that's why I wrote this book. With all the changes in technology and the media, how can middle school *not* be different than it was in past generations? With so much greater concern about bullying and terror in our schools and in our world, how can middle school kids grow up feeling safe and secure?

At the Family Achievement Clinic that I have directed for almost 30 years, I see children of all ages. In earlier years, there was a disproportionate number of clients in junior high school (grades 7, 8, and 9), but now I see more kids who are in middle school (grades 4 through 8) and even younger. In the more than 40 years that I've been a parent and a psychologist, I have seen gradual changes in adolescents and have had to modify my practice accordingly. I used to see problems in grades seven through nine that I now see in grades five through eight and sometimes earlier. Yes, the times have certainly changed—no wonder parents are baffled.

In order to advise parents in a book about the differences between their middle school years and those of their children, I surveyed more than 5,400 middle schoolers. My four-page research survey was administered to students in grades three through eight who lived in 18 different states and were from more than 50 schools: small and large, public and parochial, independent, urban, suburban, and rural. While the survey has broad representation, it cannot be construed as a random sample. It was impossible to select schools at random because it's so difficult to enlist schools' participation in surveys. Educators are unwilling to take time from children's already overloaded school days to add another project that they are required to complete. The schools that I was able to enlist did me a great favor, and I appreciate their contribution to my research.

The survey included 36 questions about children's descriptions of their own characteristics, worries and fears, family relationships, peer relations, role models, interests, activities, and self-confidence. In addition, I conducted focus groups around specific issues that worry middle school children. These groups included more than 350 children from six different cities.

I will also share research findings by other social scientists and educators that bear on this age group you're parenting now.

There are references in this book to the research in my book *See Jane Win,* which was based on an extensive survey related to the childhoods of more than 1,000 successful women. My daughters, Sara Rimm-Kaufman, PhD, and Ilonna Rimm, MD, PhD, assisted me in that research, which provides a road map for parenting girls toward success and which was hailed as groundbreaking by Oprah Winfrey and Katie Couric.

I'd like to give you some final reassurance on tackling the incredible challenge of parenting middle schoolers today. Surely you know your children well, and good common sense will help you through even this difficult stage of their development. Furthermore, there's often more than one right approach for coping with adolescent problems. Your approach will need to fit your own family, regional, religious, and cultural values. Sometimes you will find yourself wanting to make decisions based on what seems to work immediately; I caution you to think about what's best for your children's future before acting on impulse.

Please consider my advice seriously. Children's problems often surge in middle school, and despite reassurances from educators that problems will vanish with maturity, many only worsen as kids grow older. You can correct problems and give your children their best opportunities for success and happiness through good parenting. You *can* make a positive difference for your children.

It is my intense hope that this composite of quantitative and qualitative information will inspire parents, teachers, counselors, and others to understand middle school children and to guide them toward happy and healthy lives. Most important, I hope you can enjoy the challenging but exciting years ahead as you guide your children through middle school.

DEVELOPMENT

CHAPTER 1

GROWING UP TOO FAST

"When I was a kid . . ." and then it starts. My parents say how spoiled we are. They say, "When I was a kid, I didn't have this or that and I had to buy everything myself. We'd get whipped if we got in trouble or they'd pull out the belt." The first time they tell the story, it's the truth, but then it grows. They go on and on. Our parents don't understand. It's like they're looking through a blocked window.

5th-grade girl

We all like girls. We learn about everything from the movies and try out the sex we see.

5th-grade boy

Parents can't remember when they were our age. They try their best, but it's so long ago. They don't remember how hard it is to make friends and fit in.

5th-grade girl

ADOLESCENCE MARKS THE PATHWAY between childhood and young adulthood. Our world has changed so much since you, who are now parents, grew up. What you may think of as the typical behavior of your own junior and senior high school years now frequently takes place in middle school. As you recall your own maturing, you probably think of your junior high school years as early adolescence and your teen or high school years as later adolescence. Your particular junior high may have started with sixth or seventh grade and extended to eighth or ninth grade. If your school included sixth grade, you probably thought of sixth-graders as "babies" compared with seventh- and eighth-graders, but ninth-graders may have seemed pretty grown up. Back when you were in junior high, kids between 10 and 14 who weren't quite full-fledged teenagers were often called tweens. That was then.

This is now! For the most part, middle schools have replaced junior high schools. They may begin as early as fourth grade and typically extend until eighth grade. A *Newsweek* article about tweens described their age range as 8 to 14 years old, 2 years younger than they were described in past generations.[1] Today's middle school youth have a head start on adolescence. Parents had better prepare early—tweens provide interesting challenges!

Erikson's Stage Theories of Psychological Development

If you've ever taken a psychology course in high school or college, you've learned about the famous psychoanalyst Erik Erikson and his well-accepted theory of psychosocial development. He posited that children, and adults too, pass through psychosocial crises at orderly stages in their lives, and if they emerge from these stages successfully, they continue with healthy maturation. Each successful emergence provides the foundation for the next stage and solving its crises. If challenges aren't accomplished, people must unravel these crises later in life. Children, thus, build on the successful outcomes of each stage to develop into fulfilled adults.

To help you understand the stages, review Figure 1.1 and read the descriptions of middle childhood, adolescence, and young adulthood. When Erikson first described these stages in 1963, middle childhood began in first grade and extended to approximately seventh or eighth grade. Adolescence began with puberty, at approximately age 12 or 13 (seventh grade) for girls and about 2 years later, or age 14 or 15 (ninth grade), for boys. Young adulthood was initiated upon high school graduation or at approximately age 18.

My survey data, information from focus groups, and clinical observations have shown that the stage described by Erikson as middle childhood has been shortened precariously. The challenges of the adolescent stage now begin well before puberty, and kids are experimenting with some of the behaviors of young adulthood in their early teens.

Children in middle school today have blurred the edges of these developmental stages. The Girl Scout Research Institute, based on their study of girls between the ages of 8 and 12, calls the phenomenon developmental compression, or "kids getting older younger."[2] When middle childhood is foreshortened by early entrance into adolescence, there isn't sufficient time for the learning that leads to competence and confidence.

Not only have the years of middle childhood been squeezed together and shortened, but adolescents are also initiating some of the developmental tasks of young adulthood, like sex and intimacy, long before they have mastered finding their own identities. Adolescence has expanded beyond its borders, encompassing many more years of push-pull and opposition between parents and kids and limiting the years of compliance and learning of skills and information.

Adolescence has always provided the most challenge to parents, and now that it begins at a younger age, parents are becoming stressed earlier than ever and are remaining uncertain of how to treat their children for a much longer period of time. This provides good reason for a new look at parenting middle school children today. Indeed, parents have good reason to be concerned.

Interest in the Opposite Sex

We knew as much about sex in second grade as our parents knew in middle school. We know everything about sex now because we've seen it all on television and the Internet.

6th-grade girl

Interest in members of the opposite sex has forever been a marker of an important transition from middle childhood to adolescence. Theoretically, in middle childhood, girls and boys rarely play together, and girls say

Erikson's Stages of Psychological Development

Fig. 1.1

Basic Trust Versus Basic Mistrust (First Year of Life)

Autonomy Versus Shame and Doubt (Second Year of Life)

Initiative Versus Guilt (The Preschool Years)

Industry Versus Inferiority (Middle Childhood)

Building on the previously developed trust, autonomy, and initiative, children can achieve a sense of industry. In school, they learn the basic tools of literacy and cooperation that will enable them to become productive members of society. They learn the satisfaction of persisting at a task until it is completed, and of using their skills to perform according to their own and others' expectations. The dangers of this period are twofold: On the one hand, children may learn to value achievement in work above all else, alienating their peers by excessively competitive behavior. On the other hand, they may feel unable to perform the tasks required of them and develop a sense of inferiority that prevents them from trying.

Identity Versus Role Confusion (Adolescence)

Adolescents are in a period of questioning that comes with their rapid physical growth and sexual maturation at a time when they have established a first level of competence in the world of tools.

"yuck" to boys while boys call girls "poison." Many children at that age still do, but there is no doubt that some kids are starting to be interested in the opposite sex earlier than you might imagine. My survey found that as early as third grade (that's about age 8), 14.5 percent of the children worried

The chief concerns of adolescents are to establish their identity and to find a career commitment. Role diffusion may threaten among adolescents who feel ambivalent about their identity. As a result, adolescents may experience anxiety and feel incapable of making decisions or choosing roles. To compensate, an adolescent may become completely committed to some fashionable hero or ideal. Another reaction is to seek temporary relief in young love, where the adolescent seeks to define his own identity through a close relationship with a peer.

Intimacy Versus Isolation (Young Adulthood)

The young adult, having emerged from the identity crisis, seeks to fuse his identify with that of another human being. He has developed the ethical strength to make commitments—to causes, to friends, and to sexual partners. It is in this stage that true *genitality* and *mutuality* develop; with a loved partner, the individual looks forward to the responsibilities of adulthood. If the young person avoids intimate relations out of fear that they will threaten the emerging identity, isolation and self-absorption will result.

Generativity Versus Stagnation (Prime of Life)

Ego Integrity Versus Despair (Old Age)

Source: Adapted from *Lifespan Human Development* (2nd Ed.) by S. R. Ambron and D. Brodzinsky (New York, NY: Holt, Rinehart, and Winston, 1982), pp. 318, 410, and 471.

about being popular with the opposite sex. By fourth grade, that percentage increased to 17.5 percent, and by eighth grade to 36 percent. Surprisingly, more boys worried about popularity with girls than vice versa. (I'll give you more details about that unexpected finding in Chapter 10.)

Eighth-graders' worries about popularity with the opposite sex were not disturbing; they were expected. But the third- and fourth-graders' responses were certainly startling, since my survey asked students to check not only what they worried about but what they worried about *a lot*.

Kids' concern about and interest in the opposite sex is echoed again and again among my middle school clinic clients and in the letters I receive from young people. In my clinical sessions, when asked about girlfriends and boyfriends, a typical third- or fourth-grader may tell me he or she doesn't have a girl- or boyfriend, *but some kids in the class do.* If they add the italicized phrase to their answer, I know they've at least noticed the opposite sex and may or may not be thinking of a boy- or girlfriend of their own. By fifth or sixth grade, I'm more likely to hear, "I don't, but lots of the other kids do." The *some* has changed to *lots,* and it's likely they have someone special of the opposite sex in mind if they use that phrase.

Seventh- and eighth-graders often tell me that they have a boy- or girlfriend, they once did, they don't at this time but that most everyone has boy- or girlfriends, or they're thinking about one. From a very few, I may hear "I'm in love." If they say, "I'm in love," I've found that it's likely they are either sexually active or at least considering intimate, sexual involvement, which Erikson described as a developmental task of young adulthood. When your kids tell you that "everyone does" or "most kids do" something, you can probably assume they are thinking about trying or have already been involved in whatever they're describing. Your kids may use the same responses when you ask them about boy- or girlfriends. When using this phrase, their agenda is to get a read on how you'll respond without taking the risk of your teasing, criticism, or condemnation.

I met with hundreds of middle schoolers in focus groups in preparation for this book. Those students ranged from grades five through eight. Students in urban schools were more vociferous about their interest in the opposite sex, but all groups showed a similar trend. About half the fifth-graders in the focus groups indicated interest in boyfriends or girlfriends. By sixth grade, about three-quarters of the children claimed that most kids had girlfriends or boyfriends, and by seventh and eighth grade, there was unanimous agreement in the group about their interest in the opposite sex. If students weren't interested in the idea of having a girl- or boyfriend, I doubt if they would have had the courage to admit it because of the overwhelming response of the groups. Here's what one sixth-grade girl had to say about crushes (by seventh or eighth grade, kids aren't as secretive about them):

> A lot of fifth-graders have crushes, but usually they don't want to tell anyone. If it looks really obvious that a girl has a crush on a boy, the other girls will tease her. It's obvious a lot of girls in my class have crushes, but only four girls have admitted it. They don't want to be teased. I've had a boyfriend for a long time, but I don't mind kids knowing about him.

I've also received letters from parents of troubled tweens and teens and from kids themselves who are concerned about dating and relationships. Here are a few examples:

> When do you suggest letting girls talk on the phone and hold hands with boyfriends? I'm being accused of not letting my daughter do that and other things her girlfriends are doing. Am I being too strict for a sixth-grader?

> Our son has gotten into some trouble in school during the past month because he wrote some inappropriately sexual letters. In one letter, he wrote some mildly vulgar things about a girl in his class. In the other case, he had a girlfriend with whom he spoke frequently on the phone, went to junior high dances, and attended a couple of other supervised outings. They both showed a mutual interest in each other. I know the girl's mother pretty well and everything seemed innocent enough. We began finding letters that they were writing to each other,

which were completely inappropriate for seventh- and eighth-graders. The letters my son was writing were so bad that the girl's parents didn't want my husband or me to see them. We parents decided that that was enough and made the kids end the relationship. When we try to talk to our son about this, he gets very upset. He's threatened to run away. He's even mentioned suicide. We're very concerned.

My seventh-grade daughter asked me a question that stumped me. She wants to know when she'll be old enough to make out with boys. When I was her age, a boy kissed me once and held my hand, but making out was something that didn't start until high school. I'm not sure how to answer my daughter.

My eighth-grade daughter is always on the phone with a certain boy she met. Last night I heard her say, "Bye, love you" to him. I've tried to explain to her that she's too young for a steady boyfriend. At this time she's uninterested in other boys. How can I convince her that she's too young to get serious with one boy?

While straightening up my 16-year-old son's room when he was out of town, I found notes from his eighth-grade girlfriend (his first serious one). She said she was glad she could send him off without his virginity. She talked about it in a filthy way. I cried for the loss of my son's innocence and for the attitude they both had regarding sex. The girl comes from a very unstable background with no parental involvement or guidance. She's on the Pill and has had other sexual partners.

As you might imagine, talking to my son about it was an awful experience. Since then, I've questioned his whereabouts and made the rule that he can't go to the girl's home if no one is there. He's been trying to assure me that their relationship isn't just about sex. He really feels that he's in love with this girl, and they're having sex pretty regularly.

I'm so saddened by this and so afraid for my son's future. Is sex something he should be punished for? My instinct is to keep him totally away from this girl, yet I know that will only cause more problems and make him want to be with her more. What is the right way to handle something like this?

Parents are right to be worried—their tweens show concerns about girl- and boyfriends much earlier than one would expect.

"My Parents Don't Have a Clue"

My parents don't understand one thing about me. I'll paint my fingernails or streak my hair, then my dad gets really mad and yells at me and tells me all my faults. My mom lives in Florida now, but she's worse than my dad. She's a great annoyance to me. I zone them both out.

7th-grade boy

It's a typical characteristic of adolescence that kids think their parents don't understand them (see Figure 1.2 on page 12). Unlike children in middle childhood, adolescents often lose communications with their parents, keep secrets from them, and fear talking to them. Based on the results of my middle school survey, however, it looks like kids are feeling this way even earlier. The letter below from a sixth-grade girl gives an example of a middle schooler who is already acting and feeling like an adolescent.

I feel stupid asking this question, but anyway, I'm in sixth grade and I started reading your book See Jane Win for Girls. *As I was reading it, I wondered if I'm too young to start reading it. Or is it for all ages? Also, sometimes when I want to talk to my mom, I'm too scared to talk to her, and I was wondering, what do I do? Should I go to another parent or grown-up? I'm sorry if this sounds stupid, but I'm an 11-year-old who doesn't quite understand herself yet and has had many problems with friends, family, and my boyfriend. Sometimes it seems like no one ever understands me, and I don't know what to do about it.*

My survey revealed that 15 percent of the third-graders and 17 percent of the fourth-graders indicated they were already worrying about their parents not understanding them. Percentages increased progressively each year to 30 percent by eighth grade. Girls, who are typically ahead of boys in physical maturity, worried more than boys did that their parents didn't understand them. In third grade, almost twice as many girls than boys had that concern.

The early emergence of walls that separate tweens from their parents

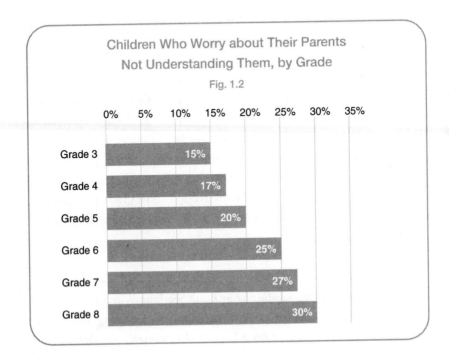

Children Who Worry about Their Parents
Not Understanding Them, by Grade

Fig. 1.2

	0%	5%	10%	15%	20%	25%	30%	35%
Grade 3				15%				
Grade 4				17%				
Grade 5					20%			
Grade 6						25%		
Grade 7						27%		
Grade 8							30%	

should remind parents how important it is to *talk* and *listen* to their children for a little time *every single day*. The listening part may seem boring to you after a long day's work, but it's crucial to your 10- or 11-year-old son or daughter. If you don't find the time, your kids will first fear talking to you, and later they'll be angry that you didn't try to understand them. They'll stop chatting with you about their lives, and then you'll wonder why you seem to know so little about them. Incidentally, one of the easiest times to get your tween talking is right before bedtime. Kids are always eager to find excuses to stay up later. Although you may be exhausted after a long day, your nighttime chats can keep you connected to what's going on in your children's lives.

Pushes for Power

My parents trust my judgment. They might give me some ideas, but I make 90 percent of the decisions.

7th-grade boy

Children love to push limits for more power. How much and how hard they press depends on both their individual temperaments and the number and severity of limits that their parents set. In childhood, stricter parents can prevent kids from pushing too much, whereas more liberal parents can have a more difficult time with their children.

Similarly, almost all adolescents press boundaries and want to be considered adults before their time. Temperament continues to affect how hard and frequently adolescents push; however, adolescents brought up in environments that go to the extremes of being strict or liberal tend to push limits more than those whose parents are more moderate. Adolescents also challenge their parents' boundaries more often when parents aren't united on the boundaries they set. The permissiveness of one parent can empower adolescents to be disrespectful and ignore a firmer parent's rules and guidelines. I will explain these situations more extensively in Chapter 14.

Peers can also influence adolescents' expectations of power. Kids compare their family rules with the rules of their friends' families to determine for themselves whether their parents are or aren't too strict. Because they want more power, they tend to compare themselves with their friends who have more privileges. I'm sure you're familiar with kids' cries of "But *all* the other kids are doing it!"

It became readily apparent from my middle school focus groups that the pushing of parental limits begins earlier in this generation than it did in the past. The groups that participated in these particular discussions were students in fifth, seventh, and eighth grades. They were asked about the share of the decisions they made about their own lives. On average, the kids for all three grades claimed to make about two-thirds of all decisions. The range for the fifth-graders was from 2 to 87 percent, 48 to 88 percent for the seventh-graders, and between 50 and 90 percent for the eighth-graders. Despite the very broad range of decision-making power these middle schoolers perceived they were given, most kids still weren't satisfied and believed they should make more of their personal decisions. Among those kids who said they wanted more freedom were middle schoolers who admitted they already made 75 to 90 percent of their own decisions. There was truly a considerable number of fifth- through eighth-graders who believed they could take adult responsibility for their lives, although they were only between the ages of 11 and 14. Here's what they had to say:

I think parents can help us make some decisions, but if we want to make them ourselves, they should just accept that and let us do it.

7th-grade girl

I really don't like when they [parents] go into something without my opinion first. Sometimes they'll go and sign me up for something, and I really don't want to do it. They don't even ask me first. One time my mom signed me up for

*an art class I really didn't want. I just went along with it
because she already signed me up and paid for it. After a
while it was okay—it's just that I didn't want to do it to
begin with. I just wish she'd ask before she signs me up.*

5th-grade girl

*Sometimes they'll ask me if I want to do something, and I
don't really want to do it. Then they say, "You HAVE TO."
Yet they asked me, and when I say no, they say I have to. It's
not really a choice, so what's the point of their asking? Then
they say, "You don't really have a choice," so why did they
give me a choice in the first place if they didn't mean it?*

5th-grade girl

*My parents won't listen to me. My dad thinks I should be
treated differently just because I'm a kid. I want the same
treatment as my parents. He says, "I'm the adult here, and I
should be treated differently because I'm older." I don't
agree.*

5th-grade boy

After the last student shared his concerns, other fifth-graders chimed in
and indicated they wanted to be treated the same as their parents, too.

When Adolescence Begins Matters to Parents

Erikson's stages of psychosocial development described earlier in the
chapter (Figure 1.1) are regularly published in psychology textbooks. His
work has influenced millions of parents and professionals. Yet current research and observations make it perfectly clear that the behaviors of
middle schoolers today more closely resemble adolescence than middle
childhood. So why does all this matter to parents and educators?

There are basically two overriding concerns for adolescence beginning

Dr. Spock Changed His Bible

Many of you who are now parents were probably raised with the advice of Dr. Spock. His *Baby and Child Care* book sold more than 50 million copies, making it second in sales only to the Bible.

Dr. Spock's first edition was published in 1946 under the name *The Common Sense Book of Baby and Child Care*. The next revised editions were identical in their advice for adolescents, as if there was no reason to revise the section because adolescence hadn't changed much in 20 years! Not until the 1977 edition, 31 years later, did Dr. Spock rewrite the adolescent section of his book, expanding it dramatically.

In the 1977 edition, the age of the beginning of girls' puberty is changed to a full year earlier (age 10 instead of age 11). Dr. Spock also added a rather large section on sexuality and romance. A section on parental guidance was also included, in which Dr. Spock points out that adults needn't take adolescents too seriously about their constant complaints of needing more freedom. He asserts that, on the contrary, most kids are relieved to know that their parents set firm limits.

In his 1992 edition, Dr. Spock added an additional section on parents talking to girls and boys about sex, another on teenage pregnancy, including the importance of informing kids about birth control, and a section on homosexual orientation, in which he asks parents to be accepting of their children should they be gay.[3] These all reflect the increasingly earlier sexual activity that he and others were observing in kids. He suggests that parents talk to girls about puberty beginning at age 10 and to boys beginning at age 12. In reading that statement, I thought about the 11- and 12-year-olds in my focus groups who claimed that they had known about sex since second grade (age 7). Dr. Spock was undoubtedly not sensitive to some of the changes in middle schoolers.

too soon. The first relates to middle childhood's developmental advantage for teaching children skills, and the second is the loss of parents' confidence and assertiveness for leading and guiding their children.

Loss of Developmental Advantage

During the stages of middle childhood, ages 6 through 12, children in the past were open to soaking up knowledge and information from teachers and parents. They were more willing to do chores at home, learn math facts, practice spelling and grammar, and study reading, social studies, and science at school. Middle childhood was considered to be a golden age of learning for children, because underachievement and avoidance of study and homework weren't typically found among third- through sixth-graders. Since children complied with rules, discipline problems at this early age were minimal. Rebellious students didn't impede the learning process and prevent other kids from gaining important foundational knowledge.

Adolescent-like behavior that begins earlier leads to more opposition at home and in the classroom. Discipline problems steal precious teaching and learning time from the classroom, causing more gaps to appear in children's basic skills. These gaps will need later remediation, burdening teachers in their efforts, as they must try to help uninterested and uninvolved students to catch up.

Closing the Confidence Gap

Much of the directions parents give to their children and the confidence they have in their parenting come from what they recall of their own childhood and adolescence. In remembering your own childhood, you may choose to repeat approaches your parents took if you valued their parenting style. For example, if you found that taking music lessons or belonging to a religious group was valuable to you as an adolescent, you'd probably encourage your kids to do the same.

On the other hand, if you were unhappy about how you were treated by your parents, you may go to extremes to parent your children differently. For example, if you were afraid to talk to your own parents, you may be more open with your own kids in an attempt to build friendly and close communications.

You may use your own adolescent experiences as a guide for when to tell your children about sex. But based on my research, you may find that you're talking about "the birds and the bees" a couple of years too late.

Understandably, parents who can't identify with their children's experiences can lose confidence in their parenting, which can cause them to withdraw in frustration—right at the time their tweens need them the most.

How My Book Will Help You

It is my intention to draw on my broad experience with middle schoolers as well as on my gathered research to help you understand when your childhood memories can serve you well and when you may need additional resources to make the right decisions. Sometimes I will ask you to think back to your own childhood, and at other times I'll inform you of critical differences between generations. Hopefully, I can reassure you enough to encourage your active involvement without also causing you undue anxiety.

It is also my hope to encourage parents to set boundaries more confidently so that they can slow adolescent-like behaviors in their middle school kids. Later in the book, I will look at various concerns that your kids have, such as drugs, clothes, terrorism, and bullying, and I'll recommend paths to helping middle schoolers handle these problems. I'll also encourage parents' support of their children's teachers to improve the learning environments in schools. When parents place a high premium on their children's education, it can postpone the tween rebelliousness that can be so disruptive to learning.

The next chapter will hypothesize the degree to which tween behavior is caused by biological changes by taking a closer look at the markers of puberty development.

CHAPTER 2

IS SEXUAL DEVELOPMENT HAPPENING EARLIER?

My 7-year-old daughter is developing prematurely. She already has breast development and the beginnings of pubic and underarm hair. The other day, she tearfully told me that a boy looked down her dress and told her she had big boobs. I reported the incident to her teacher and explained to my daughter that it was wrong for the boy to look at her breasts and to say that to her, but I also reassured her that the development of her breasts is a natural part of growing up and that all women have breasts. I feel so sad, because she seems far too young for this conversation.

Mother of a 2nd-grader

There's girlfriend and boyfriend stuff by sixth grade. "Oh, he's going out with her" or "She's going out with him. They're a good couple."

6th-grade girl

My best friend has a boyfriend. He's really stupid. He's 15 and in seventh grade. Anyway, they're going out, but it's kind of gross. They'll kiss each other in the hallway, and I'm like, "Ahh! School! Stop! Go away!"

7th-grade girl

*I really don't like people kissing in the halls. Most people
don't do that, but some do. I don't like it if it's a girl and a
guy, or a guy and a guy, or a girl and a girl. I don't think you
should kiss in public. It's more of a personal thing.*

8th-grade girl

MOST PHYSICIANS AND PSYCHOLOGISTS assume that adolescent
behaviors like those I described in Chapter 1 follow sexual maturation.
Thus, some researchers have hypothesized that kids are reaching puberty
earlier than they did in the past. In this chapter, I'll review the most recent
research on puberty development and consider the evidence for that
theory. Because large data sets take so long to analyze, you'll notice that
even the most recent data on puberty is not truly current. Data published
in 1997 was actually collected in 1992 to 1993 and is now more than 13
years old. Studies need to be ongoing if we are to truly determine whether
the beginning age of sexual maturity is declining. In this chapter, I'll also
explore the hypothesis that continuous exposure to sexuality in the media
may lead to earlier sexual development.

Girls' Sexual Maturity

*Some girls in my grade have boyfriends. They talk to each
other in school and go on dates to movies. Sometimes they
go in groups, and sometimes it's one girl and one boy. Some
girls had boyfriends in third grade.*

5th-grade girl

The earlier age of sexual maturity for girls has long been assumed to be related to their nutrition and body weight. From 1850 through 1948, the average age of onset of menstruation occurred 3 to 4 months earlier every 10
years, and this trend was most frequently attributed to improved nutrition.[1]

In an extensive study of more than 17,000 girls, reported in 1997 in
the journal *Pediatrics,* the average age of onset of menstruation was studied

both for Caucasian girls and for African American girls. Researchers looked at data that was recorded in 1948 for the Caucasian girls and data that was recorded in 1967 for the African American girls. It was found that the average age of onset of menstruation in 1997 was 12.16 years for African American girls and 12.88 years for white girls.[2] This age did not differ significantly for white girls compared with the average age in 1948, but it was found that African American girls were menstruating almost 4 months earlier than they were 30 years prior. In this study, researcher Marcia E. Herman-Giddens, PA, DrPH, MPH, and her colleagues hypothesized that the lack of changes over the past 50 years may be related to white girls having achieved reasonably healthy nutrition 50 years ago. Dr. Herman-Giddens and her colleagues also state that that may not have been the case for African American girls and that the differences between the races could also be attributable to genetics.

While onset of menstruation hasn't changed much in the past 50 years, the study in *Pediatrics* hypothesized that the start of puberty, characterized by early breast development and pubic hair growth, may be beginning earlier for girls than formerly believed. Dr. Herman-Giddens and her colleagues found that 48 percent of the African American girls and 15 percent of the white girls in the large sample of 17,000 girls had begun breast development by age 8. In contrast, classic medical textbooks document breast development, on average, beginning at age 10 or 11.

The typical amount of time from breast development to full puberty is 2.3 years, but according to Paul Kaplowitz, MD, PhD, a pediatric endocrinologist at the Medical College of Virginia in Richmond, this stage is often closer to 3 years for early-maturing girls.[3] Dr. Kaplowitz also cites frequent cases of pubic hair development between the ages of 6 and 8 for girls. Typical pediatric clinical experiences as well as my own clinical experiences, although subjective, confirm the tentative findings of the researchers that suggest puberty is beginning earlier. I don't recall *any* examples of extraordinarily early female maturity in my practice 20 years ago. Yet examples like that of the concerned mother at the beginning of this chapter are fairly common in my practice now.

Despite research that points to the idea that puberty is beginning earlier for girls, it's a difficult point to prove conclusively. The benchmark study on which the classic medical textbooks are based was done in the 1960s and was based on 192 white girls who lived in a children's home in England. Aside from the study subjects being a small and relatively homogenous group, it's been theorized that these girls may have been undernourished.[4]

Since conclusive research isn't available, scientists have repeatedly cited the need for additional studies in this area. Until that research is done, parents should be aware that their daughters may indeed enter puberty at a younger age than in the past. If this is the case, parents will need to help girls understand their sexual development as well as the differences in feelings they may be having.

Boys' Sexual Maturity

It's like, "Are you gonna kiss her? Are you gonna make out with her?" That's like kissing but a little bit deeper.

7th-grade boy

While menstruation clearly marks a beginning of sexual maturation for girls, sexual maturation for boys is much more difficult to assess. The start of pubic hair growth and genital growth are the initiating markers that begin puberty in boys. Not surprisingly, there is significantly less historical research done on this topic. In addition to the study of girls, Dr. Herman-Giddens and her colleagues also conducted an extensive study on the sexual maturity of a random sample of 2,114 boys. The study, conducted from 1988 to 1994 and published in 2001, found the average age for beginning genital growth was 10.1 for white boys, 9.5 for African Americans, and 10.4 for Mexican Americans.[5] The same study found the average age for developing pubic hair was 12 in white boys, 11.2 in African Americans, and 12.3 in Mexican Americans. The researchers estimate those ages to be 6 months to a year younger than what has been found in earlier studies. Even more remarkable are their conclusions that substantial numbers of boys in all three racial groups had signs of genital development by age 8—approximately 3 years younger than previous estimates.

Dr. Herman-Giddens and her colleagues acknowledge that some of these comparison studies have been too subjective, supporting the difficulty in assessing boys' onset of maturation. As with the girls, the common reference for norms on male sexual maturation is based on a 1969 study of institutionalized white boys, and again, this may not be the best comparison group.[6] Although the 2001 study on boys was inconclusive, the researchers suggest that earlier beginnings for puberty are likely, and they recommend further study and consideration of sex education and emotional guidance for early-maturing boys.

My Survey Findings on Early Development

My survey asked middle schoolers how they viewed their *physical* development compared with others their age. I unfortunately couldn't use the term *sexual,* because it is difficult to get schools to participate in surveys about sex. So while children may have assumed the survey meant either sexual development or height, it is the best measure of perception of development that could be obtained under the circumstances. On page 24, Figure 2.1 shows that more than twice as many girls thought they were developing early as opposed to those who thought they were developing late. For boys, the percentages were even more surprising. Four times as many boys considered themselves to be early rather than late developers.

What's Rushing Kids' Development?

The earlier maturity of boys and girls is potentially, but inconclusively, attributed by Dr. Herman-Giddens and her colleagues and many other researchers to better nutrition, obesity, lifestyle and cultural changes, exposure to chemicals in the living environment, or the use of infant

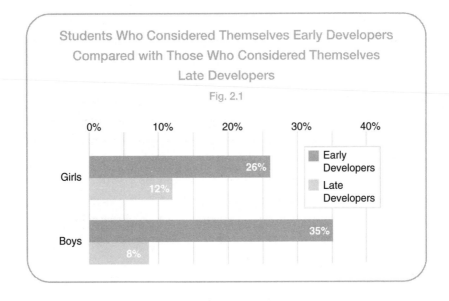

Students Who Considered Themselves Early Developers Compared with Those Who Considered Themselves Late Developers

Fig. 2.1

0%	10%	20%	30%	40%

Girls
Early Developers: 26%
Late Developers: 12%

Boys
Early Developers: 35%
Late Developers: 8%

Legend:
■ Early Developers
□ Late Developers

formula containing soy, which mimics sex hormones.[7] Dr. Kaplowitz and other experts blame early maturity primarily on being overweight.[8]

Since the percentage of children who are obese or overweight has tripled in the last 30 years, and if indeed overweight induces earlier sexual development, there would be good reason to assume that maturity does begin earlier. My survey supports this possibility. Figure 2.2 suggests that being overweight may contribute to boys' and girls' perceptions of early development. The impact of being overweight on perceptions of sexual development was much greater for girls than for boys.

Can Sexual Behavior Advance Sexual Maturity?

We sit down at the lunch table and there isn't a day that goes by that we don't talk about that S-E-X word.

8th-grade boy

Although epidemiologists have blamed earlier sexual maturity mainly on nutritional and environmental issues, it's reasonable to at least consider the idea that while sexual maturation may substantially affect sexual behaviors, sexual behaviors may also instigate sexual maturity.

There is plenty of evidence that behavior influences physiology. Virtually all physicians and educators accept that learning behavior and early exposure to enriched environments enhances brain growth during the preschool years (when brain growth is most rapid) and also during the teen years (the second most rapid period of brain growth). Learning during periods of rapid brain growth is said to provide the potential for new hardwiring of the brain. There is also evidence that cognitive-behavioral psychotherapy can change the brain's physiology: Brain scans done after psychotherapy have shown changes comparable with the alterations medications have made for obsessive-compulsive disorders.

Likewise, there is some evidence that behavior can cause developmental and sexual changes. In a study of 105 girls ages 10 years and younger who were sexually abused, Dr. Herman-Giddens and her colleagues found that 1 in 15 of them had an earlier onset of puberty, beginning before 8 years

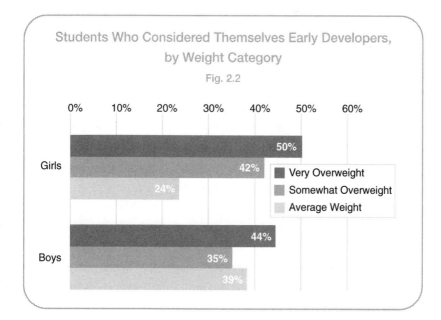

Students Who Considered Themselves Early Developers, by Weight Category

Fig. 2.2

of age, leading the author to hypothesize that early exposure to sex may accelerate sexual development.[9]

Is it possible that earlier exposure to sexuality actually affects physical maturity? Though it may be a bit of a leap to suggest that kids' earlier and more frequent exposure to sexuality via the media could in fact prematurely instigate puberty, it's not unreasonable to consider the possibility. Sexually stimulating images may actually arouse girls and boys, triggering vaginal discharge in girls and erections in boys, which in turn may quicken sexual maturation. If we could prove that observing sexualized behaviors in the media awakens sexual feelings in our children, we could take the media to task and blame it for kids' earlier sexual activity and premature puberty. Unfortunately, no such research could be conducted without harming kids. Although we can't come to absolute conclusions, parents should be aware that exposure to sexuality could be one culprit in early sexual development.

The Hazards of Early Sexual Maturity

Although we cannot conclusively prove that sexual maturation is happening earlier, current studies do point to a strong likelihood that sexual maturity begins earlier for this generation than it did for today's parents and grandparents. Early sexual maturity carries with it the likelihood of earlier occurrences of sexual activity, teenage pregnancies, and sexually transmitted diseases. For girls whose menstrual cycles begin at an earlier age, there's a greater risk of breast cancer, and for boys who mature earlier, there's a greater risk of testicular cancer.[10] All of these are worrisome public health issues for the future. They're also a source of anxiety for parents and teachers of middle schoolers who see developmental inconsistencies in their kids. The cognitive and emotional maturity that should guide sexually mature kids is simply not yet in place. Recall the sixth-grade girl's question to her mother in Chapter 1, "When will I be old enough to make out?" A child's mind is exploring decisions in an almost-adult body.

Having "The Talk"

Sexuality is a powerful distraction to middle schoolers, so parents should take heed. There's much that parents can do to protect their children from sexuality in the media without becoming the TV police. You can minimize and de-emphasize the exposure your kids receive. You can set limits by insisting they follow age guidelines for films, video games, and television. You can recommend appropriate magazines and books for their grade level. Talking with your kids about images they've seen through media and interpreting those messages will create an open discussion between you and them. More advice on media topics will be addressed later in Chapter 6.

The symptoms signaling early onset of puberty are your push to have a talk with your kids about the changes they can expect in their bodies. Your children's intellectual and emotional maturation may not be keeping pace with their sexual maturation, but definitely by the beginning of middle school, you will need to provide full explanations of menstruation and breast development for girls, genital development and wet dreams for boys, and growth of pubic and underarm hair, sexual feelings, and intercourse for boys and for girls.

Explaining sex to children has always been difficult for parents, but it becomes even more difficult when children need these explanations at younger ages. Some parents may expect to have "the talk" with their kids when they turn 10 or 12, but ages 7 or 9 may be more appropriate for some kids today. The goal of your birds and bees talk with your kids is to give them a balanced view of sex. It's important to emphasize that sex is a positive relationship between committed people and not simply a casual dallying with other people's bodies. While your own personal values must guide you in such discussions, it's important to remember that telling your kids only of the dangers may either scare them for life or tempt them more, as if sex were forbidden fruit.

Fortunately, there are now many books available to help you talk with your kids about sex, and some of these are specifically geared toward younger children. The Appendix lists books that provide appropriate vocabulary and illustrations that you and your kids can study together. First, read the books yourself to determine if you are comfortable with the values they express. Topics such as sexual protection, birth control, abstinence, and homosexuality may be treated very differently in some books. It's a good idea for your kids to know about both your values and those of others, since they will certainly be exposed to a wide range of values within their peer groups and schools.

Despite the fact that the middle school kids in my focus groups bragged about knowing everything there is to know about sex, don't assume they or your own children actually have all the facts. You don't have to immediately divulge every detail when your kids turn 7 or 8, but opening up the door to information will at least permit them to ask questions and prevent their naïveté and vulnerability around peers. While you may want to borrow and review books from the library before making your choice, after you've made your selection, be sure to purchase a few books that your kids can keep and look at when they're interested and ready. Once they have had the chance to become familiar with some of the material in the books, they will be less embarrassed about asking you questions.

The Sexual Rush

Sex is a beautiful way for responsible adults to express love and commitment. That is the most important concept about sex that young people should hear. Yet they see, hear, and feel many other intense messages that encourage them to be casual about sex without responsibilities or commitments to achieve intimacy. Indeed, intimacy, according to Erikson's stages, is a developmental task of late adolescence and young adulthood. Our middle school children are confronting the power and intensity of sexual involvement—a developmental task that many adults struggle with. Middle school kids have neither the cognitive nor the emotional maturity to cope with it.

Just Sexualized or Having Sex? That Is the Question

Kids play truth or dare on the bus. The boys dare the girls to sit on their laps and play pony so boys can feel girls on their penises. Some kids dared a boy to kiss a girl on the bus, and he kissed her on her you-know-where [breasts] in front of everyone. Those kids got into big trouble.

6th-grade girl

Many reports about middle schoolers indicate that they talk about sex, dress provocatively, and brag about sexual experiences, but very few are actually sexually active. This may not in fact be the case. Recent studies have pointed out that kids are more sexually active than parents may be aware.

A group of researchers in Washington, DC, were planning to start a school program to encourage kids not to get involved in early sexual activity.[11] Their original intention was to begin with seventh-graders, but they quickly changed plans when they discovered that many of the seventh-graders were already sexually active.

Another study, conducted by the Washington, DC–based research group Child Trends, followed 12- to 14-year-olds between 1997 and 1999 and found that 16 percent of the girls and 20 percent of the boys reportedly had sexual intercourse by age 14 (eighth grade) or younger.[12] Sixteen percent and 20 percent are a sizeable portion of our children. Another survey, The 2001 Youth Risk Behavior Surveillance, indicated that 6.6 percent of students studied nationwide had initiated sexual intercourse before age 13, or approximately seventh grade.[13] The survey also found that males were significantly more likely than females to have had sex at that early age.

Statistics from Child Trends and the Youth Risk survey apply only to actual sexual intercourse. No one seems to have dared to poll kids who are busying themselves with oral sex. Judging from the consensus that parents of middle schoolers have shared with me, by seventh and eighth grade there are definitely groups of kids who are casually involved in oral sex and explain away their activity as "not real sex." Kids assume oral sex is safer and less intimate than intercourse.

"Rainbow parties" have entered the middle school scene. At these parties, girls wear a variety of colors of lipstick to leave their special marks on the boys with whom they engage in oral sex. In a 2003 issue of *Seventeen* magazine, a favorite among middle school girls, writer Noelle Howey reported on the casual oral sex taking place among teens at parties.[14] Though the article made a sincere attempt to discourage girls from oral sex, the article's very existence acknowledges that there is, indeed, a problem.

Why the Hurry?

According to a study of young women who had sex before age 15, younger kids have sex for different reasons than older teens. This study revealed that the women attributed their sexual activity to a partner's pressure, peer pressure from their friends, curiosity, or the desire to feel grown-up.[15] Those who waited until they were 16 to 18 were more likely to say they had sex because they wanted intimacy with someone they loved. In another study of boys and girls who had sex before age 15, the researchers reported that 7 percent of their study sample said they had been forced against their will to have sex with an adult, 17 percent said they were forced by a teenager, and 19 percent indicated they felt pressured by their friends to have sex.[16]

There are definite conditions that increase the likelihood that children will have sex early, particularly the use of drugs, alcohol, and tobacco. K. Lynne Robinson, PhD, at the University of North Carolina at Charlotte, conducted a study of sixth-graders who were having sexual intercourse. Her study found smoking to be the best predictor of early sexual involvement.[17] Similarly, in a study led by Robert Valois, PhD, MPH, alcohol consumption was consistently found to be related to increased numbers of sexual partners for teens.[18] In yet another study, the Henry J. Kaiser Family Foundation teamed together with *YM* magazine on a national survey of teens. Seventeen percent of teens reported having done something sexual they wouldn't have done otherwise if they hadn't been under the influence of drugs or alcohol.[19] Another group of middle schoolers who had early sex was studied by Barbara VanOss Marín, PhD. Dr. Marín's study indicated that middle schoolers who had sex at a very young age were more likely to have had girl- or boyfriends who were 2 or more years older than they were.[20]

Fortunately, there are also conditions that lessen the likelihood of kids experimenting too early with sex. In a study of seventh-grade males, it was discovered that good grades and living with both parents made it less likely for boys to initiate sexual intercourse before seventh grade.[21] Another study found that kids who perceived their relationships with their mothers as highly satisfactory were 2.7 times less likely to engage in early sex than those who had poor relationships.[22] Additionally, if mothers disapproved of their kids having sex, teens were less likely to engage in early sex.[23] Parents, please realize that you can make a great difference in your kids' choices and behaviors by stating your opinions and setting clear limits.

There's Plenty of Sex in Middle Schools Today

What all this data on sexual activity boils down to is that there's *plenty* of sex taking place among middle schoolers today. Although alcohol, tobacco, drugs, and older peer groups increase the likelihood that kids will be involved in sex, and good family relations, sex education, and mothers' opposition decrease the likelihood of sexual involvement, kids in middle school are still at risk of having sex at a time when they have neither the intellectual nor the emotional maturity to handle it. While you may remember holding hands or sharing an innocent kiss or two at their age, it's important to remember that some of today's kids are involved in very heavy make-out sessions, oral sex, and even sexual intercourse. It's not just what kids see on television anymore. Whether they are personally sexually active or have friends who are, sexuality surrounds them in real life, and few can shut their eyes to a red-hot sexual scene.

Kids' Worries about Sex

With all the talk about sex at a typical middle school, and a fair amount of action too, certainly most kids are exposed to sexuality. Yet only a small percentage of the kids I surveyed reported having many worries concerning sex. About 12 percent of the overall group reported worrying a lot about sex, and surprisingly that percentage didn't vary much from grades three through eight, nor was it very dissimilar for boys and girls.

There were some variables, however, that made a difference. Students with good grades worried less about sex than did students with poor grades (10 percent compared with 17 percent), students with good family relationships worried less than did those with poor family relationships, (10 percent compared with 17 percent), and more students in public schools worried about sex than did those in parochial and independent schools (13 percent compared with 11 percent). Not surprisingly, only 6 percent of students in all-girl schools worried about sex. They presumably observed less sexual behavior and weren't dealing with flirtatious boys in school.

Since middle schoolers are unalarmed about their exposure to sex, should we assume that their families are providing reassuring information sufficiently early? Or are the kids so naive about sex that it hasn't occurred to them to worry about pregnancy, sexually transmitted diseases (STDs), and intense emotions, which are pitfalls of having sex too early? Should we be concerned that their emotions about intimacy are being numbed by overexposure? Regardless of the reasons for kids' apparent lack of concern, there can be some big problems when middle schoolers become sexually active.

Early sexual involvement increases the likelihood of teen pregnancy and STDs. It also distracts kids from school learning and enrichment experiences. There is no research that suggests any positive outcome stemming from earlier sexual involvement, so you should be very concerned about the pace of sexual behavior in your children.

Kids Want to Grow Up Quickly

Your middle schoolers are being pressured by their peers to join in the behaviors of sexuality. Kids want to grow up as soon as possible, and they see sex as a way to prove their maturity.

The issues kids face as they grow up are different for girls and boys. Early-maturing girls aren't exactly thrilled with their lonely beginnings of breast development and menstruation. Yet girls who develop more slowly often have some jealous feelings, which they rarely admit. Girls are often eager to wear training bras, shave their legs, use antiperspirant, and apply makeup in attempts to catch up with early maturers—even if their childish

"But *All* the Girls Wear Makeup, Mom!"

Claire, 6th-grader: Mom, all the popular girls at school are starting to wear makeup. I don't understand why you won't let me. I'm not a baby. Can't I just wear some blush or a little mascara? I hate feeling so left out.

Mother: Claire, I don't think the popular girls should set your standards. You're naturally a pretty girl and you have a very nice complexion. Makeup will make you look older than you are, and you'll be grown up for a very long time, so I'm not going to let you hurry into your teens before you're really there. I think makeup can wait until you're in high school, but I'm willing to reconsider your request again when you're in eighth grade.

Claire: But Mom, that's not fair!

Mother: I'm sorry you're disappointed, but for this year it's my absolute, final decision. You can ask me again next year. Let's go outside for a bike ride. It's a beautiful day.

bodies haven't entered puberty. Parents often go along with their daughters' choices, feeling that there's little harm in permitting their tween girls to wear adolescent clothes or to be involved in adolescent activities. They may also want to shield their daughters from feeling different or from thinking they're falling behind in the race for maturity.

For boys, peer pressure to prove their masculinity may make them want to start dating girls, because other boys are. I'll explore more of this kind of peer pressure in Chapter 3, which is about establishing

---

Daring to Date

Scott, 8th-grader (small and immature for his age): Mom, all my friends have girlfriends, and I was thinking of asking Meredith to go to the movies with me. Would that be okay, and could you drive us?

Mother: I just wonder, Scott, if you want to go out on a date with Meredith, or if you're doing it just so the guys will accept you.

Scott: I guess it's a little of both. I don't like being the only guy in my group without a girlfriend, and Meredith's been a good friend for a long time. It'd probably be cool to go with her. We could try it anyway.

Mother: Well, Meredith is a nice kid. Do you plan to go on a group date or just you and Meredith?

Scott: I don't know, but I think I could get Dan and Randy to bring girls and meet us at the movie. Maybe afterward, we could all walk over to Pizza Hut for dinner, and you could pick us up there.

Mother: I think that sounds like a reasonable plan, but I want to know what movie you're going to. It sounds like fun, and I'll be glad to drive you and pick you up.

> ## "It's Not Me!"
>
> **John, 5th-grader:** Dad, look what our gym teacher gave us. It's deodorant! She told the whole class to wear it because the gym smells bad. I get sweaty when I run around, but I don't need this stuff. I think she just wants some of the girls to wear it.
>
> **Dad:** Maybe you don't need it yet, but the teacher wouldn't have given deodorant out if she didn't think it was necessary for some kids. Since she asked you to use it, you might as well get used to it early. It won't hurt you, and if everyone uses it, the kids who need it won't feel singled out or strange. I respect your gym teacher, so you should do what she asked you to.

sexual identity, homosexuality, and the problems that immature boys often cope with.

The Slippery Slope

Your decision to let your kids go along with the crowd may not cause your children any problems, or it could be the beginning of a slippery slope. Every parent hears the all-too-familiar "All the kids are doing it!" that tweens will use to justify everything they want to do—from fashion and makeup to alcohol, drugs, and sex.

The first time you're tempted to let your kids go along with the crowd is a valuable time to begin talking with your kids about conformity and independence. It's definitely not enough just to say, "Don't conform; be independent!" Remember, there are times ahead when you will want your kids to conform, as in doing their homework, participating in school activities, demonstrating good sportsmanship, and following school rules.

So when your kids ask you for permission to do something just because their peers are doing it, you can encourage them to think about when it's all right to conform and when it's better to be independent and different. The Insets include conversations between parents and kids that you can use as an example of how to talk with your kids about these important issues. The kids are questioning their developmental readiness for something their peers are doing. The parents have responded in appropriate ways, which fit with their own personal values. You may or may not agree with the answers given, but they can be used as a guide for your own conversations with your children.

Steering Your Kids in the Right Direction

Research suggests that preventing your kids from using alcohol, tobacco, and drugs, as well as limiting their involvement with older social groups, may decrease the likelihood of them having sex too early. You'll want to do your best to promote positive family relationships and encourage your children's good grades in school, which are also likely to discourage early sexual involvement. In addition, you'll want to be clear in your message to your middle school children that sexual activity should wait until they're older, when they can appreciate its value as a commitment to a serious relationship.

CHAPTER 3

GENDER STEREOTYPES AND SEXUAL ORIENTATION

Hot for a guy is really, really cute. He's tall, his voice is a bit deeper, his hair and eye color are good, and he has muscles.

7th-grade girl

Hot for a girl is pretty and thin.

8th-grade boy

Sometimes kids will say, "He's really sexy," and that's basically the same as "hot," but uh . . . a little more than that.

7th-grade girl

No matter what your social status is, all girls get criticized by guys. It never fails. We all go through it.

8th-grade girl

If you walk around with a gay kid, the other kids say, "Are you turning gay or something?" If you hang around with skateboard people, you're known as a skateboard dude, and if you hang around gay people, you're known as a gay dude.

8th-grade boy

Some kids called me a girl and wouldn't let me sit with them. Then other kids wouldn't let me sit with them either. They totally isolated me.

7th-grade boy

TWEENS' GENDER AND AGE make a significant difference in what they think and worry about. Middle school kids continuously compare themselves with their peers, and more specifically, their peers of the same sex and the same grade level. It's therefore important for you to know the similarities and differences between girls and boys, some of which are new to this generation. Being attuned to the developmental concerns of your kids as they mature between grades three and eight will prepare you for their changing questions, interests, and behaviors. Kids' developmental push to establish their masculinity or femininity also plays a part in causing homosexual youth to experience extreme peer pressure.

This chapter will expand on gender and developmental differences to inform you of the changes that have taken place since you were in junior high school. You will also be reminded that kids' adolescent-like behaviors begin earlier than they did when you were growing up, and in turn, homophobia develops earlier among middle school kids.

Gender Stereotype Differences

The women's movement of the 1960s opened doors for women by expanding the roles that they play in society. Feminism has sensitized parents and educators to prevailing gender stereotypes and encouraged parents to envision opportunities for their kids—especially girls—beyond previously accepted norms.

Shifting Stereotypes

There have been some changes in how girls and boys describe themselves and also in the activities in which they participate. However, not all has changed.

Figure 3.1 presents characteristics that continued to be stereotypical

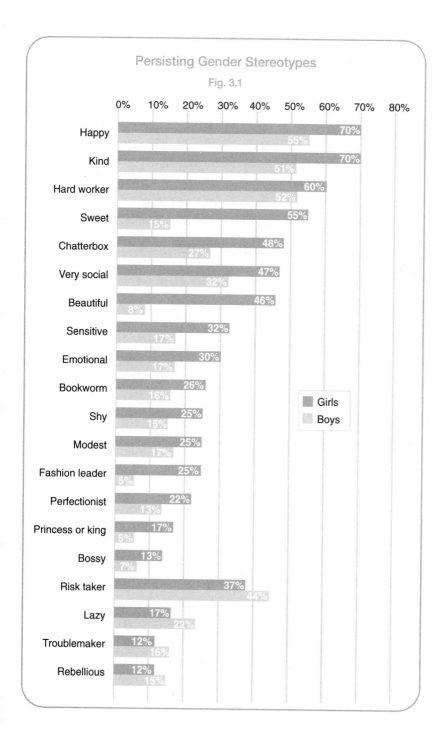

Persisting Gender Stereotypes
Fig. 3.1

	Girls	Boys
Happy	70%	55%
Kind	70%	51%
Hard worker	60%	52%
Sweet	55%	15%
Chatterbox	48%	27%
Very social	47%	32%
Beautiful	46%	8%
Sensitive	32%	17%
Emotional	30%	17%
Bookworm	26%	16%
Shy	25%	15%
Modest	25%	17%
Fashion leader	25%	5%
Perfectionist	22%	13%
Princess or king	17%	5%
Bossy	13%	7%
Risk taker	37%	44%
Lazy	17%	22%
Troublemaker	12%	16%
Rebellious	12%	15%

for the girls and boys in my study. I found that girls were more likely than boys to describe themselves as happy, kind, hard workers, sweet, chatterboxes, very social, beautiful, sensitive, emotional, bookworms, shy, modest, fashion leaders, perfectionistic, princesses or kings, and bossy. They were less likely than boys to see themselves as risk takers, lazy, troublemakers, or rebellious.

There were, however, a few characteristics that broke the gender stereotype mold. My survey found that more girls than boys described themselves as smart, creative, talented, confident, independent, and a leader (see Figure 3.2)—all of these being characteristics that were considered masculine in the past. In addition, girls were nearly equal to boys in descriptions of themselves for positive traits like being funny, gifted, cool, and courageous. These too are traits that were more common among boys in previous times.

What's discouraging is that close percentages of each gender also described themselves as lonely and mean. Past gender stereotypes would have suggested more girls as lonely and fewer as mean compared with boys. Although only 3 percent of the girls and boys viewed themselves as mean, consider that 166 boys and 166 girls voluntarily identified with that characteristic. In the past, hardly any girls would have admitted to this trait. Unfortunately, not all changes in gender stereotypes can be considered progress.

The Gender Issue of Intelligence

The findings on girls' feelings about their intelligence were somewhat confusing and even contradictory. In the general characteristics list, more girls than boys considered themselves smart, creative, and talented, and equal numbers of girls and boys described themselves as gifted, suggesting that girls have gained more confidence in their intelligence.

However, when kids were asked to rate their intelligence on a five-point scale, fewer girls (64 percent compared with 70 percent of the boys) rated themselves as above average. Puzzlingly, when the kids were asked

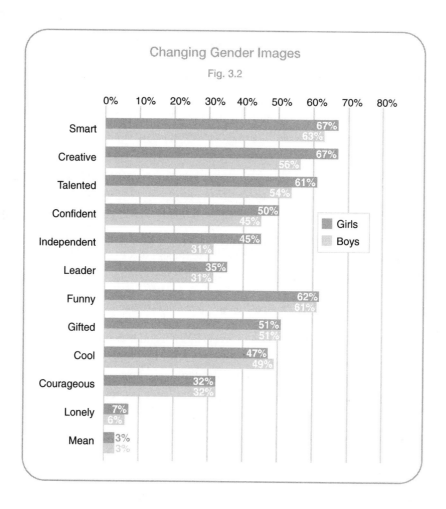

Changing Gender Images

Fig. 3.2

	Girls	Boys
Smart	67%	63%
Creative	67%	56%
Talented	61%	54%
Confident	50%	45%
Independent	45%	31%
Leader	35%	31%
Funny	62%	61%
Gifted	51%	51%
Cool	47%	49%
Courageous	32%	32%
Lonely	7%	6%
Mean	3%	3%

to describe their grades in school, 78 percent of the girls described their grades as above average compared with only 70 percent of the boys. Despite the higher percentage of girls who considered their grades to be above average, fewer thought of themselves as intelligent. Moreover, 14 percent of the girls felt they had only average intelligence despite high grades. Having higher grades didn't afford them more confidence in their intelligence. This lack of intellectual confidence in girls has been noted in past studies and apparently persists.

Gender Differentials in Activities

Involvement in school activities is important for kids in middle school not only because it keeps them out of trouble, but because it builds confidence (see Figure 3.3). The early adolescent years mark a developmental time when children begin to establish their identities. Participation in areas of interest has the potential for steering kids toward careers, lifelong recreational activities, and fulfilling lifestyles. Nonparticipation has the risk of leaving kids with too much time "just chillin." Kids who felt they were highly intelligent were more likely to participate in the activities listed on my survey than those who felt less intelligent. A similar pattern held for self-confidence: The more self-confidence kids had, the more likely they were involved in these activities.

Sports Are Finally for Girls, Too

The differences between girls' and boys' participation in their favorite activities generally followed gender stereotypes. The differences weren't as great as I had expected them to be, and they were certainly less extreme for today's kids than they were for you at that age. The most obvious and impressive change is that many more girls (a whopping 71 percent) now participate in sports. Thanks to Title IX legislation, girls have many more opportunities to be involved in sports at school.

Sports are not only important for staying healthy and physically fit, but they also teach kids important social skills, like perseverance, competition, teamwork, self-discipline, accepting criticism, coaching others, and a host of other more subtle skills that are foundational for success in many upper-level, competitive careers. In addition, the tweens in my focus groups reminded me that athletes—girls and boys alike—are more apt to be popular than nonathletes are. It's an incredible change from a generation ago, when the only sport offered to girls was cheerleading.

It's true that more boys participate in sports (77 percent compared with 71 percent of the girls) and that boys still choose to participate in a higher number of sports activities than girls do (an average of 3.1 for boys

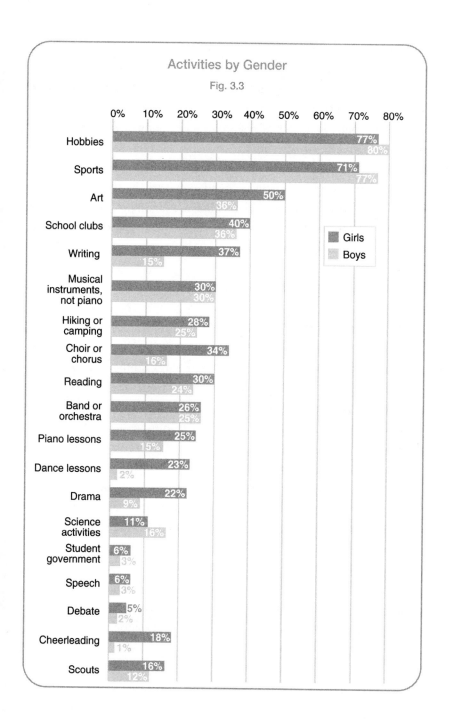

Activities by Gender
Fig. 3.3

Activity	Girls	Boys
Hobbies	77%	80%
Sports	71%	77%
Art	50%	36%
School clubs	40%	36%
Writing	37%	15%
Musical instruments, not piano	30%	30%
Hiking or camping	28%	25%
Choir or chorus	34%	16%
Reading	30%	24%
Band or orchestra	26%	25%
Piano lessons	25%	15%
Dance lessons	23%	2%
Drama	22%	9%
Science activities	11%	16%
Student government	6%	3%
Speech	6%	3%
Debate	5%	2%
Cheerleading	18%	1%
Scouts	16%	12%

compared with 2.7 for girls), but the percentages from the survey were still fairly close. While girls do have more opportunities to play sports, perhaps their lesser time commitment allows them to be involved in other activities. Significantly more girls than boys were involved in art, writing, chorus, reading, piano, dance lessons, drama, hiking or camping, speech, debate, Scouts, student government, and cheerleading. Parents should encourage their sons to join speech, debate, drama, writing, and student government activities, which were foundational for the successful women in media, government, and law in my book *See Jane Win.* Committing too much time to sports may prevent some boys from exploring opportunities in other important enrichment areas.

Enticing Girls toward Science

As in their parents' generation, my survey showed that boys were more involved (about 50 percent more) than were girls in science-related activities. Early involvement in science activities is predictive of careers in medicine, science, and nursing, suggesting that parents should continue urging their daughters to explore science fields. Although today there are as many women as men who attend medical school, there continues to be a greater percentage of men in both medicine and science, with great disparities favoring men in salaries and in the highest ranks of those fields. Many protest that women are in the pipeline for those higher salaries and ranks, but the pipeline is indeed leaking women. Many drop out of science and math as they get older—some claiming that the scientific environments are inhospitable to women. Scientific organizations are now making efforts to determine the basis for these claims.

The science field has been less hospitable to women in subtle ways. James Wagner, PhD, and Stacy Caudill, an MD candidate, discovered gender bias after studying several scientific TV series on PBS.[1] In one series, *Evolution,* there were significant differences in the amount of airtime given to male and female scientists. The males were given an average of 200 seconds of airtime; the females were given an average of only 124 seconds. The total airtime given to male scientists in the series was 153 minutes, compared with only 25 minutes for the female scientists. Furthermore, a female was never a dominant speaker in the series. Because TV is so influential to kids, this type of coverage can play a huge role in either attracting or discouraging girls from becoming interested in science or other fields.

I found another example of science targeting more boys than girls in a 2004 issue of the book series *Popular Science Almanac for Kids*. The book is a creatively illustrated compendium of scientific information and experiments for teens and tweens pertaining to earth science, biology, weather, and more. Although it includes pictures of boys as well as girls, the star of the book is Tim, who guides readers as they learn. All 16 chapters of the book begin with an illustration of Tim doing something scientific. Girls could easily assume this book is for boys because Tim is the prominent figure. However, the educational material in the book should be of interest to girls and boys alike.

There are many paths for making science appealing to girls. A natural interest of pets and other animals can lead girls to biological studies, veterinary science, or medicine. Gardening can spark an interest in botany. Watching the moon and stars through a telescope can make astronomy intriguing, or as in Space Shuttle Commander Eileen Collins's case, it can tempt one toward becoming an astronaut. Preparing food can lead to an interest in chemistry, and caring for an ill family member can inspire girls toward medicine. Even a sad or traumatic death of a family member can inspire a young person to pursue medical research in the hopes of finding a cure for a terrible illness. We assume all these possibilities for our sons, and we're certainly improving on encouraging girls toward science, but as parents, we need to believe in these possibilities for them.

Girls may encounter sexism about science as early as their middle school years from teachers who assume that boys are more naturally science-oriented. Parents can prepare girls for this type of opposition by explaining that it may take time for people to change their views about girls' potential. Reassuring daughters that they can do well in science, and explaining that it's an interesting, creative, but still pioneering career field for women, will help them to pursue their interests. As more women successfully enter scientific careers, barriers will diminish and opportunities will expand.

Girls and Boys Use Technology Differently

In my study, I found that kids spend much more time watching screens than doing homework. It's not a surprise that the boys in my study watched more TV, played more video games, and even edged out the girls a little on the Internet. There are very few video games directed at girls' interests. The fact that more boys than girls played video games may predict a greater interest among boys in computer technology careers, which are likely to continue to be in high demand in the future.

Girls from my survey used technology as a means of communication, rather than entertainment. Their use of e-mail and instant messaging (IM) was higher than that of boys, but they also invested more time in homework and study. E-mail and IM are a continuation of the communication and verbal interests girls have always displayed. Parents should be aware, however, that this technological interest doesn't necessarily lead girls to good careers. It's very worthwhile to encourage girls to explore careers in programming or Web site design. These fields continue to be less successful in attracting women.

Parents may want to suggest that schools provide optional all-girl computer programming classes, where girls can explore technology in an environment that they won't be intimidated in by techy boys whose skills are more advanced.

Gender Difference in Development

As parents, it's important to understand that children experience dramatic transitions through their 6 years of growth and development in grades three through eight. Some of their characteristics remain constant, others change only for girls or just for boys, and still others change for all kids.

In past generations, masculinity and femininity were rather narrowly defined. Women's work was restricted to nurturing roles, like being a mother and homemaker, teacher, nurse, or social worker. There were almost no women in medicine, law, science, government, serious media, orchestral music, art, or the higher echelons of business. The armed services, the police force, construction, sports, and careers that required physical strength and stamina were reserved for men as well. Furthermore, men were rarely involved in nurturing careers, and they made very few contributions to family child care or domestic chores. Women typically served men within the home, while men usually served women outside the home.

The Good News and Bad News about Changing Gender Roles

Girls are nicer to be friends with than boys. They listen and they talk, and they have better imaginations than boys. Boys are, you know, boom-boom and they're done. How can I confide in them?

4th-grade boy

While some careers and chores remain either male or female dominated, many of them now overlap. Many parents have raised children who have established their femininity or masculinity in a broad range of directions. We can consider it to be bad news for a gender if stereotypical gender roles are strongly integrated between third and eighth grade. If maturity encourages a variety of roles, without regard to gender stereotypes, we can consider it to be good news for our kids and the enrichment of their lives.

Figures 3.4 through 3.9 display the good news and bad news of kids' development. The "+" next to each characteristic indicates that the percentage of students checking that characteristic *increased* between third and eighth grade. The "−" indicates a decrease. Some characteristics are graphed only for girls, because those traits did not display any significant developmental trends for boys. And some are graphed only for boys, because there were no significant developmental trends for girls. I've labeled some characteristics "Good or Bad?" You can evaluate what category they fall into according to your own values. For example, some of you may consider it good that an increasing percentage of both girls and boys became emotional between third and eighth grade, or you may think that such an increase in emotionalism is problematic. Let's start with the good news.

The Good News

Historically, middle school has been a time when girls lose confidence. Surprisingly, and contrary to earlier studies of girls, my study found that confidence, leadership, and independence increased for girls as they matured (see Figure 3.4). It's important to note, however, that girls who adopted leadership roles were more likely to describe themselves as bossy.

There was good news for boys, too: Their confidence, leadership, and independence increased from grades three to eight (see Figure 3.5). Their percentages trailed behind the girls', however, and the changes were not as substantial as they were for the girls. Nevertheless, there was notable progress.

Earlier research has suggested that girls "lose their voices" and are less likely to speak up during middle school. That seems to have changed

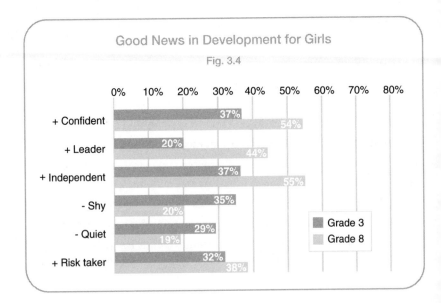

Good News in Development for Girls

Fig. 3.4

for this generation. My study showed that fewer girls described themselves as shy, with percentages decreasing from 35 to 20 percent between grades three and eight. Fewer girls also thought they were quiet, falling from 29 to 19 percent, and more described themselves as chatterboxes, increasing from 38 to 46 percent. Their stance as risk takers also increased—from 32 to 38 percent. All of this is very good news for girls who traditionally become shier during these years.

What about the boys? Shyness, being quiet, and risk taking didn't fluctuate much for the boys, but all of those traits, on the average, continue to be less of a problem for boys than for girls.

The Bad News

Although girls generally appear to be happier than boys, the percentages of girls and boys in my study who considered themselves to be happy decreased gradually from third to eighth grade, from 76 to 69 percent for girls and from 58 to 51 percent for boys (see Figures 3.6 and 3.7 on page 50). Their unhappiness may be related to the fact that kids compare themselves with others more frequently in adolescence. Peer pressure to fit in may allow slightly fewer kids to feel happy about themselves.

There was a continuously decreasing percentage of boys who considered themselves to be sweet, dropping from 21 to 15 percent, and unfortunately, their call to masculinity also seemed to cause a continuous

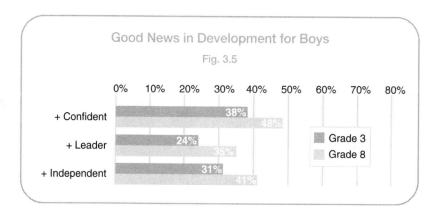

Good News in Development for Boys

Fig. 3.5

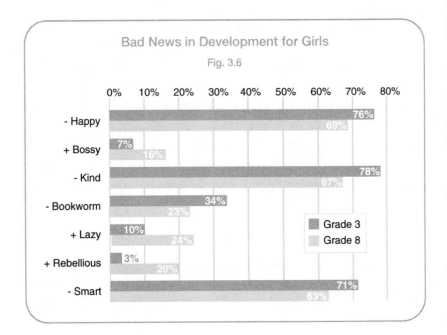

Bad News in Development for Girls
Fig. 3.6

	Grade 3	Grade 8
- Happy	76%	69%
+ Bossy	7%	16%
- Kind	78%	67%
- Bookworm	34%	23%
+ Lazy	10%	24%
+ Rebellious	3%	20%
- Smart	71%	63%

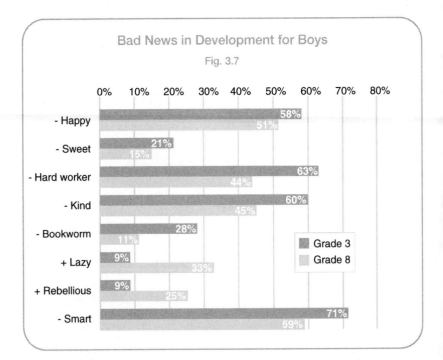

Bad News in Development for Boys
Fig. 3.7

	Grade 3	Grade 8
- Happy	58%	51%
- Sweet	21%	15%
- Hard worker	63%	44%
- Kind	60%	45%
- Bookworm	28%	11%
+ Lazy	9%	33%
+ Rebellious	9%	25%
- Smart	71%	59%

decline in their work ethic, with percentages of those who said they were hard workers falling from 63 to 44 percent. It's no wonder girls are moving ahead in academics. Percentages of girls who felt they were hard workers (varying between 57 and 63 percent) were higher at every grade level than they were for the boys. More girls just seemed to work harder.

There's bad news about kindness among girls and boys. Kids were less likely to describe themselves as kind as they got older. Girls who considered themselves to be kind decreased from 78 to 67 percent and boys dropped from 60 to 45 percent. As parents, it's important to teach your kids the value of kindness. You can help kids learn kindness by getting them involved with helping or teaching younger children or participating in a community activity that helps others. Contributing time and energy to others helps boys to value their own sensitivity, without destroying their fragile sense of masculinity. Through community projects, boys and girls can learn to be both strong and sensitive.

Kids' perceptions that they weren't smart may be related to how they compared themselves with peers. Fewer girls felt they were smart; their percentages declined from 71 to 63 percent between third and eighth grade. Boys' perceptions of being smart suffered even more than girls', with 71 percent of third-graders feeling smart but only 59 percent of eighth-graders having this intellectual confidence. Considering the boys' drop in work ethic, it's not surprising that fewer felt smart. Even so, fewer girls felt intelligent as they matured despite their continued hard work. It's important to motivate kids to work hard; as parents we can help by equating intelligence with effort. In my clinical work, I often explain to kids that the harder they work, the smarter they get and vice versa. Don't let kids' negative attitudes discourage you—making it cool to be a hard worker can seem like a near impossible task in middle school. I'll discuss other effective strategies for building kids' work ethics in Chapters 12 and 13.

Kids who described themselves as lazy also highlighted another area of bad news for both sexes. Laziness is unfortunately too acceptable among peers of these ages. Percentages of girls who described themselves as lazy more than doubled between third and eighth grades, while boys' percentages tripled. Combine those percentages with an increase in rebelliousness (3 to 20 percent for girls, and 9 to 25 percent for boys) and wow—no wonder middle school parents and teachers feel frustrated.

Is It Good or Bad News?

This third category is where I suggest that you make your subjective evaluation. You may think it's positive that kids become less sensitive and more emotional with maturity, or you may believe sensitivity should be encouraged or emotionality discouraged. Either way, your personal views will determine how you rate these qualities (see Figures 3.8 and 3.9).

As girls matured, they became more sensitive, but boys' lesser indications of sensitivity, which varied between 14 and 18 percent for all grades, showed no relationship to developmental changes. An increase in the number of girls who believed that they were fashion leaders was not

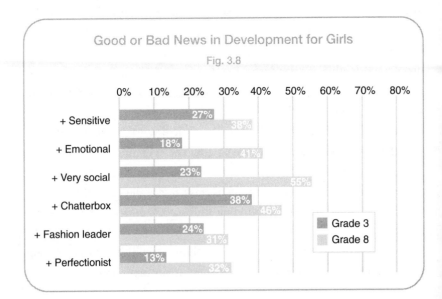

Good or Bad News in Development for Girls

Fig. 3.8

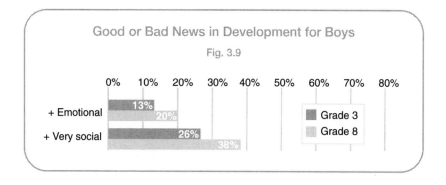

Good or Bad News in Development for Boys

Fig. 3.9

| | 0% | 10% | 20% | 30% | 40% | 50% | 60% | 70% | 80% |

+ Emotional 13% 20%

+ Very social 26% 38%

Grade 3
Grade 8

unexpected, since clothes become more of a priority as girls get older. But percentages increased only from 24 to 31 percent, hardly a substantial difference, meaning that some girls are interested in fashion very early on, but many simply aren't.

Perfectionism, which is more typically a girl's trait, also increased for girls between grades three and eight. It may be that younger children didn't know the meaning of the term, so they could have been perfectionistic without actually labeling themselves as such.

Girls also described themselves as increasingly emotional from grades three to eight. The 18 percent of emotional third-grade girls rose to 41 percent by eighth grade. In contrast, only 13 percent of boys indicated they were emotional in grade three, a figure that rose to just 20 percent by grade eight. The differences between the girls' and boys' emotionality is typical. This is usually frustrating for males and females, with boys proclaiming they don't understand girls emotionally and girls claiming that boys are insensitive to their feelings.

Girls' social lives underwent the most change. In third grade, only 23 percent of girls described themselves as very social, but by eighth grade, more than twice as many felt they were very social. Older girls may have problems attracting very social boys, since boys' gradual increase varied only between 26 and 38 percent. Again, this difference may be temporary and related to the later sexual maturity of boys. In any case, it may lead girls to be attracted to older boys, because boys their same age tend to be less social than they are.

What is obvious from Figures 3.4 and 3.7 is that in terms of development from third grade to eighth grade, there's more good news for girls and more bad news for boys. That may be because girls have been mobilized and motivated by the women's movement of previous generations. While life isn't a contest between girls and boys, and men and women, this data is gratifying in that it appears that girls have made great progress in a generation, with hopefully even more changes ahead for the future. Even so, parents and teachers should continue to bolster girls' independence and hard work. Despite the good news for the girls, like the boys, they are working less and feeling less intelligent as they get older.

Parents should also encourage boys to be hard workers and to develop their academic strengths during this trying time in their lives. Encouragement from dads and other male role models can be especially helpful to boys and persuasive to tween boys.

The Future Is Bright, But Priorities Are Different

For the most part, the girls and boys in my study were optimistic about their futures. More girls than boys (12 percent compared with 8 percent) were afraid of the future, but happily, 79 percent of girls and 80 percent of boys believed they'd have a happy future. While their outlooks were good, their priorities for their futures were drastically different. More girls were interested in having happy family lives, creative jobs, and happy personal lives and in making the world a better place, whereas more boys wanted to make a lot of money, have a challenging job, have a good reputation in the community, and become famous. Although these variations reflect expected gender differences, the actual percentages were fairly close. Thus, while there is a difference between boys' and girls' expectations, the disparity is not great.

"When I Grow Up . . ."

Career choices showed the most dramatic change for girls, although some choices continue to be as stereotypical as in the past. Medicine, law, media, and veterinary science are careers that few women would have chosen a generation ago. Now, more girls than boys are considering careers in these areas, as I found in my survey (see Figure 3.10). A generation ago, most girls would have chosen nursing, teaching, and homemaking, and few boys would have chosen these professions. Even now, more girls than boys are considering taking on careers in these traditionally feminine areas. Of

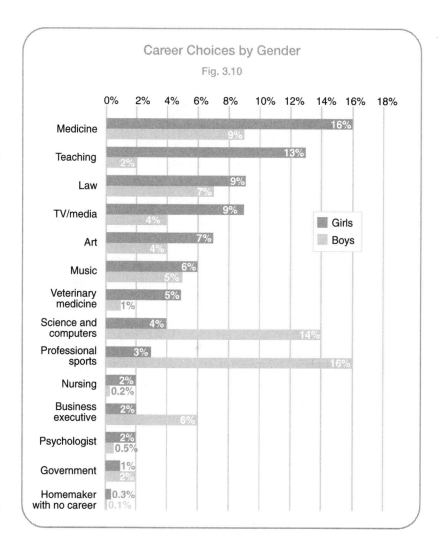

Career Choices by Gender

Fig. 3.10

course, the highest percentage of males (16 percent) is still planning on becoming professional athletes, and that dream may well have been held by their fathers, too.

For careers, it seems that many girls have raised and varied their expectations, but boys haven't changed much. We can thus expect that men will feel great competition from women in high-paying careers that their fathers—and certainly their grandfathers—didn't experience. It's also likely that girls will have to continue to struggle and work very hard to achieve careers that have only recently begun opening their doors to women. Women may have to continue to fight for equality in the workplace, and both genders may continue to feel cheated in future generations—women when they're not accepted into male-dominated fields, and men when they feel that women have received preferential treatment. Both will require resilience to cope with the competition for high-status careers.

Traditional careers for women that once offered low salaries and status will be under great pressure to attract talented and committed people of both genders. Even now, nursing, education, and mental health fields are struggling in their efforts to prevent those trained for these professions from straying. In light of the fact that these fields are critical for raising our next generations and for maintaining health for adults and children, parents should recognize that these fields could provide challenging and satisfying careers both for men and for women in the future. Girls and boys who have interests and talent in the direction of nursing, teaching, or mental health should be encouraged to choose these fields, which are likely to have a surplus of jobs available. These opportunities deserve to have their status elevated, and incidentally, they tend to be family-friendly for both genders.

Changing Marriages in the Future

An important finding of my survey is the contrast between what girls expect for themselves and what boys expect of their future wives. Ninety-two percent of the girls and 90 percent of the boys hoped for both a family and a career when they grow up. Two percent of the girls and

1 percent of the boys planned to have a family and no career, and 7 percent of the girls and 8 percent of the boys expected not to marry. Only 64 percent of the boys expected to have wives who held careers while their children were growing up. Twenty-six percent expected their wives to postpone their careers until later in life.

Boys may be in for a surprise if they don't change their expectations, because most girls are expecting to simultaneously manage a career and a family. This is undoubtedly the greatest change apparent in middle schoolers today. For some readers, this may seem like great progress; for others, it may be a disappointment. Marriage may be very different in the future, which brings us to an important discussion of homosexual issues in middle school.

The Special Struggles of Homosexuality

Robert called me gay because I wouldn't tell him who I liked. So I just finally told him I liked the hottest girl in our class, and then he stopped calling me gay.

7th-grade boy

At a time when children are only beginning to understand their own sexuality, homophobia and kids' and parents' unreasonable fears that kids may be homosexual play a large role in middle school children's development. Homophobia affects tweens' sexual identity behavior in at least three dramatic ways. First, heterosexual kids who want to appear mature feel considerable pressure to prove their masculinity or femininity, even though they may not be interested in the opposite sex yet. They may act in sexually aggressive ways or force themselves to pretend they have girl- or boyfriends to prove to their peers that they're straight. Second, kids may resolve to prove their own sexual identity by isolating and being cruel to other children of their own gender whom they suspect to be gay or questioning their sexual identities. Third, tweens who are homosexual, bisexual, or questioning may be so afraid their secret will be discovered that they isolate themselves out of fear, causing depression and self-doubt. These behaviors affect all middle school children adversely but especially those who have the least confidence in their sexual identity.

How Many Kids Are Gay?

Studies of middle school kids' homosexuality have only rarely been conducted, because schools and parents are hesitant to ask kids questions about homosexuality at so vulnerable an age. We can conclude from the studies of older teens and adults that although the vast majority of middle schoolers (probably about 90 percent) will eventually identify themselves as heterosexual, a sizeable minority of between 5 to 10 percent will mature to consider themselves bisexual or homosexual. In a 1995 study of 8,000 high school students in grades 9 through 12, 4.5 percent identified themselves as gay, lesbian, or bisexual, and another 4.5 percent indicated they were unsure of their sexual orientation.[2]

There's never before been more awareness and openness about gay, lesbian, bisexual, and transgender (GLBT) issues in the adult community. A recent survey conducted by Greenberg Quinlan Rosner Research for the Human Rights Campaign reported that more than half of the adults polled believed that the rights of GLBT people should be protected.[3] Even so, that still leaves many adults who feel otherwise, and acceptance of gays by middle school kids is much less common. The prejudice in middle schools against homosexuality is so dominant and so hateful that children who believe they may be homosexual suffer terrible emotional abuse. In my middle school focus groups, kids who accepted gays were hesitant to discuss their support of the issue. It was as if they ethically believed that gay rights should be protected, but they feared their peers might label them as being gay if they spoke up too fervently.

In addition to those kids who are themselves homosexual, some parents are either gay or lesbian, and their kids have to cope with the intolerance of their classmates for the homosexuality of their parents. The issues for GLBT or questioning middle schoolers and for kids of homosexual parents continue to be undeniably complex and daunting.

Hormones Rush In

I've seen girls kissing each other in the restrooms a couple of times.

7th-grade girl

Adolescence is rampant with new sexual feelings of every kind. Kids are often sexually attracted to actors, actresses, teachers, athletes, ministers, and adult leaders of both sexes. Popular kids of either sex may be sexually attractive to either sex. Kids' hearts skip beats, their hormones rush in, and they fall "in love" with almost anyone they dream about. Film, music, television, books, and talk all excite kids' sexuality easily.

Kids have always experimented with sexual exploration. What is frequently labeled as sexual abuse by 5- to 7-year-olds today was called "playing doctor" in past generations. Because such exploration was considered "normal," parents and kids didn't consider it a problem. Sexual exploration during middle childhood and even early adolescence was usually with kids of the same sex, because girls typically played with girls and boys with boys at those ages. Catching kids exploring in early adolescence would bring a somewhat more stern response from a parent, such as, "You're getting too old to do those things."

Those secret sexual explorations a generation ago didn't cause children to worry that they were homosexual, because the acts weren't labeled as abuse or sexual behavior. Although some of those children may have eventually determined they were homosexual, the majority probably did not. They soon found the opposite sex more attractive than their own and dismissed their childhood exploits as part of normal growing up. Not only is touching another's privates considered abuse now, but many children fear they're gay if they're either a perpetrator or recipient of same-sex touching. I remember an 8-year-old boy from my clinic telling me that he thought he was gay because his male cousin had touched his penis and he had allowed it.

Homophobia

I have nothing personal against gay guys. I just think they're so weird. They freak me out. They should make laws against them. My parents have always been real against them . . . I stay away from them.

8th-grade boy

Because most middle school children are anxious to establish themselves as masculine or feminine, they're especially afraid of another kid discovering they're homosexual, being labeled homosexual when they're not, or having any sexual feelings for others of the same sex. Being mean to gay and lesbian kids, or making derogatory references about homosexuals, can make kids feel like they're providing proof to themselves and others that they're straight. The negativism surrounding homosexuality is incredible. In fact, the term *gay* is synonymous with *lame* and is used to describe anything that's boring or uncool, as in, "That was such a gay party"—meaning that it was a dull party. Kids call other kids *lezzies, fags,* or *faggots* to insult them whether or not they're gay, and if kids are suspected of being homosexual, they're often completely isolated. Other kids fear that if they associate with kids who are rumored to be gay, they too will be labeled as homosexual. One eighth-grade girl explained it to me this way.

The girls are pretty nice to boys who might be gay, because they can be nice guys, and [the girls] aren't afraid they'll hit on them. The boys aren't usually too mean to girls who may be tomboys or lesbians for the same reason. But boys are really mean to other boys who seem gay, and girls aren't too nice to girls who could be lesbians. So it's the same sexes that are mean to each other because kids are afraid they'll get hit on or be called gay because they're with gay kids.

Parents whom I saw at my clinic shared this story of their son.

When Brett was in fourth grade, he dressed up like Britney Spears for Halloween, including a wig and breasts. He did such a good impersonation and sounded exactly like her. Although he got plenty of laughs from his peers for the day, he was teased mercilessly by the boys. Two years later, his peers wanted him to dress up as Britney again for a show they were doing. We felt it necessary to forbid him because of the cruel repercussions he had experienced the first time.

An environment that permits the bullying of gay kids can cause tweens and teens to feel insecure and take drastic measures. The 1999 Youth Risk Behavior Survey of high schoolers in Massachusetts found that 33 percent of GLBT kids reported attempting suicide, compared with only 8 percent of their heterosexual peers.[4] Another study of gay and bisexual males found that they were four times as likely to kill themselves as were heterosexual males.[5] Homosexual middle schoolers may not attempt suicide at as high a rate, but they're certainly suffering from bullying that may pressure them toward later attempts. Researchers have found that young homosexuals tend to hate themselves because of their sexual orientation and feel socially and emotionally isolated.[6] Homosexual youth often believe the terrible things with which society labels them.

Discussing Homosexuality with Your Tweens

Middle school youth may learn about homosexuality from their parents or peers before they enter middle school. As with other topics related to sex, parents and educators should share in the responsibility of providing accurate information about homosexuality. Because cruelty toward gays is so extreme in middle school, it seems urgent that children at least understand what homosexuality is, and even more important, learn tolerance and respect for sexual minorities.

Annie Wonders Why Ben Has Two Moms

Annie (10 years old): Mom, where's Aunt Lucy's husband? How come Ben doesn't have a dad?

Mother: Ben doesn't have a dad, but he does have an extra mother. When Aunt Lucy comes to visit us, Aunt Jane comes with her because they live together in much the same way as your dad and I do. Although most of the time men and women live together in a family, there are many different kinds of families. Some families have only one mom or one dad, and some have two moms or two dads. What is most important is that Ben has parents who love and care for him. Have you ever talked with Ben about his two moms?

Annie: Yes, I asked him where his dad was, and he got angry at me and said he didn't have one. Maybe he thought I was being mean to him. Some kids at school call him a momma's boy and a fag, but he gets along pretty well with most kids. Maybe he gets tired of explaining it to kids. So, does that mean that Aunt Lucy is a lesbian?

Mother: It does. Aunt Lucy wasn't attracted to boyfriends and preferred being with women, and so did Aunt Jane, so they found they were good partners.

Parents' Responsibilities

Parents need to inform their tweens about homosexuality at approximately the same time that they help them to understand heterosexuality. Parents can most easily find segues or teaching moments for such conversations based on their kids' exposure to life experiences. For example, a child who has a friend whose parents are homosexual would probably need to have an informative conversation well before middle school. If an adult friend, acquaintance, or relative is homosexual, that should also encourage parents to divulge information earlier. For instance, parents can calmly explain that a woman they know prefers having a female partner rather than a male partner. (See "Annie Wonders Why Ben Has Two Moms" and "More Questions from Annie" for sample discussions.) News on the radio or TV about gay and lesbian rights may also provide ideal teaching opportunities to introduce the concepts of homosexuality to your tweens. Be as matter-of-fact and unbiased as possible, because any of your prejudices will certainly influence your children, just as the eighth-grade boy quoted at the beginning of this chapter was prejudicially influenced by his parents.

More Questions from Annie

Annie: Mom, I was wondering, am I a lesbian because I love Aunt Lucy? She's always been a role model for me and she loves me too, so maybe it's because I'm gay.

Mother: Aunt Lucy loves you very much but not in a sexual way. Just because she's a great role model for you and you love her doesn't mean you're a lesbian. In any case, it's probably too early for you to know if you're homosexual or heterosexual. You're just beginning your sexual development, so you'll have to wait until you're older to figure out whether you are attracted to men or women. Most girls like boys better when they get older, but there's plenty of time for that. You can be assured that we'll love you with either choice though, and you'll always be part of our family, just as Aunt Lucy is.

Annie: That's good Mom, because right now, I'm not much interested in boys or girls in *that* way.

Educators' Responsibilities

Although most schools today provide sex education within the health education curriculum, there is almost no mention of homosexuality in health textbooks. James T. Sears, PhD, professor of curriculum studies at the University of South Carolina in Columbia, calls the absence of such information a "conspiracy of silence."[7] Homosexuality is simply not an open topic for discussion in most middle schools today. The absence of these discussions undoubtedly perpetuates the harassment of gay and lesbian tweens. Education about homosexuality that is free from prejudice would at least give kids a fairer picture of what some of their peers may be experiencing.

If we are to see homosexuality included as part of the sex education curriculum, it's vital that parents become advocates of this change. School boards hesitate to include homosexuality in the curriculum because they anticipate parental objections. Thus, school boards may simply be trying to avoid the controversy.

Establishing Homosexual Identity

When homosexual adults are asked when they realized they were gay, they almost always indicate they were very young when they identified themselves as "different" from others of their sex. In a study of homosexual adults, the average age that participants indicated that they had first awareness of homosexual attraction was about age 9 for boys and age 10 for girls.[8]

Supporting Your Questioning Tween

If there are indications that your son or daughter is attracted to the same sex, assure your tween that it's too early to determine for certain whether he or she is heterosexual or homosexual, and if it's clear he or she is attracted to same-sex partners later on, you will continue to love and accept him or her. If your own moral convictions oppose homosexuality, you need to state those to your child, but please offer your support during what will be an incredibly difficult time for your son or daughter. Your rejection could turn your child to alcohol, drugs, depression, or suicide.

Kids who suffer peer rejection and aren't interested in the opposite sex as soon as their peers are may assume that normal crushes on same-sex celebrities or adults prove they're gay. Encouraging them not to rush to conclusions will help. Tweens' infatuations with musicians and celebrities may have them constantly listening to music by their favorite groups, taping pictures of favorite stars all over their rooms, or even writing secret letters or e-mails to celebrities. All of these actions are normal, as long as tweens aren't obsessed and are still involved in typical peer activities. However, if they are withdrawing from school activities or social life, or seem anxious or depressed about their sexuality, then you should see these as symptoms of more serious problems. Either way, let your tween know that you can arrange for her to see a psychologist to share her concerns with someone outside of the family. Kids who think they're gay may have difficulty telling their parents for fear of disappointing them or of being rejected.

Before your child sees a counselor about sexual identity, meet with the counselor yourself to determine if his or her attitude about homosexuality fits with your personal value system. A homophobic counselor could drive your gay or questioning child toward isolation, guilt, or suicide. If a counselor concludes too quickly that a child is gay following the first office visit, it may cause the child to come to conclusions too quickly about his or her sexual identity. You have a right to know the philosophic perspective of your child's counselor and to receive continuing guidance from the counselor with respect to your child. You also have the right and responsibility to discontinue counseling if it doesn't fit with your value system.

Your Expectations Make a Difference

It's obvious that middle school is a difficult time for kids and a challenge for you as parents and teachers. With the increase of problems and concerns for kids between grades three and eight, you can hardly rest on your laurels. Although higher expectations of girls today have made a huge difference in how girls see themselves at the difficult juncture of the middle grades, parents and educators need to keep encouraging girls to be independent and strong, and to discover their identities. Boys, too, need support so that the increase of competition from girls doesn't impede their mission for adolescent independence. You know that it isn't healthy for girls to depend on popularity with boys to build their self-confidence, but neither is it healthy for boys' self-confidence to be tied to popularity with girls. All tweens are subjected to new pressures as they mature and seek their identities, and your guidance can lead them along the path to independent self-confidence. For helpful books and more information to guide you in helping your kids with gender issues, see the Appendix.

My findings should spur you to provide the support that your kids need in this increasingly difficult transition from childhood to adolescence. My further suggestions in the next chapters will provide you with more helpful advice for guiding your tweens as they navigate the environment of middle school.

⚠ ENVIRONMENTS

CHAPTER 4

THE BUZZ ON DRUGS

I have a friend who brags that she can chug a Bloody Mary in less than 10 seconds.

7th-grade girl

A couple of my friends smoke. It was their decision, and they're not proud of it anymore. They know they should stop, but it's hard. They don't pressure me or anything, but I want to be like them, so I pressure myself.

8th-grade girl

I think the media encourages us to do drugs because we see people who are famous and have been caught doing drugs in the real world. They're our role models. Like Ozzy Osbourne, for example. He's famous and he did drugs.

8th-grade boy

JUST AS THE SEXUAL ACTIVITY found in today's middle schools sounded more like what you might remember from your own high school days, so will middle schoolers' world of tobacco, alcohol, and drugs. Because these risky behaviors are also tied to early sexual activity and its repercussions, you'll want to pay scrupulous attention to the things to which your kids are exposed. Providing an environment that prevents your children's early experimentation and involvement in substance abuse is doubly important.

The Reality of Drugs and Alcohol

I know a lot of people who talk about drinking and doing drugs. One girl I know cuts school to smoke weed. Ecstasy has really increased, too.

8th-grade boy

Surveys from the National Parents' Resources Institute for Drug Education (PRIDE) provide comprehensive data on tobacco, alcohol, and drug use from the 1987–88 academic year to the present. Conducted annually, the information is collected and analyzed for grades 4 through 12.

Figures 4.1 and 4.2 show a decline in the use of tobacco, alcohol, and drugs for sixth- through eighth-graders between the 1997–98 and the 2001–02 PRIDE reports. Lest we be complacent, notice that the 2002–03

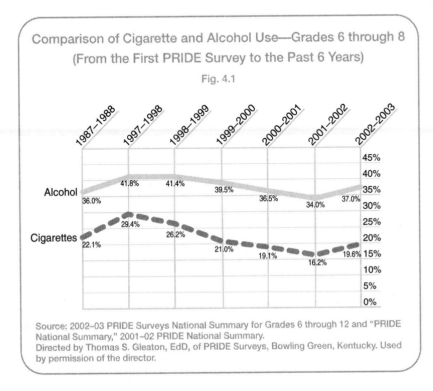

Comparison of Cigarette and Alcohol Use—Grades 6 through 8
(From the First PRIDE Survey to the Past 6 Years)

Fig. 4.1

Source: 2002–03 PRIDE Surveys National Summary for Grades 6 through 12 and "PRIDE National Summary," 2001–02 PRIDE National Summary.
Directed by Thomas S. Gleaton, EdD, of PRIDE Surveys, Bowling Green, Kentucky. Used by permission of the director.

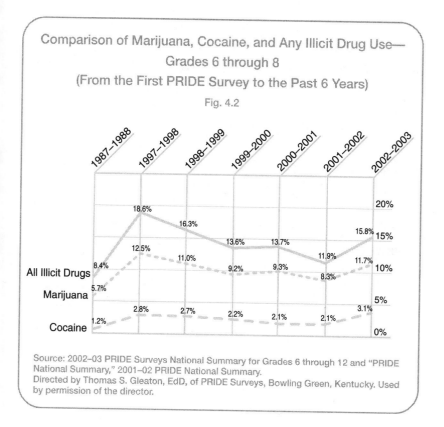

Comparison of Marijuana, Cocaine, and Any Illicit Drug Use—
Grades 6 through 8
(From the First PRIDE Survey to the Past 6 Years)
Fig. 4.2

Source: 2002–03 PRIDE Surveys National Summary for Grades 6 through 12 and "PRIDE National Summary," 2001–02 PRIDE National Summary. Directed by Thomas S. Gleaton, EdD, of PRIDE Surveys, Bowling Green, Kentucky. Used by permission of the director.

school year has again shown an increase in the use of all harmful substances by middle school children. Compared with the earliest PRIDE survey, cigarette smoking decreased only a little, from 22.1 to 19.6 percent, despite the antismoking campaigns launched by tobacco companies.

All other areas of substance use have shown increases since the first PRIDE survey in 1987–88. The use of alcohol rose slightly, but the most serious change was in the dramatic expansion in drug use. The use of marijuana more than doubled, use of cocaine nearly tripled, and use of any illicit drug from the most recent survey was almost twice as high as the 1987–88 report.

PRIDE surveys also include statistics on tobacco and alcohol use for fourth- and fifth-graders, and they show a worrisome early start. In the 2002–03 survey, PRIDE found that 2.7 percent of fourth-graders and

4.4 percent of fifth-graders had smoked cigarettes in the past year, and 6.3 percent of fourth-graders and 6.4 percent of fifth-graders reported having drunk beer in the last year.[1] Percentages were lower for marijuana use (0.7 and 1.2 percent of fourth- and fifth-graders, respectively) and for use of other drugs (1.3 percent of the fourth-graders and 1.4 percent of the fifth-graders).[2] Most startling, the same PRIDE study showed that high percentages of fourth-, fifth-, and sixth-graders reported that it was *easy* to get cigarettes, beer, and marijuana (Figure 4.3). Although the percentages of actual use of these high-risk behaviors may seem low, consider the numbers. There are approximately four million children in each age category, meaning that of the fifth-graders, 176,000 smoked cigarettes, 256,000 reported drinking beer, and 48,000 used marijuana during the 2002–03 academic year. That's a lot of very young children (8- to 10-year-olds) who have started down a self-destructive path. Presently, according to the National Survey on Drug Use and Health, an average of 4,700 teens under

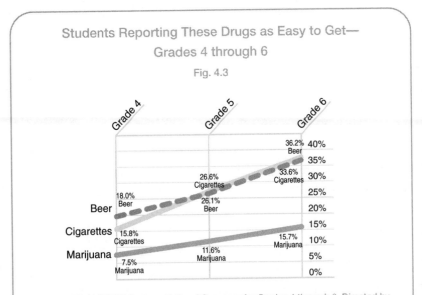

Students Reporting These Drugs as Easy to Get—
Grades 4 through 6

Fig. 4.3

Grade 4 — Grade 5 — Grade 6

Beer
18.0% Beer
26.1% Beer
36.2% Beer — 40%

35%

Cigarettes
15.8% Cigarettes
26.6% Cigarettes
33.6% Cigarettes — 30%

25%

20%

15%

Marijuana
7.5% Marijuana
11.6% Marijuana
15.7% Marijuana — 10%

5%

0%

age 18 try marijuana for the first time every single day.[3] The problem is *huge,* and parents can no longer ignore the impact on their children.

Most likely, there weren't any extensive national surveys on tween substance abuse when you, the parents of today's middle schoolers, were that age. We can, though, assume almost for certain that the percentages were far lower (at least in junior high) than they are in middle schools today.

"Just Try It"

In my apartment house, a couple of kids get high on drugs. I try and stay away from them. They bring cigarettes to school to try to get us to smoke. They also try to get us good kids to try drugs. If I bought them, I figure I'd die faster, and that's a waste of a good life.

5th-grade boy

My own survey asked middle schoolers whether or not they worried about being pressured to use alcohol and drugs. Figure 4.4 shows by grade level

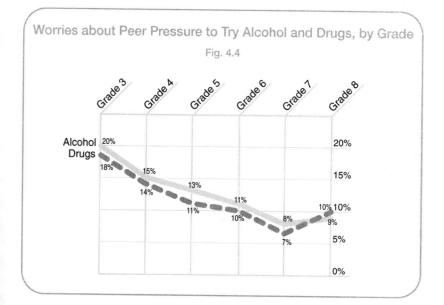

Worries about Peer Pressure to Try Alcohol and Drugs, by Grade

Fig. 4.4

the extent to which students worried about that peer pressure. It's interesting to note that worrying about peer pressure to try alcohol and drugs *decreased* significantly and consistently between grades three and seven. A slight increase among eighth-graders may be due to their concern about entering high school and the new pressures they could encounter. The 2002–03 PRIDE report, however, showed that the use of cigarettes, alcohol, and drugs *increased* consistently in grades 4 through 12. Worries about peer pressure may be a helpful deterrent to using these substances, but when kids just assume they can handle peer pressure and stop worrying about it, the actual use of the substances may increase. Read what one eighth-grade boy from my focus group had to say about peer pressure.

> *My friends were experimenting with weed and stuff like that, so my parents thought I was too. The scent was always on my clothes. My parents didn't want me to hang with them because they were afraid my friends would pressure me to do drugs. But they're my friends and if that's what they want to do, let them do it. Let them ruin their lives. I can hang with them and not do it. Peer pressure doesn't bother me.*

I would be surprised if this boy managed to avoid using drugs for any length of time. His parents were right to worry, and even though he denied using drugs, there's a good chance he had already experimented. Kids usually minimize their behavior when discussing substance abuse. Peer pressure is more powerful than young people like to believe, so don't be fooled by their reassurances. Kids who are surrounded by smokers, drinkers, and druggies almost always succumb to the pressure because they want to belong.

Preventing Tobacco, Alcohol, and Drug Use

> *I look at it like this: Some people do drugs, but I don't do drugs. Let's see who lives longer. If they die first, then I can laugh at them 'cuz they were stupid and took drugs. Every*

time you smoke, it shortens your life by 12 seconds or some-thing like that. It's really stupid that people just smoke, and smoke, and smoke. Yeah, it's addicting, but why'd they start in the first place?

7th-grade girl

PRIDE surveys provide a good understanding of the kinds of activities and behaviors that are likely to lessen the chances that your middle school children will become involved in tobacco, alcohol, and drug use. The surveys leave little doubt that parents and schools *can* and *do* make a difference in decreasing these risky behaviors.

Just Say NO!

Dad: Do you know if any of the kids at school smoke marijuana?

Scott, 8th-grader: I'm not sure. Maybe some kids do, but none of my friends.

Dad: I'm glad your friends don't, and I hope you won't become friends with druggies in the future. I'm counting on you to never use drugs. They're illegal, and I can't ever support you when you do something against the law. They're also just bad for you in every way.

Scott: Dad, don't worry so much. I'm no druggie.

Dad: I hope you aren't, but there are plenty of kids out there who will try to pressure you. I want you to know exactly how Mom and I feel. Sometimes you could be tempted to experiment, and some parents may not mind that, but we do and we hope that's clear. We believe you're strong enough to resist temptation, and we want to be able to trust you.

The Benefits of Positive and Active Interests

There are no surprises in what prevents substance abuse. Participation in community and school activities like Scouts, Girls and Boys Clubs, religious youth groups, community work, sports, music, and school clubs makes a huge difference in whether kids use tobacco, alcohol, and drugs. Positive activities and outlets decrease drug use and use of alcohol and tobacco.

Kids who don't participate in any community and school activities are certainly more bored, and it's been shown that boredom invites trouble. A study by the National Center on Addiction and Substance Abuse (CASA) at Columbia University found that 12- to 17-year-olds who were frequently bored were 50 percent more likely to smoke, drink,

Having a Blast without the Beer

Scott: You've made it real clear how you feel about drugs, Dad, but what about alcohol? You have beer when you watch a game, and you and Mom usually have wine with your dinner, so when can I have a drink or two?

Dad: Alcohol is different in some ways, but in other ways it should be treated just the same as drugs. Alcohol isn't illegal or unhealthy for adults in moderation, but it isn't healthy for growing kids, and it isn't legal for kids to drink unless they're in the presence of their parents. Your mom and I are moderate in our drinking, and when you're an adult, you can make your own judgments about alcohol. I don't mind if you take a small sip of my beer or have a small glass of wine with us on the holidays, but you can't drink alcohol regularly. You definitely can't drink at someone's party, not even a sip, because that's against the law. Not only that, you don't belong at parties where there's alcohol. You'd be taking a chance that something bad could happen. You'll save yourself a lot of trouble if you stay away from those types of parties. Scott, if you ever find yourself at a party where kids have beer, just pretend you're not feeling get drunk, and use illegal drugs compared with those who rarely felt bored.[4] Just hanging around with nothing to do but "chill" may seem cool, but it isn't healthy for otherwise energetic young people. Throw money at your kids, and the risk also increases. The same CASA study found that kids who had $25 or more spending money a week were twice as likely to abuse substances. Kids with unsupervised time are three times more likely to use marijuana or other drugs as kids who are supervised.[5] Keeping kids positively busy makes good sense.

Good grades make a powerful psychological difference as well. In fact, they make even more of a difference than kids' involvement in activities. Very few students with good grades used drugs frequently, per-

well or something and give us a call. We'll come right over and pick you up. No questions asked.

Scott: You know, Dad, that's going to be hard once I get to high school. Most of those parties have beer, and a lot of the kids get drunk. The kids already drink at eighth-grade parties, and it's even some of the smart kids and the jocks.

Dad: That does make it hard, but Mom and I plan to call the parents before you go to any parties so we can make sure there won't be any drinking. If all the parents call each other, none of the kids will have to feel embarrassed, and the parents won't feel pressured to provide beer. Other parents are concerned, too, so we're getting together because we want to keep our kids safe and healthy. We want you to have fun but not to get into trouble. Why don't you have some kids here for a party? We'll get pizza, soda, and some snacks, and you can dance or watch a movie in the family room. You have nice friends, and we'll be glad to have them over. Their parents will probably let them invite you to their houses, too. You don't need to get drunk to have fun.

haps because they were smart enough to know that drugs would harm them (see Figure 4.5). Although it's important to expect good grades, it's just as important to be realistic. Good grades can mean As and Bs for some kids and Bs and Cs for others. Ds and Fs are usually the dividing line between good grades and poor grades. For most kids, getting good grades is merely a matter of developing intellectual confidence and a work ethic. I'll talk more about how you can help your kids with their motivation in school in Chapter 13.

Parents' Commitment Counts Too

Parental involvement is important for preventing your kids from using drugs. The 2002–03 PRIDE survey found that when parents talk to their kids about the dangers of risky behaviors, when they set clear rules for their children, and when they enforce rules with reasonable consequences, kids are less likely to use drugs. That may seem ap-

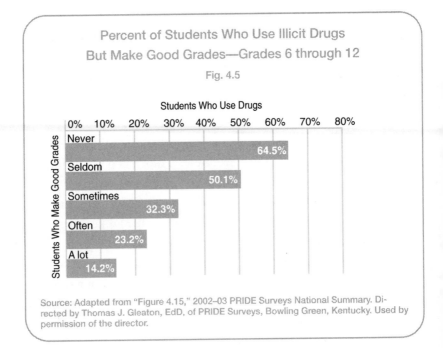

Percent of Students Who Use Illicit Drugs
But Make Good Grades—Grades 6 through 12

Fig. 4.5

Source: Adapted from "Figure 4.15," 2002–03 PRIDE Surveys National Summary. Directed by Thomas J. Gleaton, EdD, of PRIDE Surveys, Bowling Green, Kentucky. Used by permission of the director.

parent to you, but it isn't obvious to all parents. Examples of effective and ineffective punishments are listed in "Dealing with the Consequences."

Many parents are so determined to be close to their kids that they're too lenient and understanding when their kids experiment with drugs or alcohol. They may feel too intimidated to give a firm *no* that sets clear limits. Unfortunately, kids don't understand what "experiment a little" means. What does "just a little marijuana," "a little cocaine," or "a little heroin" mean for the future of an adolescent? Kids don't just sip a glass of wine to socialize, or take a drag to fit in. They drink to get drunk and do drugs to get high, so they can do and say things they wouldn't have the

Dealing with the Consequences

When middle schoolers disobey their parents' rules about alcohol, smoking, or drugs, it's time to have a serious discussion and apply punishments. However, when punishing kids, it's important not to take away the activities that will keep them involved with *positive* peer groups. It's also more effective not to take things away for too long, or kids tend to feel angry and discouraged. They lose hope that they can earn privileges again. A reasonable amount of time for taking away a privilege or an activity is a day, a weekend, or a week. Any more than a week can cause kids to rebel and defy you again to get even.

Effective punishments can include taking away video game, TV, bike, or computer privileges, or forbidding your tween from attending a party, a dance, a date, movies, or sleepovers. You can also consider taking away part of your tween's allowance.

Ineffective punishments include actions such as taking away sports, music, art, drama, school clubs, or other extracurricular activities, and forbidding parent-child trips, babysitting jobs, volunteer opportunities, or religious groups.

Smoking Is for Losers: Don't Be a Loser

Mom: I found two cigarettes in your desk drawer while I was putting your things away. I've noticed your clothes smell smoky lately, too.

Kayla, 7th-grader: The cigarettes aren't mine! Melanie just asked me to hold them for her. She's trying to stop smoking, but she didn't want to throw them away. She smokes after school sometimes; that's why I smell smoky.

Mom: Kayla, I'm not sure I can buy your story. Melanie wouldn't be asking you to hold her cigarettes if she was planning to stop. I threw the cigarettes away. They're bad for you, and they're bad for Melanie, too. Don't even start the habit. You know smoking is addicting. You watched your aunt die of lung cancer at 50. Those cigarettes probably stole at least 25 years of her life. When Aunt Alice was a teen, they didn't know tobacco caused cancer, so many more young people smoked then. Now we know for sure, so only losers get started, and you're no loser.

Kayla: Melanie's not a loser either. She's a good friend. She just wanted to try it, and now she's hooked.

Mom: If she's a good friend, she'll understand that you can't hang around with her if she smokes. Dad and I want to be very clear with you. Kids who smoke, drink alcohol, and do drugs are off-limits. You can talk to them in school, but you aren't allowed to go to their houses or have them here unless they quit. If you're really close with Melanie, and if she really wants to be your friend, she'll get the message. If not, you'll have to find a different crowd. I bet the kids in soccer or band are just as much fun—without the cigarettes.

courage to do otherwise. There are too many parents who ignore the law and host teen parties where beer is served. They may think that there is no harm, as long as their kids aren't driving. While these parties are more common in high school than in middle school, I've heard stories from parents at my clinic about eighth-grade parties with alcohol at homes where parents should know better. Some examples of conversations on how to talk to your kids about tobacco, drugs, and alcohol are included in "Just Say NO!" on page 75, "Having a Blast without the Beer" on page 76, and "Smoking Is for Losers: Don't Be a Loser" on page 80.

Even something as simple as serving regular family dinners can make a difference. CASA researchers found that when family dinners occurred only half the time, which becomes more common as kids get older, teen substance abuse increased sevenfold.[6] Though this study applied to both middle and high schoolers, it's important for parents to realize that families start to be too busy for a daily dinner together when their kids are in middle school. Mealtimes provide for valuable family conversation and listening. They're opportunities for kids to share their daily lives and for parents to offer guidance. Values can be reinforced through talking and laughing together. Families who eat together are more likely to have kids who care about their parents' values and expectations and are less likely to abuse substances. Kids who see their parents daily are also more likely to internalize the belief that their parents care about their well-being.

Schools Can Do Their Share

Teachers and schools also have an impact on kids' drug use and abuse. As shown in Figure 4.6 on page 82, teachers are a powerful influence on children. When teachers take the time to discuss the dangers of drugs, many students listen and believe them.

School-wide programs on substance abuse prevention also make a difference. With the installation of a drug and alcohol abuse prevention program in its fifth- through eighth-grade middle school, York Middle School in York, Maine, reported a below state-average for the frequency of substance abuse by their students.[7] Similarly, Project ALERT, a drug

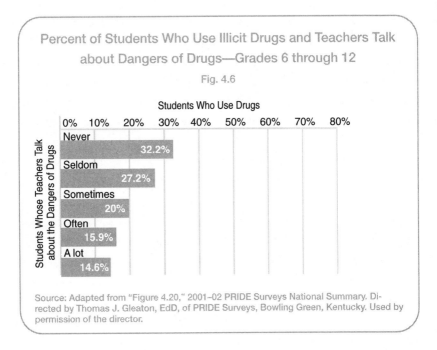

Percent of Students Who Use Illicit Drugs and Teachers Talk about Dangers of Drugs—Grades 6 through 12

Fig. 4.6

Students Who Use Drugs

Students Whose Teachers Talk about the Dangers of Drugs

Never	32.2%
Seldom	27.2%
Sometimes	20%
Often	15.9%
A lot	14.6%

Source: Adapted from "Figure 4.20," 2001–02 PRIDE Surveys National Summary. Directed by Thomas J. Gleaton, EdD, of PRIDE Surveys, Bowling Green, Kentucky. Used by permission of the director.

prevention curriculum for middle school students, was administered in 55 South Dakota middle schools between 1997 and 1999.[8] Evaluated 18 months later, fewer students in the program were involved in risky behaviors than students who weren't part of the educational program. Project ALERT not only targeted prevention but subsequently caused a decline among students who had been former users.

School prevention programs are much more likely to be implemented if educators and parents both get on the bandwagon and make them happen. Your job as a parent is to let school board members and administrators know that you want alcohol and drug prevention programs in your children's schools. You can't assume your kids are immune to the abuse of drugs. Temptation surrounds them—wherever they go to school.

While your parents were worried about tobacco, alcohol, and drugs when you went to high school, your concern should start much earlier. The next chapter will focus on another topic your parents probably worried little about—technology.

CHAPTER 5

TECHNOLOGY IS KEEPING KIDS BUSY

We just click a mouse and everything's right there.

6th-grade girl

I'm going to be 13 on my next birthday, and I still won't be able to watch PG-13 movies unless my parents approve. It's no different than being 12.

6th-grade boy

My parents make me play soccer, but I don't really like it. I like to read, play with radio-controlled cars, and watch TV.

Overweight 4th-grade boy

I kind of trick my parents into letting me see R-rated movies. I say I watched it on TV and already saw most of the violence on there, so let me see the real movie. I did that with The Matrix. At first they wouldn't let me watch the real movie, but then they did.

6th-grade boy

TECHNOLOGY LITERALLY DOMINATES middle school kids' activities. My survey and interviews with my focus groups showed that kids spent much less time on physical activities and more time in front of TV and computer screens. The kids I talked with were more vocal about

TV, music, movies, and the Internet than they were about extracurricular or physical activities. The fact that kids are so much more immersed in media than in their communities is a great cause for concern. Research from the National Parents' Resources Institute for Drug Education (PRIDE), which was detailed in Chapter 4, confirms that kids who are active in community and extracurricular activities are less likely to become involved in high-risk activities, like smoking, drinking alcohol, and doing drugs.

The Omnipresent Screen

Technology makes things easier for us 'cuz we can type stuff up on the computer and print it out. We can use scanners and the Internet and get any information whenever we want it. It makes school a lot easier.

5th-grade girl

Kids spend a great deal of time watching, playing, communicating, and working in front of a screen. A 1999 survey by the Henry J. Kaiser Family Foundation compared kids' screen time to a full-time job, noting that the average American child between the ages of 8 and 18 spends more than 40 hours a week in front of a screen.[1] My survey's results were similar, showing that the kids spent an average of 6.9 hours *a day* watching TV or using computers. That total doesn't count other screens, like those on their cell phones or at the movies. Multiplying their daily screen time by 7 days brings us to 48.3 hours a week. That number may be slightly inflated because kids may have checked more than one box if they played games, e-mailed, or did homework on the Internet. Nevertheless, their average screen time is at least equal to a full-time job, plus overtime!

Finding a home without a screen for kids to watch, especially a TV, is pretty rare. Only 2 percent of the kids I surveyed indicated that they didn't have a TV at home, and only 4 percent said they didn't watch TV on a daily basis. Seventy percent of homes now have access to cable TV. Although one in three kids didn't use computers at home, schools in the United States (along with Australia and Latvia) have the highest student-to-computer ratio, at 5:1.[2] It's possible that kids who don't use computers at home use them in the classroom, but they're definitely doing more than just homework. Use of e-mail, instant messaging (IM), and the Internet increased with each grade. Seventh- and eighth-graders spent twice as much time on e-mail and the Internet than did third- and fourth-graders. Overall, middle school kids spent more than four times as many hours watching TV and computer monitors as they did completing homework. It's no wonder they talk much more about media stars, violence, and sex than they do about social studies or science.

IM Supersedes the Old Telephone

While middle school kids are still using the telephone and now cell phones to talk with friends, according to a report in *TIME for Kids,* middle schoolers prefer IM for chatting with friends.[3] IM lets them talk to more than one kid at a time. It's also playful and creative; kids can change fonts and colors for emphasis and even add a variety of smiley faces called emoticons to express their feelings. According to the Pew Internet and American Life Project, one in three kids surveyed said they use IM every day.[4] "IM Conversation" and "Cracking the IM Code" on pages 86 and 88, which were prepared by my grandkids, Ben, Dan, and Rachel, show a sample of the coded dialogue kids are using online. IM's shortcut spellings and symbols are leading many teachers and parents to worry about children's grammar and spelling.

There's tacit agreement among kids that IM language is secret. Notice how quickly they change the screen when you enter the room. Kids in this generation guard their IM messages much like you guarded your telephone calls when you were growing up. It adds a tone of conspiracy, and it's ironic that kids who can't remember their homework or their foreign language vocabulary are able to easily memorize a long list of abbreviations and symbols that most parents struggle to decipher.

(continued on page 88)

IM Conversation

CurlyGirly1919: Hey ken!

sportskid6597: Hi Amanda

sportskid6597: supCurlyGirly1919: uhh n2m u

sportskid6597: nm

sportskid6597: hey did u start ur essay for ms b. yet

CurlyGirly1919: Yea im almost dun

CurlyGirly1919: its long

sportskid6597: cool

CurlyGirly1919: did u start

sportskid6597: im not even near done

CurlyGirly1919: oOo!!!!! thats not good

CurlyGirly1919: :-(

sportskid6597: still 5 more paragraphs

CurlyGirly1919: brb!

sportskid6597: k

CurlyGirly1919: k im back

sportskid6597: o

sportskid6597: what took u so long

CurlyGirly1919: sorry i had to feed my dog

sportskid6597: o

sportskid6597: loil

sportskid6597: *lol

sportskid6597: i c

CurlyGirly1919: So whatd u get on ur science quiz?

sportskid6597: not sure

CurlyGirly1919: o we got ours back today

CurlyGirly1919: i got a 98

sportskid6597: Mr. Balie didnt give us r's back yet

sportskid6597: nice job

CurlyGirly1919: oo

CurlyGirly1919: thanx

CurlyGirly1919: !

sportskid6597: :-D

CurlyGirly1919: do u know saras sn

sportskid6597: nope

sportskid6597: sorry

CurlyGirly1919: o cus i needed to ask her a questin

CurlyGirly1919: I g2g

CurlyGirly1919: bye

sportskid6597: ask Joe

sportskid6597: o

sportskid6597: ok

CurlyGirly1919: cya 2morro!

sportskid6597: l8er

CurlyGirly1919: ttyl

sportskid6597: bye

Cracking the IM Code

NM = not much

JC = just chillin'

SOS = same old stuff

NMU = not much, you?

TTYL = talk to ya later

TTFN = ta ta for now

POS = parent over shoulder (don't talk)

9 = parent over shoulder

CTN = can't talk now

BRB = be right back

SUP = what's goin' on?

GGBB = gotta go bye bye

G2G = got to go

GG = gotta go

BBL = be back later

BBS = be back soon

NMJCSOSED = not much just chillin' same old stuff every day

LOL = laughing out loud

JK = just kidding

ROTFL = rolling on the floor laughin'

The Mini Screen: What's That Ringing?

As popular as IM is, it's still cool to talk on the phone—as long as it's a cell phone. Cell phones now include mini screens, which offer games, text messaging, and even e-mail. Kids persuade their parents to get them cell phones with all kinds of excuses. "What if there's an emergency? You want me to be safe, don't you, Mom?" "What if my plans change? I could just call!" or "I could've told you I'd be late if I had a cell phone." All of these are justifiable reasons for a kid to have a cell. Furthermore, service providers now offer affordable family calling plans, so getting a cell phone for your tween can seem like a relatively good investment.

Before you sign on the dotted line though, you should address the responsibilities associated with having a cell phone. While cells may indeed be handy for keeping in touch with your kids and vice versa, they won't be worth the money if your kids ignore the call waiting signal when you're trying to reach them. If their primary goal in getting a cell phone is to do more chatting or text messaging with their friends, there's probably no harm in it, provided it doesn't interfere with school or homework and their chatting isn't excessive. Many schools have prohibited cell phone use in the building because it disrupts class time. Not only that, but camera phones also pose the possibility that kids will take inappropriate photos, especially in locker rooms. If you don't absolutely trust your kids, however, cell phones become even riskier because they are the easiest way for kids who sell drugs to contact kids who want to buy them.

The Big Screen

Although I didn't survey the middle schoolers about movies, the kids in my focus groups had lots to say about what they learned from the big screen. Most kids acknowledged that their parents used ratings to guide what movies they could see. Some kids accepted guidelines from their parents, but others fought their parents on their use of ratings, and still others managed to see inappropriate movies without their parents knowing. Some told me that their parents were stricter than actual ratings, preventing them from seeing PG-13 movies even after they turned 13. Others bragged that their parents ignored ratings altogether and that they could watch even R-rated movies.

There's no scientific doubt that the violence and sex kids see in movies affects their feelings, actions, and activities. (I'll discuss this further in the next chapter.) Here are some suggestions for helping you to determine if certain movies are appropriate for your middle school child.

- Respect the rating scale as a guide for your children.
- Be willing to make an exception only if you believe the film is especially worthwhile and your children are close to the age requirements.
- Talk to other parents so you can stay united in allowing your children to see only those movies within rating guidelines.

- Use the Internet to find out more about the movies you're letting your children see. (See Web sites in Appendix.)
- Attend movies with your children so you can gauge their responses and explain things they don't understand.
- Be selective in your choices so your children will also learn to be selective.

Home Alone

My parents trust me and let me stay home by myself after school. They let me go to the movies as long as there's not extremely bad words or a whole bunch of violence.

6th-grade boy

The time kids spend viewing screens may also be time they're spending alone. In fact, kids are spending plenty of time home alone these days, and its impact is damaging. My survey gave kids the opportunity to indicate the number of hours they spent alone each day, though it's uncertain how they interpreted *alone*. They could have defined *alone* as spending their time independently and not socializing with peers (but with adults present), or they could have been totally alone (with no adults around). It's healthy, normal, and a sign of independence for middle school children to be spending *some* time alone, with or without adults nearby. However, it's somewhat worrisome that the kids I surveyed spent an average of 1.8 hours alone each day. The amount of time kids spent alone increased with grade level, with children as young as grade three spending 1.5 hours alone and eighth-graders spending 2.2 hours alone.

Feelings of confidence and the quality of family relationships were the most powerful predictors of how much time kids from my study spent alone. Children with below-average self-confidence spent more time alone (2.8 hours), as did children with below-average family relationships (3 hours). Feelings of intelligence also had an influence. Children who considered themselves to have above-average intelligence spent less time alone

(1.8 hours) than did children who considered themselves to have below-average intelligence (2.3 hours). In all of these cases, it was evident that the children equated the word "alone" with "lonely" time.

The fact that overweight children spend more time alone shouldn't come as a surprise; many tend to be incredibly lonely. As you'll read in Chapter 11, overweight children watched screens for more hours and were less involved in sports and extracurricular activities than other kids in my study. Spending time alone may even contribute to overweight problems. In a 2003 study, Deborah Vandell, PhD, and her colleagues at the University of Wisconsin, Madison, studied the after-school habits of 191 eighth-graders. The researchers found that the kids who were enrolled in after-school programs were more likely to be doing homework, enrichment activities, sports, or volunteer services and less likely to be eating or watching TV than those not enrolled. This research suggests that the loneliness of the kids who are not involved in activities or the community contributes to overeating. Undoubtedly, the food is comforting. The study also showed the importance of habits—those enrolled in programs were typically unaccustomed to eating during programming and were then less likely to eat at home even on days when they weren't in programming.

After-School Advantages

After-school care seems a healthier alternative to leaving kids at home alone. Consider whether your kids should be in after-school programs or with a neighbor instead of at home alone. Most after-school programs have an incredible amount of work and play activities; you often hear that humming sound of happy involvement when you visit the school. Even if children are indoors, they'll be doing homework or working on crafts, talking, and busy doing things together.

The U.S. Department of Education cites further reasons to avoid leaving kids at home alone. They found that kids in quality after-school programs have better academic performance, behavior, and school attendance, and greater expectations for the future.[5] On the flip side, kids who don't participate in after-school programs are more likely to be involved in violent crime, substance abuse, or antisocial behavior; have poor academic performance; and drop out of school.[6]

As a result of these findings, the national 4-H organization has launched 4-H Afterschool, an after-school program for urban, suburban, and rural school children. 4-H has a longtime national reputation for providing excellence in youth programming. Their expansion to providing after-school programs should facilitate healthy opportunities for kids. Check the Appendix for the Web site of 4-H Afterschool and other after-school programs for kids.

If your children do have to spend time alone after school, make the time productive for them and you. Along with an emergency contact list, leave a list of chores and activities that should be completed before you arrive home, along with occasional parental love notes. Reward your children with special family game nights if they can accomplish their chores. Let them know you appreciate their efforts and that their help affords you the extra time together. Also, be sure to fill the refrigerator with fresh fruits and vegetables instead of stocking your cupboards with junk food. Hopefully, you'll find chores accomplished and your children eating fruits or veggies instead of cookies and chips when you return.

Keep 'em Busy!

Keeping kids busy with wholesome activities is positive for kids in many ways. Perceptions of intelligence, self-confidence, and family relationships seemed to make the greatest difference in how much time kids spent in front of a screen. In all cases, children who perceived their intelligence to be below average devoted more of their time to monitors than children who considered their intelligence to be average or above average. One might assume that the more intelligent kids were spending greater amounts of time on their homework. But as you can see from Figure 5.1, it wasn't homework that diverted these kids from screens. They spent no more time on homework than kids did who had less confidence in their

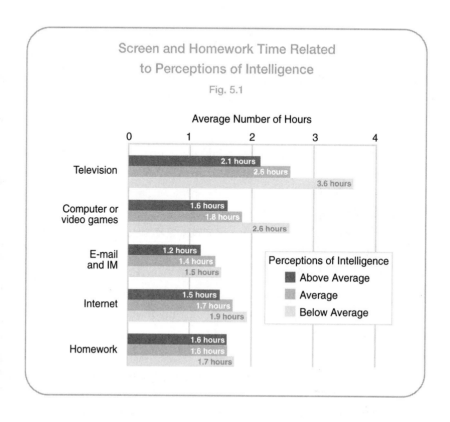

Screen and Homework Time Related
to Perceptions of Intelligence
Fig. 5.1

Average Number of Hours

Perceptions of Intelligence
- Above Average
- Average
- Below Average

Category	Above Average	Average	Below Average
Television	2.1 hours	2.6 hours	3.6 hours
Computer or video games	1.6 hours	1.8 hours	2.6 hours
E-mail and IM	1.2 hours	1.4 hours	1.5 hours
Internet	1.5 hours	1.7 hours	1.9 hours
Homework	1.6 hours	1.6 hours	1.7 hours

intelligence. Kids who described their intelligence as above average had more hobbies and were involved in more sports and school clubs than those who perceived themselves as having average or below-average intelligence. The larger number of school activities in which kids participated was what kept them away from screens. In other words, confident and smart kids are more likely to be busy and active!

Busy Kids Are Confident Kids

Kids displayed a similar pattern of time spent on screens, homework, and activities related to their general self-confidence. Children who indicated they had above-average self-confidence were less likely to be in front of a screen and more likely to be involved in hobbies, sports, and extracurricular activities.

Relationships between intelligence and confidence don't necessarily infer causation. The relationship is much like the proverbial chicken and egg; the study doesn't tell us whether kids' active involvement provided them with confidence and feelings of intelligence, or if children who believed they were intelligent and confident participated in activities instead of deferring to the TV or monitor.

When I encourage kids in my clinic to become actively involved in sports, hobbies, lessons, and clubs, it's apparent that their activities increase their intellectual and general self-confidence, and their involvement often generalizes to improving their academic achievement. Mind you, it's not always easy to convince them to become involved, especially if they lack confidence. The most common excuse kids use for skipping activities is that they think they'll be bored. Once they're involved, however, they halt the excuses and learn to just have fun. I guarantee that your kids' confidence will grow if you get them actively involved. There's no reason to allow kids to choose inactivity.

Family Relationships Affect Activity Too!

Kids' perceptions of the quality of their family relationships are also tied to screen time and activity time. Kids who described their family relationships as below average spent more time in front of a screen and were involved in fewer activities than kids who perceived their family relationships as above average (see Figure 5.2). Oddly enough, those with poor family relationships spent almost twice as much time on homework as kids with average and above-average family relationships. Perhaps television and even homework provided an escape for these children who found themselves lonely and unhappy.

Tweens, Sports, and Exercise

Although the majority of kids I surveyed indicated that they participate in a sport, other surveys have shown a definite lack of involvement among

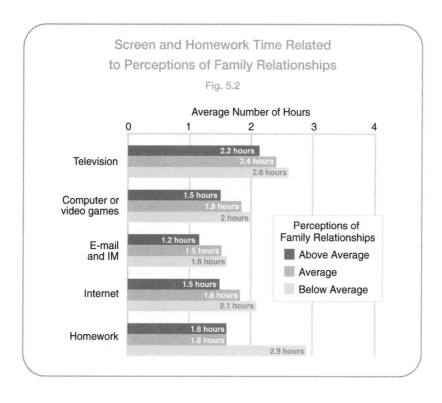

Screen and Homework Time Related
to Perceptions of Family Relationships

Fig. 5.2

Average Number of Hours

0   1   2   3   4

Television
2.2 hours
2.4 hours
2.6 hours

Computer or video games
1.5 hours
1.8 hours
2 hours

E-mail and IM
1.2 hours
1.5 hours
1.6 hours

Internet
1.5 hours
1.8 hours
2.1 hours

Homework
1.6 hours
1.6 hours
2.9 hours

Perceptions of
Family Relationships

■ Above Average
■ Average
□ Below Average

kids in physical activities. In 2002, the Centers for Disease Control and Prevention (CDC) conducted the national Youth Media Campaign Longitudinal Survey of children 9 to 13 years old, along with the kids' parents. When the kids were asked about their participation in organized physical activity in the preceding 7 days, only 38.6 percent of the girls and 38.3 percent of the boys indicated participation.[7] However, they took part in more free-time physical activities (74.1 percent of the girls and 80.5 percent of the boys). Although the percentages of participation were high, children weren't asked how much time they invested in these activities, so we can't be assured they met the surgeon general's recommendation of at least an hour of exercise a day.

Furthermore, a substantial percentage of kids from the CDC survey didn't participate at all in physical activities. When kids were asked what prevented them from taking part, the greatest barriers were expense

(46.6 percent), transportation problems (25.6 percent), lack of parents' time (21 percent), lack of opportunities (20.1 percent), and lack of neighborhood safety (16.1 percent). Of course, these were reasons given by children. We don't know whether they were real or were only excuses for kids who felt too awkward to join in or who would rather sit in front of a screen.

The dramatic difference between the CDC study and my survey, where I found so much more participation in sports (71 percent of girls and 77 percent of boys), is that I asked kids to indicate if they participated in a sport at any time. Every sport has a season, and it may be that some kids who answered the CDC survey participated in a sport that wasn't currently in season, so they didn't include it. Even so, if they participated in one sport or season, they were sitting around or watching TV during much of the rest of the year. Thus, at any one time, a much smaller percentage of kids may have been physically active.

What Parents Can Do: High Fives for Exercise

Children are unlikely to believe that physical activity and exercise are important for them unless they are praised for their athletic skills. It obviously is much more difficult to praise athletic skill when children are poorly coordinated, self-conscious, reluctant to play sports, or fearful of losing. Children in my focus groups frequently mentioned that kids who were awkward or overweight were often laughed at by peers and even gym teachers and coaches.

Encouraging praise for physical activity should start very early, when young children are still oblivious to whether or not they are awkward. If you voice your delight at your child's performance, she'll keep dancing, but if you're disappointed at her lack of gracefulness, she'll feel helpless to do anything about it and will likely drop out. Young children rarely compare their own grace with that of other children; they compare only the compliments they receive. Some parents are so worried that their children aren't as graceful or as well-coordinated as others that they won't enroll them in classes at all, meaning that these kids miss out on important opportunities to learn the skills to play a sport. Sadly, parents continue to refer to their kids as klutzy, clumsy, and awkward, and children internalize those as characteristics; they think they can do nothing about it.

Physical activities such as soccer, gymnastics, dance, and swimming should be introduced early to all kids, but especially to kids who are poorly coordinated or have genetic tendencies toward being overweight. If you missed the opportunity to introduce these activities when your kids were younger, it's not too late. Small classes in dance, gymnastics, or swimming that don't require performances in front of large audiences can entice middle school kids to discover new skills. Even private swim lessons can be found—similar to arrangements for private piano lessons or tutoring. When tweens discover that their activity causes them to improve their coordination, lose weight, or make friends, they'll be more likely to get into the exercise habit. Like tutoring, small group or private classes may actually help your tweens to catch up on skills and develop enough confidence to join a large group class later on.

Some praise is good, but praising kids to an extreme can cause them to feel pressured, or it can even seem unbelievable. Moderate, noncompetitive praise works best. Phrases like "Hey, you're pretty good," "You've got rhythm," "You're really learning," "You hit that ball hard," "Terrific flexibility," "You're running faster," and "What fun you're having" are general but honest and encouraging compliments to keep your kids active. If you can't in good conscience praise your child's performance, perhaps you can at least comment positively on her improvement and effort. You don't need to tell her she's the best dancer, gymnast, or soccer player to keep her active, only that she's getting better. If you overpraise your child and she can't attain the competitive goals you set, she's likely to feel pressured and drop out. Children don't have to be the best at sports, but they should learn to *try* their best.

Parents are busy in their own careers, and attending every sports event their kids play in may not be possible. Your occasional attendance is enough to let your children know you care, and in some ways, your occasional absences may even relieve some pressure for kids who aren't stars. They won't have to be worried about their parents noticing their mistakes, and they'll be happy to come home and brag about the hit, catch, or special play they made. Asking your child about his game without prying into details gives him the chance to brag without feeling the pressure to impress you if the game didn't go too well. Parents can offer a little consolation from time to time, as long as losses aren't taken too seriously.

There's a Sport for Everyone

For children who hit the home runs, score winning baskets, are star ballerinas or gymnasts, or catch a fly ball in the outfield, motivation comes more easily. Many kids are deprived of winning experiences because they have poor coordination, or because their parents assume they lack skill or aren't interested. Parents fear these activities will further damage their children's self-esteem.

It's best for parents to assume that there are sports for all children. With reasonable practice and opportunity, all kids can have winning experiences even if they're only part of a winning team. Remember, you'll have to be sure to provide opportunities for your kids, and that will mean some financial and time commitment on your part.

The Rimm children were told early on that no matter how good they were at an activity, there would always be some kids who were better and, fortunately for them, some who were worse. As long as there are kids who are worse, it's possible for all kids to win, if only occasionally. Fortunately, kids who are worse at one activity may be better at another. More than one child has glumly acknowledged that their team lost every game of the season. Perhaps a losing season now and then builds resilience and teaches kids that they can try again next season.

The popular team sports—baseball, soccer, hockey, and basketball—may not work for your overweight or awkward child. But he or she may be very well-suited to individual pursuits—like swimming, track, tennis, skiing, golf, or karate—which have the advantage of being lifelong sports that can be enjoyed through adulthood. While cheerleading, gymnastics, tumbling, and dance may be gender stereotyped for girls, they can be great for boys, too, since they teach competition and self-discipline. Camping, hiking, biking, and canoeing aren't team sports, but they require teamwork, provide plenty of exercise, and bring families and friends together. These are particularly good fits for tweens who might feel it's too late to join a competitive team sport filled with highly skilled peers.

Your kids aren't required to be passionate about sports in order to participate in them. You may be surprised to find that once they've given a sport a fair chance, they'll be excited to participate. If they stamp their feet and refuse to join, you may not be able to force them. You may have to settle for convincing them to ride their bikes, climb some trees, or walk the dog several times a day. At least that will get your kids actively out and about. But make no mistake about it—walking the dog around the block is not enough exercise for a middle schooler. It's only a start. Don't give up on convincing them to find more-vigorous physical pursuits.

Kids' Favorite Activities

Mostly the boys play baseball, basketball, football, or soccer.
5th-grade boy

Involvement in school activities is important for middle school kids because it keeps them out of trouble and also builds their confidence. The early adolescent years mark a developmental time when kids begin to establish their identities. Participation in areas of interest has the potential for steering kids toward careers, lifelong recreational activities, and fulfilling lifestyles. Nonparticipation has the risk of leaving kids with too much time "just chillin'" without opportunities for building self-confidence and trust in their intelligence.

Plenty of kids from my survey had hobbies (see Figure 5.3 on page 100). Almost three-quarters were involved in at least one sport. More than half the kids were involved in a school club. Quite a few participated in music: 26 percent were in band or orchestra, 20 percent played the piano, 30 per-

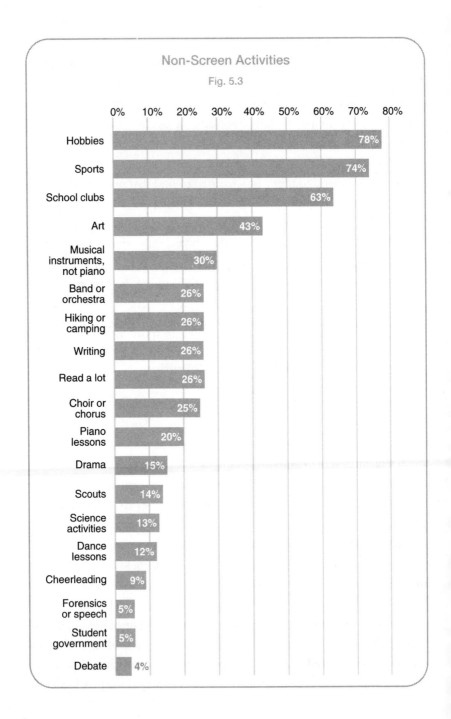

Non-Screen Activities

Fig. 5.3

Activity	Percentage
Hobbies	78%
Sports	74%
School clubs	63%
Art	43%
Musical instruments, not piano	30%
Band or orchestra	26%
Hiking or camping	26%
Writing	26%
Read a lot	26%
Choir or chorus	25%
Piano lessons	20%
Drama	15%
Scouts	14%
Science activities	13%
Dance lessons	12%
Cheerleading	9%
Forensics or speech	5%
Student government	5%
Debate	4%

Are Your Kids' Sports Dominating Your Family Life?

The daily discipline of practicing a sport can encourage both perseverance and healthy exercise, but before you sign your kids up for a sport that requires practicing 5 days a week, you should think seriously about the other activities they could miss. Consider, also, the impact on their academic enrichment and the unscheduled time that kids need for relaxing and having fun with their family. Each family needs to make a personal decision, but it's important to stop and think through all the options rather than let your kids' immediate exhilaration and excitement dominate their childhoods.

Parents need to project into their children's futures to determine if concentrating so much time and energy into sports will serve their children's best interests. Before you invest full time and energy with a sports team, consider how many millions of kids expect to get sports scholarships or aspire to be professional athletes and how few actually qualify. Moderate involvement with sports can be good for all children, but total immersion in sports may indeed obliterate their chances for other learning opportunities.

cent played other instruments, and 25 percent sang in a choir or chorus. Art attracted 43 percent of kids, but schools often teach art as an elective.

Other activities, like Scouts, attracted only a small percentage of students. Although Scouts was a very popular activity for today's parents in their youth, only 14 percent of my surveyed students were involved with the organization. Scout programs continue to provide a variety of interesting and challenging activities in single-sex environments, and I encourage you to persuade your kids to select this activity. Parent leaders can make a huge difference—your volunteering to help lead can benefit many kids' confidence and interests.

Parents' Prodding and Nagging

Many parents who come to my clinic worry that although their children are involved in extracurricular activities, they aren't passionate enough about any one activity. They complain that their talented kids take lessons but don't voluntarily practice without being nagged, or if they do practice on their own, they invest only a minimum amount of effort. Parents often wish that their middle schoolers would immerse themselves in a talent that might eventually lead them to a career.

Although adults may look back to their early adolescence and recall when their talents became more than just a hobby, intense dedication to an activity only rarely shows itself as early as middle school. Most middle school kids still need to be prodded to practice, and very few find their hobbies or extracurricular activities to be intrinsically rewarding. Even when kids seem self-motivated, they're more likely to push themselves for a specific goal, like a performance or winning a contest. It's difficult for kids in middle school to find the initiative to practice just for the sake of improvement.

The earlier maturity that middle school kids exhibit is related primarily to social and sexual behavior; it doesn't seem to generalize to their dedication to activities. Most middle schoolers haven't yet identified their passions. They instead seem to want to dip into many activities, and they're still finding themselves more or less skilled as they explore activities. By high school, many more will discover their specific talents, drop some activities where they feel less capable, and become more intensely involved in their favorite ones. Though some kids become passionate and motivated about their interests in high school, others may take until college or beyond before they actually discover what they love to do.

In the middle grades, parents need to continue to carry a fair amount of the responsibility for guiding kids toward interests and involvement in extracurriculars, and that holds for physical activities as well. Your interest and your praise will lead your kids to healthy involvement, which will eventually permit them to discover their long-term interests, talents, and passions.

The Family That Plays Together Stays Together

I like to read, but my dad taught me to play baseball and basketball, too.

5th-grade girl

From board and card games to backyard baseball and hula hoops, the family that plays together cements a bond that preserves family relationships. Actively playing together rather than merely observing a screen or only passing each other on the way to work establishes an empowering family relationship. Parents can coach sports, Scouts, or activities so that children are able to learn many new skills while spending time together.

Families also communicate more during play. They talk through the rules of the games they play and the contests they organize in the same way that they solve problems about the rules for living life itself. Kids learn about good sportsmanship and competition, being kind to younger siblings, collaborating as a team, and most of all, taking active control of their lives. From their improvement in family games, they learn to think, plan, strategize, laugh at their mistakes, apologize, and persevere. In my own family, board games and Ping-Pong tournaments were regular nightly features while our children were growing up, especially during winter when outdoor activities weren't as feasible.

Families will have to be cautious about being too competitive when playing games, particularly if one child is less coordinated than others. Teaming up the members of your family so that the more coordinated parent allies with the poorly coordinated child may make for a more balanced team and less embarrassment for the child with less skill. That may hold true for younger and older children as well, because older children are likely to be more skilled at many games and activities, even if those activities are not physical. Younger children may need handicap points to encourage them to join in.

Family Fitness

Exercising with the whole family is beneficial for encouraging kids to adopt a healthy lifestyle. From a national study of 700 parents and 372 kids ages 10 to 17, it was found that 69 percent of kids whose parents exercised with them had healthy weights.[8] Additionally, 76 percent of the kids either liked to or would like to exercise with their parents.

If you aren't accustomed to physical activities, your involvement with your kids is long overdue, but it's never too late to start. If you haven't thrown a football or basketball since middle school, don't know how to keep score for tennis or bowling, or hate sports in general, try jogging, skating, walking, or biking. Order pedometers or speedometers to count your miles and chart your distance. Simulate a walk to California or Florida or only to a near city or park by plotting your weekly distance on a map. Establish a family reward system for each person who arrives at a destination, whether he gets there first or last. You can double the credited miles for younger children just as the airlines do for frequent fliers. When weather is a factor, visit a nearby gym or a local YMCA. Perhaps some family friends can join you to make the excursion into a party. Exercising with others for companionship and support will prevent you from backing out at the last minute. The concept that play is exercise and exercise is play will teach children to make exercise a healthy lifelong habit.

Making Changes Together

Schools feel a great deal of pressure to accomplish almost everything for children, from basic skills to enrichment, special education, and counseling. Some activities are dropped from school schedules and from the budget because of overload and financial restrictions. Physical education, sports, and even extracurricular activities have been eliminated or cut back in many schools without complaints from tweens or their parents. Tweens may not consider gym, chorus, or band to be cool, and their parents may be worried about school taxes. In light of the importance of physical education classes, sports, and extracurricular activities, you should attend school board meetings to make your voice heard—especially if your school has cut any of these programs. Your presentation or petition to the board can keep quality activities in your school.

I served on a board of education for 12 years, but it was rare for us to have observers or participants. Occasionally, when a parent would call the board of education office to request that a topic be placed on a meeting agenda, we board members would take notice and be anxious to hear the parent's concern. You may never have attended a board of education meeting before, but you can still be powerful in bringing about healthy change to your school. Your voice will be heard even better if others join with you. Prepare handouts and take the time to review why you believe activities are critical to the well-being of kids.

CHAPTER 6

SEX AND VIOLENCE IN MUSIC, MOVIES, AND MEDIA

If actors in a movie are having sex with someone or smoking, it doesn't necessarily mean the actors do that in real life. They were paid to do that and that's their job. Some kids go out and actually do that stuff because they saw people do it in a movie.

8th-grade girl

Believe it or not, what celebrities do affects the way some kids think. If you think a movie star is so great and you want to be like her when you grow up, you're going to do everything you can to be just like her.

8th-grade girl

If you look at the news, you'll see things that are 10 times worse than PG-13 movies.

7th-grade boy

The violence that's portrayed in music is one reason why there's so much suicidal stuff. The number one reason why teenagers die is suicide, and then it's drugs. Those are all portrayed in music, so it's a really big influence.

7th-grade girl

AS OF 1998, 98 PERCENT OF HOMES with children had television sets, 97 percent had VCRs, 90 percent had CD players, and 89 percent had either personal computers or video game equipment.[1] The use of portable DVD players is on the rise, and kids are able to select almost whatever they wish from the big screen to privately watch on a smaller screen. Teen fashion magazines are readily available at every grocery or drug store counter, with headlines like "476 Ways to Look Sexy for Spring" and "The Sexiest Hairstyles; The Sexiest Jeans." As a result of this media exposure, our kids are being brought up in a culture saturated with sex, violence, and an emphasis on fashion and appearance. Regardless of the limits you set for your tweens, they'll eventually be exposed to this culture through their peers or unintentionally through computers. Parents have a responsibility to talk with their kids about sex and violence in the media.

The Sexual and Violent Appeal of the Media

On TV, people are always having sex with a one-night stand. There's more sex, more cussing, drug dealing, and violence now.

8th-grade boy

Craig Anderson, PhD, and Brad Bushman, PhD, analyzed 202 independent studies of the effects of media violence with a sample of 43,306 participants. They concluded that the relationship between violence in the media and aggressive behavior can be considered in the same light as the relationship between cigarette smoking and lung cancer.[2] The surgeon general's warnings, successful court cases, increased prices and taxes, and many years of public education have finally managed to decrease tobacco use among adults, but one wonders what it will take to decrease media violence, which has such a negative impact on our children and society.

The predominance of celebrities as role models among the kids I surveyed provides further cause for concern. Kids' choices of celebrity role models far exceeded choices of presidents of the United States, religious leaders, scientists, or any other category for adult role models. Forty-one percent of the girls selected men and women as role models whom they could have known of only from publicity on screen and in magazines. Forty percent of the boys selected celebrity role models, but the breakdown showed that the majority of boys looked up to male athletes.

Unfortunately, not all celebrities live ethical lives, and not all professional athletes are good sports; if they were, there would be less to worry about. Because celebrities and athletes are in the limelight, details of their personal and professional lives are sensationalized, and their use of foul language, abuse of drugs, infidelities, and criminal histories make the headlines. These behaviors teach kids that macho men break laws, are disrespectful to women and families, and are bullies, preying on those who are weaker. Kids learn that celebrities are admired and paid extraordinarily well—despite their unscrupulous behaviors.

Kids are powerfully drawn to admire athletes and celebrities. From kids' perspectives, these stars earn incredible salaries, live glamorous lives, and are always the center of attention. In one of my small focus groups of six kids, five were hoping to win the *American Idol* contest and thus achieve celebrity status. One also wanted to be a professional soccer player. The influence of celebrity role models is incredible, drawing kids to imitate the sexuality and violence that they associate with celebrity images.

The violence, aggression, and sexualization of our children will continue unless parents are willing to protest against the media and vote with their wallets. In other words, as long as parents allow kids to buy videos, DVDs, and CDs emphasizing violent and sexual themes, poor role models will thrive. As long as violent and R-rated films rake in cash at the box office, talented young people will deliver sex and violence to our children. The power of the media can be shifted to the hands of parents, but only if parents make their voices heard.

Captivated by Cable

If you haven't seen MTV, you're missing out on what your middle school kids are watching, with or without your permission. MTV is seeping into prime-time television as well. Remember Janet Jackson's flashing episode at the 2004 Super Bowl? Michael Powell, then chairman of the FCC, named it a "classless, crass, and deplorable stunt" and called for an official inquiry into the production that was sponsored by MTV. Although not all MTV projects are bad, too many of them include tweens and teens in extremely sexually provocative dance or drama. Skimpy clothes, piercings, and heavy makeup are pervasive, and although inappropriate language is bleeped out, the bleeps are so frequent that it appears that "cool" tweens curse nearly every word.

Here's a letter I received from a parent who is concerned about the media's negative influence on her daughter.

Dear Dr. Sylvia:

My 9-year-old daughter flirts with her uncle, her dad, and other adult men. They find it very annoying, as she won't leave them alone. I don't believe she's the victim of sexual abuse. I think she idolizes the blatant sexuality in the media and thinks that by flirting she'll gain approval. Do you have any suggestions as to how we can correct her behavior?

My response:

You've asked a very serious question that is, unfortunately, directly related to today's media, although flirtatious behavior should be evaluated carefully because it can be a symptom of sexual abuse. More and more parents are observing the problem you've described, and they have a serious responsibility to at least correct it for their own children, although my wish is that the media be corrected for the sake of society.

This is what I suggest you say to your daughter privately. "I know you love your uncle and your daddy, and they love you, too, but I see you acting toward them like women on TV act toward men. That's called 'flirting,' and it's the way some women act when they want to attract a boyfriend. It isn't the way young girls are supposed to behave, and if you act that way around teenage boys, they might not understand that you're just being friendly. Daddy and Uncle Dan like you to be your real self and not like the actresses on TV." Then you could show her some of the wrong kinds of flirtatious behavior you've seen her do. That would make it very clear to her.

I'd also suggest your daughter not be allowed to watch inappropriate cable television. That may be difficult to monitor, but 9-year-olds should be watching only an hour or so of television a day, and parents should know exactly what their kids are watching.

I was asked a similar question by a mom and dad at my clinic about their 8-year-old daughter, who was forbidden to watch MTV and denied having ever watched it. Sure enough, her parents discovered she was secretly watching MTV at her friends' homes. Very young girls who watch highly sexualized dancing simply assume that girls should act flirtatiously toward men. Boys will copy the macho, aggressive postures of the men in the sexual dancing they observe. Unless parents take time to interpret and teach more-appropriate and natural childlike behaviors, tweens and even younger children will imitate the sexualized interactions they see and assume they represent normal, healthy communications.

Magazine Messages

There are dozens of teen magazines, but almost all of them are directed toward girls. And although these magazines are theoretically targeted to teens, there's no doubt that they encourage and attract tween readers as well. Four best-selling teen magazines that target girls are *Seventeen, Cosmo Girl!, J-14,* and *Teen People.* Headlines from these magazines emphasize fashion, clothes, sex, makeup, celebrities, being hot, and finding boyfriends. Most of the photographs are of stars in sexy poses, and the advertisements show models in flirtatious and suggestive stances. Paradoxically, intermixed with the seductive models and celebrities are photographs of tweens and teens who look wholesome, attractive, and normal, permitting readers to see kids like themselves in juxtaposition to celebrities and models.

What's different in girls' magazines now is the premature emphasis on using sex to attract boys. When your daughter brings home teen magazines—and she will—there will be a lot to discuss with her. Although these magazines contain quizzes, craft projects, activities, stories, and even some good advice, most teen magazines perpetuate the idea that appearance, sexual allure, and having a boyfriend are what's most important for girls.

By valuing quality articles in magazines and discussing your issues with the rest, you can give your daughter a balanced view of the material

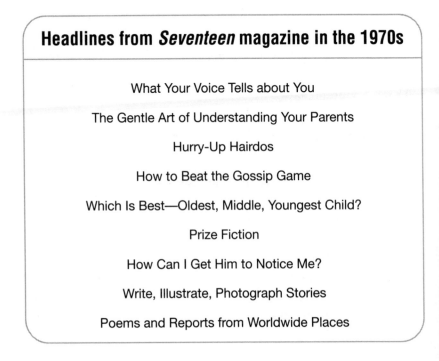

Headlines from *Seventeen* magazine in the 1970s

What Your Voice Tells about You

The Gentle Art of Understanding Your Parents

Hurry-Up Hairdos

How to Beat the Gossip Game

Which Is Best—Oldest, Middle, Youngest Child?

Prize Fiction

How Can I Get Him to Notice Me?

Write, Illustrate, Photograph Stories

Poems and Reports from Worldwide Places

she may be reading. Occasionally reading these magazines isn't likely to be detrimental for girls who already have a confident self-image. However, you should review any magazines your kids read and consider their appropriateness before buying subscriptions. Also, discuss their underlying messages with your daughters so they don't get sucked into pervasive and condescending messages. Make it clear that a girl is much more than a pretty face, thin figure, or provocative fashion showpiece. Remind them that their intelligence, creativity, hard work, and personalities will provide the lifelong opportunities they'll want.

Not all girls' magazines focus on sex, fashion, and boys. *American Girl,* aimed at 9- to 12-year-olds, conveys lots of positive values and messages, and it offers ideas for crafts, hobbies, and developing new interests. *New Moon,* edited by a panel of young girls, is superb for empowering and encouraging girls to be strong and smart and is free of advertisements. Written by teens, *Teen Voices* is instructive for more-mature

Headlines from *Teen* magazine in 2004

The Sexiest Hairstyles; The Sexiest Jeans

On Girls, Geeks, and Going All the Way

How to Be Happy, Calmer, and Hotter

203 Ways to Look Crazy Good!

438 Ways to Meet Tons of Guys

Turn-On Secrets He'll Never Tell You

Get a Better Body in Two Weeks

476 Ways to Look Sexy for Spring

Hot! Sexy-Guy Postcards Inside

tweens. *Girls' Life* is written mostly by adults, but it includes some teen writing as well. Although it includes references to fashion and appearance, it doesn't have the pervasive sexual message that many other magazines do. This magazine is also more appropriate for mature tweens.

The effects magazines have on boys aren't as negative as they are for girls, primarily because boys tend to read magazines that focus on their interests. The only popular, general magazine for boys is *Boys' Life*, which is distributed by the Boy Scouts of America to members of the organization. The magazine includes positive interests, activities, and of course, humor, which seems to keep boys interested. *Sports Illustrated, Sports Illustrated for Kids*, and other specific sports magazines encourage boys' admiration of athletes—for better or worse, depending on their heroes of choice. Other interests like music, photography, computers, fitness, video games, science, travel, and cars are targeted by magazines like *Popular Science, Popular Mechanics, DRUM!, Popular Photography,* and *National Geographic*. Magazines geared both for boys and for girls, like *Junior Scholastic* (distributed in schools) and *National Geographic Kids,* stress education and teach kids about science, math, and social studies. The Appendix lists several more magazines that may intrigue your tweens.

The Lowdown on Logging On

Middle schoolers are often much more Internet savvy than their parents are. You may feel out of the loop, especially since computers and the Internet constantly change. Kids are usually willing to show you the ropes, but you may not be able to keep up with their instruction. This may be because they zip through the steps, showing off their expertise. However, they also may be reluctant to fill you in too much, knowing that your newfound knowledge could infringe on their privacy or access to Web sites.

What's Popping Up?

Incredible frustration best describes my feelings on the occasions when, despite all blocking attempts, Internet pop-ups and search results tell me how to have "the biggest penis" or "the longest-lasting erection." I wonder how young boys feel when they read such unsolicited messages. Do they think they have to be studs? If late-maturing boys see these ads, do they question their own sexual competence? I hope that by the time this book is published, pop-ups will be under better control, but right now, even with pop-up blockers, many continue to invade the screen.

Junk mail advertising Viagra or pornographic sites is just as horrendous. Tweens who are searching the Internet to understand their sexuality likely stop to study and interpret what these ads mean to their own experiences and relationships. The advertising world is urging them to rush into sex, whether they're ready or not, stealing their innocence and naïveté.

Pornographic Web Sites

In June of 2000, the National Center for Missing and Exploited Children (NCMEC) reported that within the previous year, one in four children had unwanted exposure via the Internet to pictures of naked people or people having sex.[3] There's no way of knowing how many more children actually visit pornographic sites intentionally, since few households (only 34 percent, according to NCMEC) used filters or blocking software on their computers.

While researching my book *Rescuing the Emotional Lives of Overweight Children,* I used the Internet search engine Google.com for accessing information on overweight teens. I typed in "fat teens" only to see a long list of pornographic sites with headings like "They're Hot, They're Horny, They're Huge! Explore all the woman these women have to offer." This caption was mild compared to most, which I feel embarrassed to repeat on this page. What would happen to a naive overweight tween who did such a search? Overweight kids struggle with so much already, without having to view Web sites parading them as pornographic prey.

Parents may think filtering software for computers is unnecessary because they trust their kids, but even trusted children can be drawn into these sites. Pornographic sites are like a sport magazine's swimsuit issue that boys sneak looks at out of curiosity. Innocent kids are sucked in by pornography's sexual imagery. While these images may disappear from the computer screen, it takes much longer for them to disappear from your tween's brain. The repeated visuals will provide either premature sexual stimulation or disgust, depending on the images and how they affect a particular young person. A child may be hesitant about discussing the experience with an adult for fear of punishment. While kids may ask their friends about what they've seen, the resulting discussions may only worry kids further.

At the very least, parents need to provide filtering controls on their home computers. More than 30 million children under 18 in the United States use the Internet, and this number will only increase in the future.[4] If you're not certain how to install blocking devices, your computer store consultant can help you, or your computer-savvy kids can show you. Taking a proactive approach will emphasize to your kids your determination to protect everyone in the family from viewing inappropriate Web sites.

The Risks of Sexual Solicitation

Prior to the year 2000, one in 33 children was sexually solicited via the Internet.[5] One in 17 children was threatened or harassed.[6] Solicitors aggressively pursued children by requesting to meet them, calling them, or sending them mail, money, or gifts. It's critical to stress to your kids the importance of not giving out their real names, addresses, or telephone numbers to protect their safety while online. Kids should choose appropriate screen names, avoiding any that sound sexy or inviting to predators. "Sexy Sarah" or "Mac Daddy" is an open invitation to trouble. It's also important that kids know to tell their parents about any e-mail or message board content that appears personally or sexually threatening so that it can be reported to the police. Sad to say, predators abound.

The Songs Kids Sing

Kids make fun of the country music I listen to; they just like rap and rock. Rap music has bad language, and somewhere along the line, kids'll start using that language too.

> 8th-grade girl

Most kids today believe, as kids always have, that the music lyrics they sing, dance to, and watch acted out on screen will have absolutely no impact on them, except to provide relaxation, fun, and laughter. Song lyrics from popular artists show clear ties between lust, violence, and sex. Parents should become aware of the works their children are listening to and singing. For example, in a popular song titled "Kim," by Eminem, the word *fuck* is repeated seven times. *Bitch* is repeated five times. Hate and love are paired continuously. A 4-year-old boy is described as dead with a slit throat. A woman is heard choking and is told to bleed. All this is within one short and horrible verse.

The word *bitch* is so common in current music that you'd think the women's movement had never existed, yet many adolescents aren't bothered by the insults. Girls don't protest—they may be used to hearing it, or they lack enough gumption to express their concerns for fear it will harm their popularity.

According to a study that was published in 2001, violent lyrics increase aggressive thoughts and feelings in young adults.[7] The Recording Industry Association of America insists on the right to free expression and only voluntarily labels CDs that contain extreme profanity and sexual lyrics, but they don't label albums that contain sex, violence, and strong language. These CDs need to be classified, since parents can't take the time to listen to every CD their kids buy. Reasonable labeling, at least, permits parents to set boundaries for their kids.

I urge you to make it clear to your kids that they aren't allowed to buy inappropriate music, even with their own money. While there's little chance you'll be able to control all of your kids' access to music, especially on the Internet or at friends' homes, they may at least listen with the understanding of the impact lyrics can have on them. Furthermore, kids are less likely to listen to violent and sexual music if they don't own those types of CDs. Review and discuss lyrics with your kids and help them understand that sexual and violent lyrics numb kids' emotions, spread aggression, and represent terribly unhealthy values and emotions.

The Real Influence of the Reel World

Celebrities have always been magnets to kids. However, cable TV's expansion of the sexuality and violence portrayed by these celebrities causes serious endangerment to our children. The television and motion picture industry proclaims that the "reel world" only mirrors real-world violence and sexuality, but former chairman of the FCC Reed Hundt disagrees: "If a sitcom can sell soap, salsa, and cereal, then who can argue that TV violence cannot affect to some degree some viewers, particularly impressionable children?"[8]

Balancing Your Kids' Screen Time

Television sets should be located in rooms with full family access and shouldn't be turned on merely for background noise. Watching television should be a family activity. Kids shouldn't watch TV in their bedrooms in order to fall asleep or to entertain themselves when they can't sleep. Kids who get in the habit of watching TV during the night become "night people"—they stay awake watching TV even when their parents are asleep. They then don't function very well at school during the day. When parents tell me their kids feel entitled to a TV in their bedrooms because their parents have one in theirs, I recommend that parents respond with "When you're a responsible adult, you too can have a TV in whatever room you wish." Computers should also be placed in common areas. It's important for parents to know what kids are viewing online but without kids feeling as if their parents are snooping.

Television and the Internet can be overstimulating, hypnotic, and addictive, and they can cause children to have trouble concentrating in school, where teachers don't provide background noise. While children can learn a lot from TV and the Internet, being hypnotized by a screen won't help them build confidence, find their identities, become interesting young people, or burn calories. Here are some helpful guidelines for you and your kids to follow to monitor screen time.

- Keep computers and television sets in family-accessible rooms and not bedrooms.
- Limit TV time and computer use to 2 hours total each day.
- Don't watch television during family meals.
- Limit programming to that intended for the whole family.
- Spend time watching movies and TV with your kids so you can discuss and explain things they see.
- Set and enforce guidelines for cable channels.
- Don't leave the television on just for background noise.
- Enforce rating guidelines for video games, movies, and videos.
- Make exceptions to rating guidelines only if you're certain your kids can handle the content.
- Use your children's computers intermittently so you're aware of what they're seeing.

If you follow these guidelines, you can surely make occasional exceptions when world events, sports specials, or a particular film or dramatic production invites a little extra screen time. Your own family values will guide you in setting limits, so it's important that both parents talk through those guidelines and stay united in enforcing them.

CHAPTER 7

YOUR KIDS ARE WATCHING YOU—AND PLENTY OF OTHERS

I'm like both parents—like my mom because we're both female and my dad because we both like sports.

5th-grade girl

I'm like my mom and my sister. My sister likes computers too, and my mom and I have a lot of the same opinions and morals.

8th-grade boy

I'm more like my dad because we both love art.

7th-grade girl

I'm like both of my parents. My dad has a large sense of humor and he likes interesting facts. I'm like my mom in that we both like to go to plays and enjoy music.

8th-grade boy

I'm like my cousin. He's a police officer and a detective.

6th-grade boy

ADULTS DON'T REALLY HAVE THE CHOICE of being role models or not. Children and adolescents learn about the world by watching adult behaviors and the consequences for those behaviors. Kids may unconsciously copy behaviors that they see being rewarded, or they may avoid behaviors that they see being punished.

Model Parents

Parents are critical role models, but they're certainly not the only adults kids emulate. Students who took my survey were asked to select three of their most admired family role models, and another three people they knew and admired. They were also given the opportunity to name up to two famous

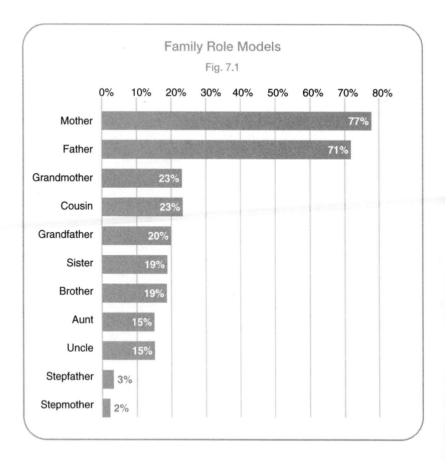

Family Role Models

Fig. 7.1

people they viewed as role models. Figure 7.1 shows that parent role models won out among the family members, although grandparents, cousins, siblings, aunts, and uncles collected their share of admirers. Gender made slight differences as well; girls were more likely to select female role models, and boys were more likely to choose male role models.

While the prevalence of parent role models among kids should encourage parents to construct positive images for their children, parents should also be aware that they're competing for their position with peers, teachers, and other adults. Other than family, peer friends were chosen most often as role models, with teachers and adult friends ranking close behind (see Figure 7.2). Singers, actors, and a host of athletes are also important role models for kids, though some of them may not represent the kinds of values you'd like your kids to embrace. Furthermore, the older kids in my study were less likely to select their parents, teachers, and Scout leaders as role models. Thus, it's important to establish yourself as a role model early on so you can maintain a positive influence on your kids as they get older.

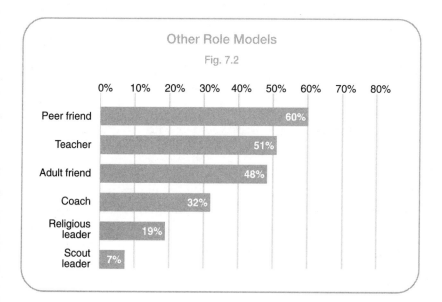

Positive versus Negative Parent Role Models

Fathers and mothers who feel good about their accomplishments can be positive models for their kids. If parents value education and hard work and respect and value each other, their children will see them as supporting partners in a healthy marriage. Positive parent role models help each other grow separately while they build a life together. Neither parent is all-powerful, and their lives fit together like pieces of an interlocking puzzle to make a complete family picture. They have a sense of progress as a family and a solidarity that provides a clear picture of their unity, which can be readily emulated.

So much for the ideal. We know that love, virtue, and achievement rarely continue as flawlessly as this image. Life is full of hurdles, and problematic patterns occur, sometimes deliberately, but more likely without the family's awareness of them. Unfortunately, at varying times, parents may act in ways that negatively influence their children. Recognizing these patterns is the first step toward correcting them and establishing yourselves as achieving, well-adjusted role models.

Remember, you're models for your children only part of the time. The productive work you do in your job and the loving words you say to your spouse in private go unobserved by your kids. However, your kids hear very clearly your tired sighs at the end of the day or the angry demands you make of your spouse. Your first task is to become more aware of *how* and *when* your children observe you. This may feel a bit like playacting, but your kids see you only when you're on your home stage.

Examine the following two scenarios to see if they sound familiar. You may feel a little guilty if you see yourself in these instances and realize that your negative influences could inhibit your children's achievement. By recognizing problem behaviors, however, you can change them. The changes you make may not be all that difficult and could actually make you feel better about yourself.

"I Didn't Like School Either"

School isn't a positive experience for all kids, and you may indeed have some bad memories. In your efforts to empathize with your struggling children, you may think it helpful to share your unfortunate experiences. You may tell of the amusing times you outsmarted your teacher, the pathos of your boredom, your perceived inadequacy of your school's curriculum, or the problems caused by your own underachievement. Although confiding these stories may help you relate to your kids, it also conveys the message that it's okay and to be expected for your kids to outsmart their teachers, be bored with school, or underachieve.

If you've already shared negative stories about yourself, try to undo the damage by reiterating how you turned those problems around. Tell your kids that you hope they won't repeat the errors that complicated your life and made it more difficult. Kids listen more to brief stories you share about yourself than to long discussions or "lectures," so cut down on the latter and give positive, partial views of the former. There's no advantage for either you or your kids in exaggerating your history as an underachieving troublemaker. Though it may seem good material for family humor, if your kids try to surpass your tricks, you won't feel very pleased with yourself for having shared your most mischievous stories.

"I Really Don't Like My Job"

Lazy or disorganized parents are surely inappropriate models, so you'd assume that hardworking, industrious parents must be positive role models. Not necessarily. Overworked parents who come home exhausted, or complain continuously about the stresses of their jobs, the unfairness of their salaries, the unjustness of their bosses, or the job itself model negative attitudes about the world of work. Furthermore, if one parent complains that the other parent works too much, or if either parent doesn't find time for play or pleasure, they're hardly providing a good image of work.

Kids whose parents constantly complain about work will also complain about all the hard work their teachers (bosses) give them. And kids who have parents who work too much will see them as "doing nothing but working" and insist that this certainly isn't the lifestyle they wish to have. They'll say, "Get a life!"—and there may be some relevance to their advice.

An almost certain way to prevent a child from respecting his or her parents is for one parent to complain that he or she hates the other parent's career, or that the career has taken that parent away from the family. If either parent has returned to school for an advanced degree and complains continuously about study overload, or if a parent denigrates a spouse's education as a waste of time, it's very likely the kids will learn to be negative about their school experiences, too.

How Hardworking Parents Can Be Excellent Role Models

How can hardworking parents manage to be positive role models for their kids when their careers consume so much of their family time? Sharing positive work experiences and describing your responsibilities will give your kids a good model to follow. Because it's not possible for most kids to see their parents in the workplace, parents need to talk about their jobs with their kids. To convey an upbeat work image, be enthusiastic, and emphasize the challenge and satisfaction you derive from your career.

It's realistic and honest to admit discouragement, frustration, and failure in your work, but if you always describe your job negatively, there'll be no reason for your kids to be inspired toward effort. They'll see only a negative achievement model, and they'll use it as a rationale for either rejecting their parents as role models or for adopting their parents' unenthusiastic attitudes. They will become antiwork kids and will convince themselves that they don't want to work hard because they prefer a "fun" and happy-go-lucky lifestyle.

I had a very busy lifestyle when my kids were growing up. I returned to graduate school while raising four children, and when my youngest daughter Sara was a teenager, I started my career in psychology. When I returned from a typical 10-hour day to Sara, impatiently waiting for one or both of her parents, I (usually) gathered up all my energy and my positive recollections of the day and greeted Sara with, "You just won't believe what an interesting day I had today." I continued with a description of the latest child I'd helped (no names given, of course), and we shared insights into our cases. I say "our cases" because Sara had learned to share with me her own psychological insights on friends and the kids she babysat for. I was sometimes astonished at Sara's insights of her teenage friends. Sara, who is now a developmental psychologist, always said that she was "born into it."

Many parents aren't happy with their work, but they have no alternatives for earning a livelihood. They may feel as if they're in dead-end jobs, but they still accept their responsibilities. They can't honestly express satisfaction that they've derived from accomplishments. However, that doesn't mean they can't project an image of achievement. Parents can tell their kids about projects they contribute to or share with them the pride they take in being responsible. Parents who arrive at work on time and are committed to performing well on the job are good models for accepting responsibility. If parents haven't had the opportunity to continue their own educations, acknowledging that they may have had more career choices if they had worked harder can encourage kids to study more in school in order to broaden their own opportunities.

Stepparents Count Too!

You may have noted that in Figure 7.1 on page 122, very few children selected stepparents as role models. Stepparents can be appropriate models, but the blending of families makes it challenging for kids to admire them. If the opposition that caused the parents' divorce prevails, kids are more likely to reject stepparents as mentors. If children's birth parents criticize and belittle stepparents, kids will feel guilty about accepting them into their lives. Kids can look to parents as well as stepparents as role models if all the adults involved respect each other, which certainly provides a more satisfactory relationship for kids.

Unfortunately, a parent's jealousy of a spouse's remarriage may prevent kids from admiring a stepparent. In a blended family, it's better if the birth parent becomes the chief disciplinarian while the stepparent works hard to bond with the kids through positive experiences. This can help kids move beyond the resistance they feel. With time and acceptance, parents and stepparents can share in united discipline.

Role Models among the Relatives

My grandma and I are a lot alike. We like to talk about art.
I'm like my uncle, too. He was a really good artist. I don't
talk to my dad that much 'cuz he's working all the time.
When I'm in the car with my dad, we both want to listen to
music, but I can't take his music. I just laugh at it.

7th-grade boy

Other relatives, including grandparents, uncles, aunts, and cousins, may be very good role models. Time spent together during the holidays, or conversations shared over the phone, can instill positive encouragement. Even deceased grandparents can be good role models for children. Stories about a grandparent's achievement, perseverance, or risk taking can inspire kids to live up to their standards. Some kids recall inspirational stories about a grandparent for whom they were named but never met.

Teachers Inspire Many Young People

Teachers are especially valuable as models. Kids often report the special admiration they feel for a particular teacher. They may spontaneously choose one as a model. It takes a very special teacher to win the admiration of a student, however, and only exceptional teachers invest the time and effort to guide youths who identify with them. Teachers can make positive differences to hundreds of kids during their careers, although their day-to-day routines and responsibilities may prevent them from sensing the impact they're making. Kids hardly ever thank their teachers for their efforts, because it may be years before they understand and appreciate a teacher's impact on their lives. Below is a letter I received from a school nurse on her observations of teachers who cared about and influenced kids.

Dear Dr. Sylvia:

I was touched by the principal, who's dedicated to helping his school's children achieve and improve behaviorally and academically. As a school nurse, I, too, work with abused children coming from families impacted with the pain of alcoholism, incest, and drug addiction.

Please be assured, principal of these children, you and the educators in your school do, and will, compensate for the parents. Because of their addiction, pain, and lifestyle priorities, they are not providing their children with the love and direction they need.

I've worked with a vice principal who treated parents of these children with respect as they entered his office. I've seen their anger dissipate and their defensive attitudes quelled, thus the parents became open to listening. A tiny seed was planted.

I've witnessed a shop teacher put his hand on a student's shoulder and say, "You did a good job." I've watched his hyperactive students become calm. I've seen their sense of pride from realizing that some human being noticed that what they did was of value. That child, each time this teacher did this, knew that he could succeed at something, someday.

I've worked with a guidance counselor who transcended the scars placed on these hurting children. I watched him give them back their dignity.

I've worked with a teacher of the emotionally disturbed who supplied these children day after day with peace, consistency, structure, fairness, and care.

Dr. Sylvia, will you tell these "inspiring educators" and every principal to never doubt what an impact they and their staffs are making on the children who enter their buildings? They have earned the title Teacher.

In almost everyone's life, even when there are wonderful parent role models, there are important teachers who positively influence kids and build their skills and confidence. For children without good family role models, teachers are even more important for filling that void. In a society where the structure of marriage is so precarious, positive and caring teacher models become even more critical to children.

The Value of Volunteering

Community leaders can also be good role models. Adults who volunteer to help with Scouts, 4-H, church youth groups, or athletic coaching can make their time commitment more valuable to kids if they understand the importance of role model identification. As adults take a special interest in young people, those adults become effective models. Although communities frequently find a scarcity of volunteers to lead youth, those who accept these opportunities can make major contributions for kids searching for role models. If you serve in the significant role of a youth leader, and you communicate the value of achievement, you can be pivotal in the lives of many kids.

Role Models from History and Biographies

I'd like to be Ben Carson. He's a surgeon in Boston that works on tumors. I read a library book about him.

6th-grade boy

Fiction, history, films, and biographies can provide effective models for many kids and are rich with descriptive material to inspire youth toward perseverance, education, and heroism. When kids identify similarities between their lives and those of their heroes, and when they learn how those achievers met failure and overcame it, they will begin to understand the pairing of struggle and success. Seeing the extensive time that heroes invested in work and practice will help kids to understand the amount of effort required to accomplish serious goals. Identifying with such heroes should help young people to realistically assess their own efforts and talents and can provide positive models for success. In guiding kids to adopt heroes as models for achievement, parents can emphasize the values that they hope kids will choose to follow. For example, biographical discussions of Olympic athletes usually emphasize perseverance and resilience—positive qualities that can encourage your own kids.

Sibling Role Models

I'm like my older brother. He's gifted in a lot of ways, too.

5th-grade boy

Older siblings can be effective role models. Younger kids typically admire their older siblings, and it takes only a small step beyond admiration to build that important role model identification. However, when parents make comparisons deliberately, they'll quickly be told, "Don't always compare me to my sister/brother." And if the older siblings have not yet managed to focus their own lives, identification with them can bring problems.

Parents have good reason to worry that a younger sibling will follow in the footsteps of a rebellious adolescent who has dropped out of high school or used drugs. If this is the case, parents should help the younger sibling realize the mistakes of the older sibling by pointing to the negative consequences of rebellious behavior. For example, parents could say, "Drugs have prevented your brother from playing sports and from getting a college education. If he hadn't used drugs, he would have been a really good basketball player and would now be a sophomore in college. He could look forward to a happier life."

Whether the older sibling is a positive role model or a negative one, it's important for parents to remember that the older sibling appears to be very powerful to a younger sister or brother. With my own kids, I remember younger brother Eric asking wistfully how his older brother David knew how to do everything so well. Eric is no longer quite so awed by his older brother, but they remain close friends.

The Power of Peers

Peer models have a greater influence on kids if the kids haven't already identified with adult role models. Peer imitation can be problematic when the peer group is antischool and antiparents. Ironically enough, even negative peer groups like gangs can occasionally provide good role models for some young people. Here's a case example.

Reverend Frost was a leader in the African American community and was certainly an appropriate role model for the kids he was trying to help. He was an authority on gangs because he had been a gang member as a kid. As he discussed his own childhood role models, he explained that he had watched one of his friends, with whom he had always felt competitive, leave the gang and go on to college. When he realized his former friend had completed his first year of college successfully, he was encouraged to try college himself. Thus, this initially negative peer was the first model who inspired him to leave the gang and go to a very different lifestyle and educational opportunity.

Positive peer groups that provide a pro-academic message and encourage enthusiasm for study and learning make parenting easier. Peers may also serve as models for appropriate social behaviors, although it's difficult to point out another young person for imitation to a tween without engendering competition and resentment. If your child already admires a positive peer, however, you can point out that there are great advantages in learning from good friends.

Magical Role Models

Sometimes, the models kids choose may not be appropriate. Kids may choose TV stars, sports heroes, and multimillionaires about whom legends of miraculous and magical success are woven. They imitate these unrealistic models in their dress, musical preferences, and fantasies. "Real people" seem inadequate by comparison, because they're not as prestigious as the stage and sports idols who seem to have made it to success effortlessly. Kids tend to select these idols as models without any understanding of the process by which the person has achieved fame, and without any conception of the many thousands who have fallen by the wayside in competition. They'd rather fantasize about the miraculous discovery of their own hidden talent than invest in the more mundane efforts that it would take to build their skills toward a realistic goal.

Hero fantasy is not harmful in itself, if those heroes lead exemplary lives. When hero worship becomes a substitute for effort, however, or when heroes use drugs or commit crimes, it can prevent kids from learning necessary skills that lead to real-life success. Fantasy then becomes an excuse for avoiding responsibility, abusing drugs, or harming others.

Avoiding Negative Role Models

Unfortunately, when children are underachieving, have poor self-concepts, or are oppositional, they're likely to be attracted to inappropriate models who share the same experiences and oppositional attitudes. You may recall from earlier in this chapter that sixth-, seventh-, and eighth-graders in my study were less likely to choose their parents and teachers as role models and more likely to select other adults. Thus, young adults who may not have established their own identities, or who may be confused about their own direction in life, may be readily available models for underachieving middle schoolers. Because these young adults are older and appear more experienced, powerful, and exciting, middle schoolers are quite attracted to them. Young adults may think they can help these kids, and the helping process gives them a sense of self-importance. However, because neither truly has a sense of realistic direction, they may flail and fail together.

How can you avoid these negative identifications? Protect your kids from the vacuum that evolves when potentially appropriate models no longer see anything positive in the child. When parents and teachers continually criticize a child, the child won't select these critics as models. Avoid this negative cycle, so often generated by rebellious adolescents. Be a coach and search for the positive in your kids. They'll be more likely to follow your guidance and select environments where they'll be surrounded by appropriate role models. Also, if you know other adults who share your child's interests and are likely to be good role models for him, encourage your child to seek them out as mentors. For example, if your daughter is interested in architecture, you may know an architect who would meet with her. A child interested in animals could volunteer at a pet shelter and meet a good role model who works there. It's natural for maturing kids to look beyond their homes for other adults to provide inspiration, and fortunately there are many successful, happy adults who are willing to give their time to mentoring kids.

How You Become a Role Model

I do homework after school at home, and my dad comes home first, so I get a chance to talk to him more, so I'm like him.

6th-grade boy

Social learning theory tells us that three variables—nurturance as a special warmth by an adult, similarities between a child and an adult, and perceptions of an adult's power—increase the likelihood that children will emulate the behaviors they observe. Thus, people who kids perceive as powerful, like presidents, senators, business leaders, teachers, athletes, doctors, celebrities, film stars, and Nobel Prize winners, all have the potential to influence middle schoolers. Kids are even more likely to look up to role models if they see shared similarities, talents, or interests.

For girls, there remains a paucity of female world leaders, prominent business executives, or Nobel Prize winners. Although there is an increasing number of prominent women in all fields, media and film provide the most powerful and obvious role models for girls. For a girl who sings well or gets a part in a school play, it's only a small leap for her to believe she will be the next Britney Spears or Julia Roberts. Perhaps that helps to explain the overwhelming number of girls who viewed their future as being a media or film star. While that is slowly changing, you may need to help your daughter find positive, professional role models other than celebrities for inspiration.

Stop and think about what your kids hear you say about your career, education, and chores. Don't get in the rut of repeating the same complaints. Optimism and resilience are contagious and cause you to seem powerful. Your kids are more likely to learn these qualities if you press yourself to act those parts. Furthermore, the more you act, the more natural the optimism will feel.

To maintain your optimism, you'll need to set priorities. Parents, together or singly, simply cannot find enough time to accomplish all the tasks that could be handled by a full-time homemaker. But there's no need to feel guilty. If you bake cookies with your kids every 3 months instead of every week, they'll still experience the fun, warmth, and good taste of cookie dough and see you as a parent who has many talents.

You can also help encourage your kids' identification by pointing out similarities between them and you. "When I was your age, I remember having some of those very same feelings" may be the sincere statement that ties a child to an adult. For a child, this makes the grown-up human and approachable and encourages the child to identify with that adult. It's different from the lectures of "When I was a kid . . ." or pointing out how "today's kids are spoiled," which my focus groups resented. If you emphasize your differences instead of similarities, your children will be less likely to see you as a role model.

As I pointed out earlier, the variables that lead to unconscious copying of an adult model are nurturance, similarities, and power. When deliberately selecting role models, similarities between an adult and child are helpful; however, it's certainly wiser to look for *positive* similarities.

Many parents tell me they don't want to impose their own values on their kids or expect them to follow in their footsteps. They want their kids to be free to select their own interests, values, and careers. That's partially faulty reasoning because giving your child such a strong message to *not* follow in your footsteps makes sense only if you're unhappy with your life. If you have a good career and good relationships in your life, and your kids share your genetics, talents, and interests, why insist that they find their own *different* direction? For some kids, that may rule out what may have been their first-choice interest and present them with an absence of a role model when you could have been such a good one.

Of course, it isn't appropriate to pressure your kids to follow in your footsteps if they have entirely different interests and talents than you do, but if you share similarities, what a wonderful opportunity your kids have to learn from you. Parents who have their acts together and go about influencing their children in "friendly ways" can be the very best role models for their children.

⚠ WORRIES

CHAPTER 8

BULLYING IN OUR SCHOOLS

If you're a foreign kid and come from a different country, they tease you and call you Japanese or Chinese. I'm from Korea. Kids make fun of my language and culture and say I'm weird.

5th-grade boy

A fifth-grade boy came up to me once on the bus and slapped me and called me a bitch for no reason. First I laughed it off, but he had no right to do that. I kicked him and stuck out my feet as he was running by.

7th-grade girl

My parents are from Lebanon, but I was born here. When I tell someone my name, they say, "Do you like Osama Bin Laden?" or "You're in league with Saddam Hussein." It doesn't make me feel good.

6th-grade boy

MOST MIDDLE SCHOOLERS FEEL SAFE most of the time. Based on an analysis of the rate of violent crimes committed during and after school hours, school hours are the safest time of day for adolescents.[1] In their 2002–03 survey, researchers for the National Parents' Resources Institute for Drug Education (PRIDE) asked the question, "While at school, have you been afraid a student will hurt you?" About three-quarters of students, ranging from grades 4 to 12, reported that they had never been afraid.[2, 3]

Despite school hours reportedly being the safest time of day for kids, PRIDE surveys revealed that there was still a sizeable group of students at all grade levels who *did* feel afraid in school. Furthermore, it was the middle school years when most children felt afraid. Bullying and violence underlie most fears in our schools. Understanding bullying, helping children who are bullies, and protecting children who are victims of bullying is the important goal of this chapter.

How Prevalent Is Bullying?

According to Tonja Nansel, PhD, and colleagues, about 30 percent of 6th- through 10th-graders surveyed by the World Health Organization (WHO) in 1998 had been involved in bullying, with the frequency of bullying higher for 6th- through 9th-graders than 9th- through 10th-graders.[4] Thirteen percent of the students polled had bullied others, 10.6 percent had been victims of bullying, and another 6.3 percent had both been bullies and been bullied by others. Boys' attacks were more physical (fighting, slapping, kicking, and pushing), while girls tended to use verbal or psychological forms of bullying, such as name-calling, teasing, spreading rumors, making sexual comments, and rejecting others. The boys were more likely to bully girls and boys, while girls usually bullied only other girls. A British study of 23 schools identified boys as being both perpetrators and victims of bullying more often than girls.[5]

Adolescence is typically a greater time of conflict than middle childhood or adulthood, but bullying goes beyond simple conflict. Dr. Nansel and her colleagues classify bullying as behavior that is intended to harm or disturb, occurs repeatedly, and involves a more powerful person or group attacking a less powerful one.[6] Behaviors may be verbal, like name-calling or threats; physical, like hitting, pushing, or kicking; or psychological, like rumors or shunning others. The most frequent type of bullying identified by the WHO survey was related to belittling looks or speech. Following in order of frequency were sexual comments or questions; rumors; hitting, slapping, or pushing; and finally, though much less common, belittlement based on race or religion.

During the middle school years, when kids are particularly concerned about popularity, appearance, and sexuality, bullying undoubtedly threatens not only those who are victims, but onlookers as well. So if kids hear a classmate being taunted about being fat, dumb, or gay, they might worry that they also appear fat, dumb, or gay and may be the next to be ridiculed. Although there have always been bullies, kids in my focus groups believe that there are more now than ever before and that they're also a lot meaner.

Characteristics of Bullies

The troublemakers determine who's in and who's out.
They're tougher and meaner and confident that they're the
best. The most extreme ones are bullies. They bully kids who
are short or fat or get all A's.

6th-grade boy

Surprisingly, most kids who bully others tend to be confident and have plenty of self-esteem.[7] They have little difficulty making friends, but those friends usually share pro-bullying attitudes and problem behaviors, including smoking and drinking.[8] Bullies tend to get into more trouble at school and do poorly in their academic work. They often come from homes where their parents provide little emotional support or involvement and where discipline styles tend to be either extremely permissive or excessively harsh.[9]

There is a strong and frightening relationship between bullying other students and experiencing legal and criminal problems later on as an adult. One study found that 60 percent of the people surveyed who were considered bullies in grades six through nine had at least one criminal conviction by age 24.[10]

Although parents and educators should understand the need for bullying intervention, it's also important to recognize that even some perfectly healthy kids occasionally get caught up in bullying behavior. When this happens, it's necessary for parents to label the behavior as bullying and be sure to correct it, but they shouldn't assume an incident or even two predicts a future of violence and crime.

Characteristics of Victims

When I got into the gifted school, I told my friends at my apartment house. They started pushing me around and calling me "nerd" and stuff. They say I'm weak because I'm smart.

5th-grade boy

Kids who are victims of bullying tend to have social adjustment problems. They're more likely to have low self-esteem and feel anxious and insecure.[11] They rarely defend themselves, and male victims are usually physically weaker or smaller than their peers.[12] Kids who are bullied may be isolated and lack social skills. Dr. Nansel and her colleagues discovered that the most common reason why kids were bullied was that "they just didn't fit in." Children who are bullied may feel anxious, fearful, and have a hard time concentrating on schoolwork. Worrying about being harassed by their peers may also make them afraid even to go to school. The effects of being bullied can last long after school years: Researchers have found that adults who were bullied frequently as youth had higher levels of depression and lower self-esteem than other adults.[13]

That is not to say, however, that all people who are bullied suffer long-term consequences. Quite a few of the successful women whom I interviewed for my *See Jane Win* research were bullied, but they overcame bullying and its effects during their adolescence. Martha Aarons, for example, is now a flutist with the Cleveland Symphony Orchestra. In our interview, she described how she was bullied in junior high and eventually succeeded in overcoming her trauma. Critical to her overcoming the bullying was the discovery of a peer group with like interests who valued and accepted her, as she describes below.

In junior high, I was teased a lot because kids were fast in Los Angeles, and I wasn't. In my sixth-grade photographs, you can see the girls already dressed sexily; they hiked up their skirts and had their hair draped over their eyes. They wore stockings and makeup, and shaved their legs. My mother didn't want me to be like that, so she wouldn't let me shave my legs or buy sexy clothes.

I was a good student in school and loved classical music, so I had all the ingredients for being teased. They called me "Hairy Legs" and "square." I'd come home crying every day. My mother was there to comfort me and say, "You'll see. Those kids will turn out to be a mess. You'll be smart, happy, and successful." I didn't believe her, and I was pretty disconsolate when I wasn't accepted by the cool group.

The semester after junior high, I attended music camp and made good friends who loved music and shared my interests. That gave me social confidence, and when I entered high school, somehow my problems disappeared. My trauma in junior high motivated me to figure out how to make and keep good friends, and the result of that is that in my highly competitive career, friends have been my best support. I'd say I'm popular in my professional life. People seem to think I'm nice and I'm a good person, and that's always been important to me.

Being a Bully and Being Bullied

Students who were both bullies and victims seemed to have the most-serious behavioral and emotional problems, as shown by the WHO survey. These students made up 6.3 percent of the population studied. Social isolation, lack of success in school, and behavior problems combined to make them an especially high-risk group. It is most likely, according to Dr. Nansel and her colleagues, that these youth were first bullied and then imitated the bullying behavior, although it's also possible they bullied first and were later retaliated against. Either way, these kids exhibited social-emotional adjustment problems typical of bullies as well as victims, making it unlikely that they will be resilient enough to adjust to a healthy lifestyle without effective intervention strategies.

Bullying by School Employees

Up until this point, I've discussed only bullying caused by kids. But when adults are the perpetrators, the balance of power is completely lopsided and kids often feel powerless to seek help. Abuse by adults in schools leaves kids feeling totally unprotected. A recent survey commissioned by the American Association of University Women Educational Foundation found that as many as 9.6 percent of students have been sexually harassed or abused by school workers at some point during their school lives.[14] Though teachers were the most common offenders, coaches, substitute teachers, bus drivers, and teacher aides were also found guilty of sexual harassment and abuse. The abuse of children by more-powerful adults is the worst kind of bullying, and the author of the study, Charol Shake-shaft, professor at Hofstra University's School of Education in Hempstead, New York, maintains that 4.5 million students have been affected.

The sexual abuse discussed in the report included language, gestures, notes, sexual jokes, and sexual pictures as well as fondling and forced sex in one all-inclusive spectrum. Lumping together these various categories fails to distinguish the severity of some actions over others. While some behaviors may simply be attributed to poor judgment, others represent serious criminal actions. The report also points out that these adult bullies often target vulnerable students who might be afraid to report the offenses or might not be believed if they complain. If schools are to remain one of the safest places for children to be, staff training, awareness, and supervision are sorely needed.

Worries about Bullying

The popular kids scorn me because they see me as unfit to talk to. I try to say hi, but they don't recognize my existence in the universe. I don't exist. They ignore me, or sometimes they call me a fag. My old friend won't talk to me anymore. He's become popular, and being friends with me threatens his popularity. High school won't be much better because there will be the sports jocks, and they'll be even more ho-mophobic and make me seem like even more of a nerd. I'm not looking forward to it.

8th-grade boy

My survey provided important insights about the extent to which middle school students worried about being bullied. Although the PRIDE data I shared earlier showed fairly consistent numbers of students who were actually bullied, my survey showed there was a decrease at each grade level of students who worried about being bullied. Students in third grade were the most concerned about bullying, with 24 percent reporting that they worried about it. This rate dropped steadily each year, to a low of 8 percent for eighth graders, suggesting that kids improve their skills for coping with bullies as they mature. A study presented at the annual National Association for Gifted Children (NAGC) conference in 2003 confirmed this trend, noting that gifted students who were bullied improved their coping skills as they got older.[15]

Self-confidence and intelligence make a big difference in whether or not kids worry about bullying. Interestingly enough, those with very good or low self-confidence worried more than those with average self-confidence (Figure 8.1 on page 146). Those who perceived they had far above-average intelligence and those who considered themselves to have below or far below-average intelligence worried more than those with average or above-average intelligence (Figure 8.2 on page 147). Perhaps bullies tend to select victims at the extremes and are less likely to bully average kids, who seem less threatening or who are not easily victimized.

Certain characteristics did make a difference in whether or not the kids from my study worried about being bullied. The type of school that kids attended is one important factor. Students in public schools and all-boy schools showed the greatest worries about being bullied (14 percent), with kids in parochial schools (13 percent) and kids in independent schools (12 percent) showing a little less concern. Surprisingly, gender made almost no difference in worries about bullying. According to my survey, 13 percent of the girls and 14 percent of the boys worried about bullying.

Helping Bullies

Some kids who instigate bullying haven't experienced consistent family love, nor have they learned to respect boundaries. They may be brought up in environments where they aren't taught self-control or respect for others. Some kids who are bullies have also been bullied in their own homes by family members, or they may copy bullying they have observed. Parents of kids who bully may need classes on managing their own anger and on parenting strong-willed children to help curtail their children's aggressive behaviors.

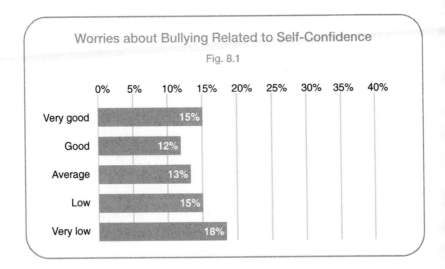

Worries about Bullying Related to Self-Confidence

Fig. 8.1

Very good	15%
Good	12%
Average	13%
Low	15%
Very low	18%

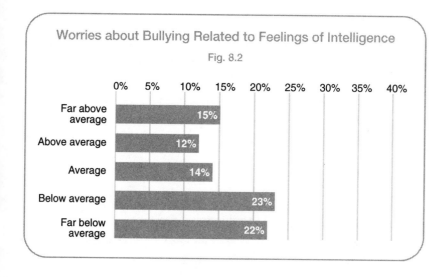

Worries about Bullying Related to Feelings of Intelligence

Fig. 8.2

Far above average	15%
Above average	12%
Average	14%
Below average	23%
Far below average	22%

Overempowered kids learn about limits and respect only when parents and schools set clear, reasonable rules and consequences. On the other hand, even when parents have tried to set boundaries and have modeled respectful behavior toward others, there will be times when normal kids will try bullying others. In this case, parents and teachers will need to take steps to stop the behaviors.

Being Clear about Bullying

You will need to be assertive and clear that bullying—either physically or emotionally—is unacceptable. If you spend enough time around middle schoolers, you're bound to hear kids insulting or harassing others because they're different in some way. Take that as a teaching opportunity to have a private discussion with your children afterward. Remind your kids that if they go along with the crowd and insult someone by using racial slurs, or if they refer to people as gay, fat, or geeky in a derogatory way, they're contributing to the abuse of other young people.

Passive inaction can also be psychologically damaging. Kids may purposely not invite a classmate to a party or other social event because he or she is "different." In a situation like this, you can discuss with your kids your disappointment in them for not accepting people with differences as friends and for perpetuating the prejudice against them. Be clear when telling your kids that your family accepts individual differences, including people of different shapes and sizes, religions, races, or sexual orientation. If they belong to a crowd of kids who are mean to others, stress that they're in the *wrong* crowd.

What Schools Can Do to Control Bullying

Schools also have the responsibility of teaching kids about respect as well as addressing the issue of bullying through intervention programs. While programs that target only individual bullies haven't been effective in curtailing bullying, school-wide approaches have been proven to reduce bullying by 50 percent.[16]

Linda Berg-Cross, PhD, believes that teaching kids problem-solving strategies can curb aggression.[17] Other useful strategies include encouraging kids to pledge that they won't bully others and that instead they will help others who are bullied. Schools can lead a *No Name-Calling Week,* a national campaign that began in March 2004, which strives to eliminate bullying by educating students on its effects.[18] School programs can provide an atmosphere where a social norm against bullying prevails. Some states have attempted to pass legislation (like New York's Dignity for All Students Act) to prevent student harassment and bullying. As a parent or educator, you can encourage school programs and legislation, which provide legitimacy and clout for preventing bullying.

Helping Victims

Antibullying programs in schools can be highly effective in providing protection for kids who are being bullied. They can also teach social skills to victims so that they don't act in ways that encourage bullying. From my own clinical work, I've found that kids often don't realize that their own sarcastic comments may arouse bullies' anger—leading to aggression later on. Though sometimes victims are part of the problem, it's important to remember that all too frequently they are helpless and unwilling participants.

Assuming that children can handle their own problems is a mistake that too many parents and teachers make. Milwaukee's WITI FOX 6 News did an investigative report of bullying on playgrounds in the five largest school districts in Wisconsin.[19] Students were videotaped punching and kicking each other at more than two-thirds of the 52 school playgrounds observed. Plenty of the bullying resulted in kids getting hurt. Teachers and

I Remember Bullying

I remember when my daughter Ilonna was bullied in the seventh grade at her junior high school. Initially, she was taunted because of her height. She was very small, but she soon learned the quick response "Good things come in little packages," and that was enough to diminish some of the teasing.

Being taunted for being a "brain" was harder for her to handle. There was one particular boy who sat behind her in social studies class, and he was most unpleasant and mean. I remember reassuring Ilonna by pointing out that perhaps his meanness was a response to his own personal problems. He was a poor student and had plenty of other behavioral problems. A meeting facilitated by the school counselor seemed to resolve the constant conflict between the two kids for a while.

About 10 years later, I read about a man who had hanged himself while imprisoned for drug trafficking. Since he had graduated the same year as Ilonna, I asked her if she knew him. Sure enough, he was the same young man who had made her life miserable for a few months in the seventh grade. Ilonna's story may not reassure your child who is being bullied, but it should remind all of us how serious bullying is and why preventive measures are essential.

supervisors, who were in scarce supply, never seemed to notice the rough activity or the bullying assaults. Unfortunately, Wisconsin schools aren't alone with this problem. Supervising playgrounds, hallways, cafeterias, parking lots, and buses should be part of antibullying programs.

Teaching Tweens to Handle Bullies

When I was bullied, my parents were really helpful. They said I should walk away from the bullies and ignore them, and it worked.

5th-grade girl

Even tweens with good self-esteem may wither on the vine from continuous taunting and teasing by powerful, popular kids or obnoxious bullies. They will have to do more than just cry about the problem, although a few tears when they come home distressed are justifiable and should receive your support and an understanding hug. Beyond comfort, your children will need some tools for coping that will diminish the problem. There is no easy way to stop taunting, but there are some approaches that have proven to be effective for children.

If your children are tormented, teased, threatened, or physically harmed, here are some ways they can protect themselves and avoid dangerous situations.

Walk away. The oldest recommendation for dealing with bullies is to ignore the taunts and walk away. It's preferable for kids to be able to join a group of other friends, but that's not always possible. It's also important for victims of bullying to understand that it's not their fault and that they shouldn't blame themselves. Self-talk like "What's his problem? I'm okay" helps victims cope with the emotional pain of teasing. Kids in my focus groups told me that ignoring bullies can actually be effective some of the time.

Discover a strength. Kids who are stars of a sport, speech, drama, or math team soon find allies. Teammates don't pick on one of their own if they want someone on their team, and bullies don't taunt kids when they're surrounded by friends who will defend them. Very few of the boys in my focus groups who were active in sports suffered much taunting. Although not all children can count on being team players in sports, interests in speech, drama, or band can also offer opportunities for kids to discover support groups in and out of school. When your kids sing solos or receive trophies for a math meet or wrestling match, the taunting can diminish a little while admiration grows. Every little bit helps.

Find a peer ally. If kids have friends among the leaders of the class, having them privately tell the leaders how much the teasing hurts is a good plan. Kids will feel better if they communicate directly to friends and are successful in saving themselves. A prestigious friend may help to stave off bullies.

Help a friend in need. Teachers may be able to help kids who are bullied by appointing them to tutor someone who needs help with homework or to assist a physically handicapped child with activities. Not only will that build their self-esteem, but it will help them to concentrate their energies on caring about others. Although there is no guarantee that the bullies will back off, even bullies can't help but admire kids who go out of their way to help people with handicaps.

Learn a sharp response. A sharp response pointing out a taunter's weaknesses may incite fear in a taunter, which will eradicate any further slurs. "You're so small I could put you in my back pocket," "My 6-foot brother is on the football team, and he doesn't like it when little squirts like you call me names," "Coming from you, I consider that a compliment," or "Haven't you learned your multiplication facts yet?" were effective for some kids in my focus groups. You'll have to determine your child's own courage level before you recommend he try to thwart bullies with a mean comment. That kind of response can backfire when kids fear their taunters may take them on physically. In these situations, it may be better for kids to ignore the taunts, find a friend to play with, or talk to a teacher for protection from the bullies.

Fight back. Though I don't recommend fighting back, many parents do, and I have to admit that it may be effective for some kids. Victims may actually put a stop to bullies by giving them a kick in the shins or a punch in the nose. However, I don't encourage hitting back for two reasons. First, it teaches kids to be aggressive in response to aggression, which can lead to problems down the road. Second, the victim risks being physically beaten and feeling worse than before. Verbal assertiveness is much safer.

Keep emotions under control. Bullies see tears as weak, stupid, silly, and babyish and assume that your "wimp of a kid needs a lesson," which they will deliver mercilessly. If kids lose their tempers when provoked, that rarely helps either. Explain to your kids that while it may be hard to walk away when they're angry, this may be the best alternative. If victims can't control their emotions in front of peers, they may require some adult intervention. Here are some suggestions to offer your kids.

- Try to control the tears or anger until you're at home so that the bullies don't have another reason to tease you.
- Walk away, ignore the taunts, and tell yourself, "Don't cry, don't cry."
- Change the tears to laughter, or make a joke and disarm the crowd while also relieving some of your own tension.
- Find a close friend who will support you and walk as far away as possible.
- Talk privately to a teacher or principal who is in a powerful position to change the bullying behavior by speaking with your class or group.

While it's important to offer your kids advice on how to deter bullying, they'll also need your understanding and reassurance. Here are some suggestions for parents whose kids are being bullied.

Reassure your children. Your kids deserve reassurance that they are good, smart, and effective people, despite what others may say or do. They also need to learn coping strategies so they don't play the victim. You should be supportive of their feelings, but be careful not to host a daily pity party. It's not helpful to your kids to allow them to dwell in self-pity. Sometimes kids learn they can get plenty of attention from a parent when they describe how mean others are. Of course, if they truly are hurt, they need you to believe them, but they also need advice that will move them forward to their strengths and interests. Helping your kids develop their personal strengths can guide them toward positive accomplishments that will eventually build their self-esteem.

Appeal to kids' sensitive sides. Kids who taunt and insult others aren't necessarily mean kids. That is, they may not realize that they're hurting others. Adults, like teachers, can take bullies aside privately, appeal to their sensitive sides, and get them to stop the teasing. This approach may be more effective with girls than boys, but it's worth trying for both. You should realize, however, that addressing the matter in front of peers could embarrass the leaders, causing them to unleash their power to taunt even more.

Deal with depression. If your child seems depressed, schedule an evaluation by a psychologist. Depression can be a serious problem and should not be ignored or dismissed. Symptoms of depression such as excessive sleeping, having difficulty waking in the morning, refusing to go to school, complaining of stomachaches or headaches, withdrawing from social or school activities, and getting lower grades should alert you to seek professional help.

Rely on an authority. If your child feels threatened, it may be necessary for you to report the problem to the appropriate authorities, even if your child is afraid that he'll be called a tattler. Explain that there's a difference between tattling and reporting: Tattlers tell authorities just to get another person into trouble, but reporters believe they or others may not be safe. Reporting problems to authorities can sometimes prevent disasters. One eighth-grader told me about his fears that bullies who hunted with their dads had access to guns and might use them on him if provoked. I encouraged him to be sure to report his concerns to his parents and his school's principal if he was ever actually threatened with a gun, and I encourage parents and teachers to report threats to the police if appropriate.

To be effective, an authority will need to investigate in order to label the behavior as bullying. That may not be easy, because bullies usually take action out of sight from adults. Once bullies are identified, the school must clearly state that bullying behavior isn't acceptable and make that

Sam Is Saved by the Principal

Bullies would surround Sam, a seventh-grader, while he waited near the school for his bus. Sam was young in his class and small. At first the boys just made fun of his size, until eventually they physically attacked him. After reporting the problem to the principal, there was an effort made to catch the bullies in the act, but the boys attacked Sam only when he was alone. Although Sam reported names to the principal, the boys denied any wrongdoing and Sam didn't have proof. Finally, the principal pulled a trick. He brought the bullies into the office and claimed that he had watched them from his office window and had seen them hit and kick Sam. The bullies crumbled, apologized, and claimed they were only having fun and meant no harm. They served detentions, and Sam was finally safe.

statement for any child physically hit or belittled in inappropriate ways. If schools follow through and require a visit to the principal's office, a conference with the parents, and an appropriate punishment, the bullying will diminish and kids will be safe. These actions may not prevent an occasional insult, but hopefully kids who feel safe can manage to ignore less-threatening taunts.

Bullying Leads to Violence

There are effective ways for changing a threatening atmosphere at home and school, but bullying evolves into violence when there are no interventions. Coping with violence has become a family, school, community, and societal problem and will be discussed further in the next chapter.

CHAPTER 9

TERROR IN OUR WORLD

I was in gym running laps. All of a sudden the announcement came on the loudspeaker: "Everyone report to your homeroom immediately!" We changed our clothes and ran to our homerooms. TVs were on in every classroom. We saw smoking buildings, fire, dead bodies, firemen carrying people and running everywhere—I'll never forget it. I was really scared and mad.

7th-grade girl

TV affects your imagination a lot. I wouldn't be scared of a lot of stuff if it weren't for TV. If I didn't watch TV, I wouldn't really think about a gunman coming up behind me and just shooting me. I wouldn't really care. TV invites your imagination to scare you.

8th-grade boy

Our parents see all this stuff on the news and that makes them more worried. We don't have as much freedom as they did when they were little. My mom and dad used to ride around on their bikes and play in the street until it got dark. They could go places by themselves. Now parents are so overprotective. Every kid has a cell phone. They [parents] have to know what their kids are doing and be in touch with them at all times because they're so paranoid by what's going on in the media and what they think is going on in the world.

8th-grade girl

My mom was freakin' out when Elizabeth Smart was kidnapped. Then she started these weird safety measures in our house. She's like, "In the house, lock the doors and don't go outside until I get home."

7th-grade girl

YOUR CHILDREN ARE NOT SAFE *anywhere, at any time.* This chilling statement was announced on television and headlined in newspapers in the fall of 2002 after a sniper's bullets had killed 10 and critically wounded 3 people, including a middle school boy on a playground. Before the arrests of John Allen Muhammad and Lee Boyd Malvo, no perpetrators had been identified and a whole nation was terrified of the sniper killers. Accounts of Elizabeth Smart, who was 14 years old when she was snatched from her own bed in June of 2002, were just as frightening for children who would normally feel safe in their own homes. The 2004 abduction of Carlie Brucia, an 11-year-old middle schooler, caught on a video monitor in broad daylight, added to parents' and kids' fears, especially when she was later found murdered.

News reports of murders and violence committed by teens and tweens on school grounds have stolen our confidence in the safety of schools. In an Arkansas middle school in March of 1998, two boys shot and killed four students and a teacher as classmates looked on, and at Columbine High School, two boys terrorized and killed 12 students and a teacher before taking their own lives in April of 1999. Even at Southwood Middle School, a magnet school near Miami that specializes in music and art and had no history of violence, an eighth-grade boy was charged with murdering a classmate in the school's bathroom in February of 2004.

As if the violence on the news and in schools wasn't enough to frighten our children, on September 11, 2001, our nation was terrorized to an extreme no one can previously recall. Students were dismissed from school early, only to watch surreal television imagery of airplanes flying into the Twin Towers, people jumping out of windows to escape the raging flames, and masses of frightened people running blindly through darkened New York streets. Although earlier generations of Americans may have witnessed violence during World War II or other wars in Korea, Vietnam, or Iraq, previous generations have never witnessed such horrors in their living rooms through the television. The TV coverage of September 11 etched horror into the brains of a whole generation of young people. Kids may be either terrified or numbed by their exposure to violence, but they cannot be unaffected. It's no wonder that the middle school youngsters in my focus groups, when asked about the most important differences between their generation and their parents', responded with a single word—*terrorism*.

The Effects of Terrorist Attacks

I was born where a sniper shooting was, so it really scared me. It happened a block away from where we used to live. To think that if my dad hadn't gotten a new job here, I could still be living there.

8th-grade girl

Between January and May of 2002, approximately 6 months after the terrorist attacks on New York and Washington, DC, children in grades three through eight responded to my survey. My survey included a checklist of things kids might possibly worry about. Most of the items checked were typical for tweens, like worries about popularity, not feeling smart enough, or being too fat, but kids also had fears of a terrorist attack on our country (30 percent) or on their families (22 percent), and a fear of flying (10 percent). Kids reported being worried about a terrorist attack on our country more than anything else, and half the children felt less safe than they did before September 11.

Certain characteristics played a part in how afraid children were of terrorism. Girls proved to be more fearful all around: 58 percent of girls reported feeling less safe, compared with 42 percent of boys. This fear decreased with age, with 61 percent of kids in third grade reporting that they felt less safe, as compared with 40 percent in eighth grade, showing that with developmental maturity, kids can make intellectual assumptions about our country mobilizing forces to make us safer. Surprisingly, more children who described themselves as having very good family relationships tended to worry about terrorist attacks than those who described their family relationships as very bad. Those children with very good family relationships also indicated they felt less safe than those children with poor family relationships (52 percent compared with 35 percent, respectively). We can probably assume that where there were better family relations, there was also more communication about safety concerns, which may have unintentionally increased worries in children.

There's Confidence in Our Country

Despite feelings of insecurity overall, 82 percent of the children indicated having the same or greater confidence in our country than before the terrorist attacks. Confidence in our country increased continuously with children's grade in school, with only 34 percent of third-graders but 53 percent of eighth-graders having more confidence (Figure 9.1). The increasing confidence in our country with each older grade also explains why there were fewer older kids who were afraid of terrorist attacks.

Also, kids who had advantages, like better grades or better family relationships, had more confidence in our country after the terrorist attacks. Fifty-five percent of children with better grades had more confidence, compared with only 36 percent of students with poor grades. Likewise, kids with better family relationships had more confidence than kids with poor family relationships (50 and 45 percent, respectively), indicating that in families with good relationships, parents were more able to reassure their children.

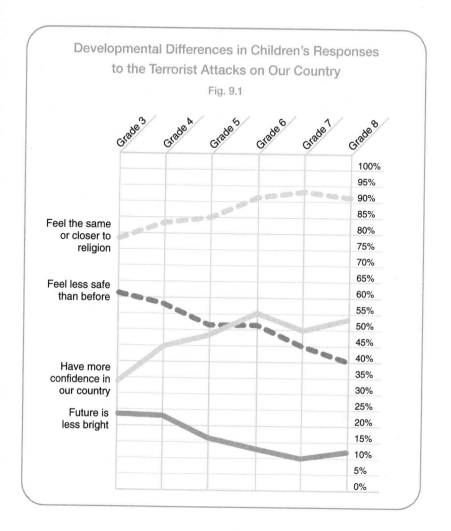

Developmental Differences in Children's Responses
to the Terrorist Attacks on Our Country

Fig. 9.1

The Future Looks Bright

Most children (81 percent) believed that the future would be as bright as
or brighter than before our country was attacked by terrorists. Eighth-
graders were more optimistic about the future (79 percent) than were children in third grade (69 percent), and children with very good grades were
more optimistic about their futures (85 percent) than were children with

poor grades (73 percent). Family relationships also affected children's optimism about their futures. Eighty-three percent of kids with very good family relationships thought the future could be as bright as or brighter than before, while only 69 percent of children with very bad family relationships indicated such optimism (Figure 9.2).

Children's perceptions of their own intelligence also played a part in their coping with fears of terrorism and their optimism about the future. Kids who perceived themselves as having above-average intelligence were

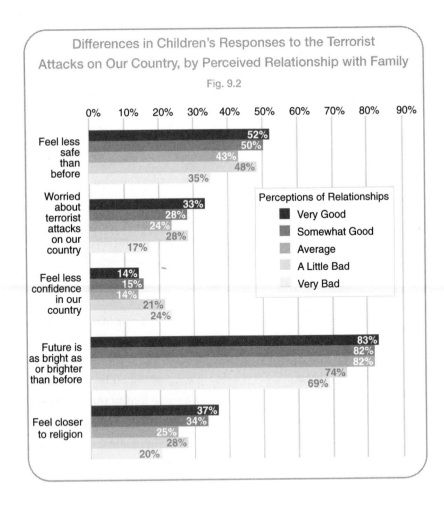

Differences in Children's Responses to the Terrorist Attacks on Our Country, by Perceived Relationship with Family

Fig. 9.2

likely to feel safer and to be more optimistic about the future than those who perceived themselves as having average or below-average abilities.

Relying on Religion

Religion may have also played a part in increasing a sense of optimism and security for these kids. Thirty-four percent of the children indicated they felt closer to their religion as a result of the terrorist attacks. Not surprisingly, kids in parochial schools (49 percent) indicated more frequently that they felt closer to their religion than did those in public schools (33 percent). Also, girls (37 percent) felt closer to their religion than did boys (31 percent), kids who earned excellent grades (39 percent) felt closer than kids who earned poor grades (20 percent), and kids with very good family relationships (37 percent) felt closer than those with very bad family relationships (20 percent).

Terror in School

This seventh-grade boy wanted a date and he e-mailed me and said, "I want to do it with you all night." Now he keeps saying he'll beat me up if I don't go on a date with him. I've told him I can't date anyone yet. He scares me and I don't know what to do.

6th-grade girl

To parents and educators, world and community terror may seem more extreme than school terror. To kids, however, the terror in school may be even more frightening than an attack on New York or Washington, especially if children have been victimized or have observed violence firsthand.

Despite the fact that children seem to be safe during the school day (see Chapter 8), the percentage of middle-school children threatened or hurt by other children while at school is alarming. Data from two different surveys conducted by the National Parents' Resources Institute for Drug Education (PRIDE) was used to compile Figures 9.3 and 9.4.

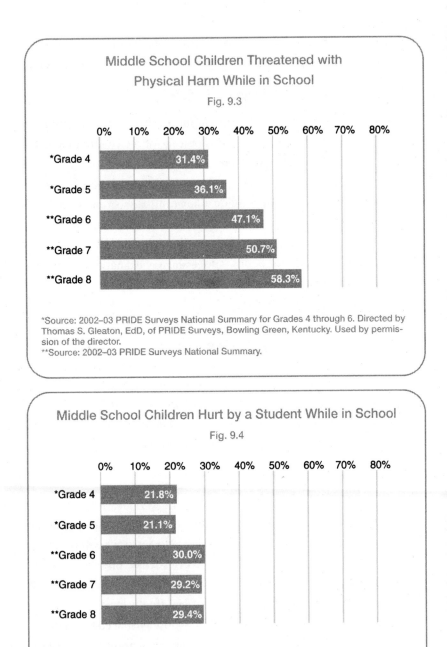

Middle School Children Threatened with Physical Harm While in School

Fig. 9.3

Grade	Percentage
*Grade 4	31.4%
*Grade 5	36.1%
**Grade 6	47.1%
**Grade 7	50.7%
**Grade 8	58.3%

*Source: 2002–03 PRIDE Surveys National Summary for Grades 4 through 6. Directed by Thomas S. Gleaton, EdD, of PRIDE Surveys, Bowling Green, Kentucky. Used by permission of the director.
**Source: 2002–03 PRIDE Surveys National Summary.

Middle School Children Hurt by a Student While in School

Fig. 9.4

Grade	Percentage
*Grade 4	21.8%
*Grade 5	21.1%
**Grade 6	30.0%
**Grade 7	29.2%
**Grade 8	29.4%

*Source: 2002–03 PRIDE Surveys National Summary for Grades 4 through 6. Directed by Thomas S. Gleaton, EdD, of PRIDE Surveys, Bowling Green, Kentucky. Used by permission of the director.
**Source: 2002–03 PRIDE Surveys National Summary.

Younger children in grades four and five were asked if they had ever been threatened or hurt by another student. Sixth- through eighth-graders were asked if they had ever been hurt by a student with hits, slaps, or kicks, and, in a separate question, if the abuse was enforced with a gun, knife, or club. Of the sixth-, seventh-, and eighth-graders, 11.6 percent were threatened with weapons and 3.4 percent were physically hurt with weapons.[1]

Despite the much smaller percentages of actual physical violence compared to threats of violence, large numbers of middle school children are affected. And if you conclude that these dangers are present only in large cities, you are only partially correct. Although there's more violence in urban areas, most of the school shootings that received national media attention occurred in small town or suburban schools. TV's focus on these horrific events can make them feel close to home for all kids.

Violence on the Way to and from School

Sometimes I see someone walking down the street with a
bandana around their leg, and I think they're drunk or have
a gun. I get nervous even if I'm in the car with my family.

6th-grade girl

Children are not only threatened with violence in school but also on their way to and from school. The U.S. Department of Education's Office of Safe and Drug-Free Schools (OSDFS) is becoming more concerned about the increasing amount of violence and serious crimes that affect kids as they're on their way to and from school, at bus stops, on street corners, and in parking lots. William Modzeleski, associate deputy undersecretary of the OSDFS, notes that crimes may happen after school hours, when principals and teachers lose control of most kids.[2] While educators can't assume responsibility for safe passage to and from schools, they are concerned with the increasing violence. Some of the violence has been instigated by individual students and gangs, but other crimes have been committed by adults near schools.

Violence around Schools

Below is a sample of violent and sometimes fatal incidents that have endangered children in and around schools.

- A 16-year-old student and a school police officer were wounded in a shooting at a city bus stop located 150 yards from Charlestown High School in north Boston. (September 2003)
- Three teenage students were injured in a drive-by shooting at a bus stop near Taft High School in the San Fernando Valley area of Los Angeles. (September 2003)
- A 15-year-old student was shot to death while waiting at a bus stop near Crane High School in Chicago. Gang members gunned down the teenager, who had no known gang affiliations, mistaking him for a member of a rival gang. (September 2003)
- A man opened fire on a group of parents and children waiting at a neighborhood school bus stop in Meraux, Louisiana, killing a 39-year-old father, wounding the man's 2-year-old son, and injuring a third person. (August 2003)
- An elementary school student was dropped off at a bus stop by a school bus when he was approached by another student who had previously threatened him. To avoid an attack, the student ran away from the bus stop and into the street. He was hit by oncoming traffic and sustained serious brain and spinal injuries. (September 1999)[3]

Predicting Violence

Violence that is not easily predictable is not easily preventable. That holds for attacks within our country, our communities, our schools, and our homes. It's easier to look back and identify the characteristics in terrorists or individuals that we should have been able to recognize than to predict who will be the next to wear a shoe bomb or attack a child at school.

Identifying students who have the potential to be violent in school is at least as difficult as predicting terrorism in our nation. After the school shootings in West Paducah, Kentucky, and Littleton, Colorado, it was difficult for the public to understand how the obviously troubled kids who committed the crimes weren't noticed earlier, before they caused such incredible tragedies. Schools have set policies of zero tolerance for weapons, installed metal-detection systems in urban schools, mandated uniform dress-code policies to cut down on gang identification, and asked kids to report other students who act or dress oddly, are loners, or seem to raise suspicion.

The great problem pointed out by Edward Mulvey, PhD, and Elizabeth Cauffman, PhD, of the University of Pittsburgh, is that the signs of distress, behaviors, and attitudes that these "killer" youngsters show are similar to those of many other adolescents who are no threat to other students but are simply going through a difficult stage in their lives.[4] Even characteristics that identify psychopathology in adults, like impulsivity and little concern for the future, are common characteristics in developing adolescents who are still struggling with self-control and searching for their identities.[5] We're faced with a double bind as a nation and as educators. Do we steal freedom of expression and overreact to strange behaviors to protect our country and our children, or do we preserve the freedom and dignity our nation represents at the risk of terror to our children and our world?

Preventing Violence

We'll watch the news and see a boy who took a gun to school. My mom threatens me, "If you ever take a gun to school, I'll bang your head against these four walls!" I've never had a gun or even seen one.

        7th-grade boy

There are some important things we do know about juvenile crimes that may help us prevent them. Kids who commit crimes are almost always with peers, and there are almost always bystanders.[6] Aggressive adolescents tend to form cliques, groups, or gangs.[7] Violent events in a school are typically part of a chain of actions and reactions, including taunting, being left out or shunned by others, or rejection by girlfriends or boyfriends.[8] Thus, the same preventive measures that school programs take against bullying can be enforced for preventing violence. Every parent and educator shares in the responsibility for making schools bully-proof and violence-free, and programs that educate all students on non-violent behaviors provide our best hope for safe learning environments.

How Parents Can Help Children during Fearful Times

As adults, we too have been traumatized by the changing times and by terrorism. We don't necessarily have answers for all our children's questions. It's difficult to respond to a 10-year-old child who says she can't believe someone could be mean enough to kill so many people, or a 9-year-old who says he can't understand how Osama Bin Laden can escape from so many people, airplanes, and guns trying to catch him. It's not easy to convince a 12-year-old who can't sleep that a kidnapper won't try to steal her away in the middle of the night, nor is it simple to explain to kids that they can no longer play on playgrounds or walk to school because there's a risk that a sniper may shoot at them.

It appears from my survey data that communication between parents and kids is helpful for combating fears. Although talking too much about fears may increase kids' sense of danger, discussing their fears also seems to give children greater hope for their futures and more confidence that their country will keep them safe. The overall objectives for parents are to make kids aware of the potential violence that can occur in homes, schools, communities, or the world; to permit kids to think through possible dangers; and to help them believe that they can continue to feel relatively safe.

Here are some tips you can use when communicating with your middle schoolers as they face dangers in their school, community, or world.

- Communicate daily with your tweens. When something bad has happened, explain the circumstances in terms that your kids can understand. Be realistic, but don't overtalk, which can make your kids more anxious.
- Watch news on television or listen to it on the radio with your tweens. The media can provide useful tools to help them understand the seriousness of the situation. Watching the news can help your kids verbalize their questions, giving you a chance to explain information that they may not understand.
- Limit excessive media viewing. While some television gives pertinent information and can be reassuring, repeated viewing of fearful incidents leaves traumatic visual imagery.
- Encourage questions. Unanswered questions will leave kids fearful. Assure them that no question they have is too silly to ask.
- Reassure tweens of their day-to-day security. Kids should go on with their lives whenever possible. Concentrating on their daily activities will help them cope with their fears.
- Explain that their school, community, or country will respond and protect them. Even if you have lost some of your own confidence, your tweens will benefit from your reassurance.
- Remind them that criminals are almost always caught. You may wish to cite examples, like the snipers who terrorized the United States but were eventually captured and punished, or you may want to cite other times in history when this country was attacked and rose to victory.
- Consider your tweens' developmental and intellectual abilities. Don't burden kids with information they can't comprehend, but don't underestimate your children's ability to know and understand. Be sure that you have answered their questions to the best of your ability, but acknowledge that you don't have all the answers.

- Help your children find some way they can contribute to others. Serving food to the poor, contributing birthday money to a charity, sending packages to soldiers, or tutoring a young child are all activities that teach kids they can help the world to become a better place. Doing something effective also prevents feelings of helplessness around terror.
- Don't teach children to hate. Crimes committed by minorities can inflict repercussions (specifically prejudice and hate crimes) against innocent individuals who are of the same religion, color, or ethnicity as the criminals. Minority children especially need understanding and support during times of school or world conflict.
- Play with your children. You can play outdoors when the weather is good, or you can play board games indoors when the weather is poor. Playing together permits parents to answer questions informally that children might not ask otherwise.
- Encourage children to explore creative outlets for expressing their fears, emotions, or distress. Art, music, poetry, or stories permit children to share their feelings instead of internalizing them and becoming more anxious.

Worries about Terror Rival Popularity Anxiety

While more kids in my survey worried about terror than anything else, recall that my survey took place 6 to 9 months following the terrorist attacks on New York and Washington, DC, when the aftermath of 9/11 was still very fresh in their minds. Even now, kids are still worried about terror, but their second most frequent worry—popularity—is edging near the top of the list. Middle school kids worry a lot about whether or not they're popular, and we'll discuss that in the next chapter.

CHAPTER 10

FITTING IN WITH FASHION AND FRIENDS

People judge by first appearances too much. It's totally by the way you look. It could have to do with anything physical. You could be too fat, too thin, too tall, too short, have ugly hair, or whatever.

8th-grade girl

The popular people are the classifiers. They walk around the school and put scorn on you if they see you as unfit to be talked to. They either insult you or turn up their noses and walk away.

7th-grade boy

I wear what I want to, whether people think it's too baggy or too small. I don't care what people think. If they like me, they like me for who I am and not what I wear.

8th-grade boy

I went to a uniform school. Kids asked, "What brand are your pants? Are they Abercrombie or Gap?" One time a girl looked at the label on my shirt. Kids checked your labels to see how much money you spend on clothes. They put you on a ladder and decided where you stood compared to everyone else. Then they decided if they should be friends with you or not.

8th-grade girl

My mom and I have lots of arguments about clothes. She says my clothes are too sexy, and she calls me "scarlet woman."

7th-grade girl

Kids are piercing earlier, like piercing their belly buttons. A girl in our class even got her tongue pierced.

6th-grade girl

The brand name of clothes is important, and you have to have a perfect body like Britney Spears.

5th-grade girl

THE PRESSURE TO BE POPULAR has always been an issue in middle school, but kids today are absolutely certain the problem is more intense for their generation than it was for their parents'. Kids told me that the right clothes and labels, makeup, piercings, and appearances are the most critical ingredients for achieving popularity (Figure 10.1).

Students in my focus groups said that popular kids shunned less popular kids. They believed that popular kids even had control over some teachers and that teachers believed what popular kids said about other students. As I will show you in this chapter, my survey findings dramatically support what the focus groups had to say about the pressure to be popular.

Popularity: Middle Schoolers' Biggest Worry

The students in my survey ranked popularity as their top concern—tied only with fears of a terrorist attack on our country. Thirty percent of middle school kids who completed my survey worried often about being popular with girls, followed closely by worrying about the pressure to have nice clothes (24 percent) and being popular with boys (22 percent). Physical attributes are often determining factors for status, so it was no

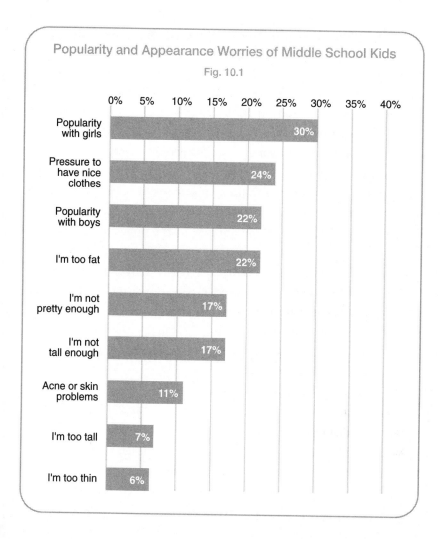

Popularity and Appearance Worries of Middle School Kids

Fig. 10.1

Category	Percentage
Popularity with girls	30%
Pressure to have nice clothes	24%
Popularity with boys	22%
I'm too fat	22%
I'm not pretty enough	17%
I'm not tall enough	17%
Acne or skin problems	11%
I'm too tall	7%
I'm too thin	6%

surprise that 22 percent of students also worried about being too fat, 17 percent worried that they weren't pretty enough, and another 17 percent felt they weren't tall enough. Being thin is definitely "in," and kids also seemed to prefer being tall. Because the weight issue is so traumatic for adolescents, I've devoted the next chapter to that issue alone, and in this chapter I'll discuss other appearance issues that drive popularity.

Early Worries about Popularity with the Opposite Sex

In Chapters 1 and 2, I pointed out that during middle childhood, girls prefer playing only with other girls and boys with boys, as kids usually think the opposite sex has "cooties." Early adolescence changes all that, and kids become curious of, interested in, and friendly with the opposite sex to the point where kids may admit or privately boast that they have boyfriends or girlfriends. As I explained in Chapter 1, my survey showed that kids become interested in the opposite sex at a very early age. As early as third grade, 13 percent of the girls and 16 percent of the boys were concerned about being popular with the opposite sex. By sixth grade, the percentages more than doubled—28 percent for girls and 34 percent for boys. The percentages increased only slightly thereafter, with more than a third of each gender being worried quite a lot about popularity with the opposite sex by eighth grade.

Surprise! Boys Worry More Than Girls

Popular boys go with popular girls.

5th-grade boy

Most astounding was the fact that, at every grade level, boys were slightly more worried about popularity with girls than girls were with boys. This is contrary to what has been developmentally accepted or expected in the past. Girls physically develop earlier than boys do, suggesting that hormonal changes should invite them to notice boys sooner than boys notice them.

It used to be assumed that boys were more interested in being active, developing their identities, and being independent and unencumbered by girlfriends. Thus, I expected to find significantly fewer boys worried about girls than vice versa. It was surprising to find that boys who hadn't even begun physical puberty were nevertheless attracted to girls. This premature sexual attraction preceding puberty may be driven by media exposure to sexuality and could take a toll on boys' confidence and learning. Boys may also feel they must attract girlfriends to prove their masculinity, fearing they'll be labeled gay unless they have a girlfriend. They may need assurance from their parents, especially fathers, that there is no need to hurry to attract a girlfriend.

I discovered other significant differences between girls and boys in my survey. Girls were more concerned about being popular among other girls than they were among boys, but the boys didn't worry as much about being popular with other boys (Figure 10.2 on page 176). Boys and girls both were a lot more worried about popularity and appearance than they were about being smart enough or having self-confidence.

Parents may need to reassure their sons even when boys haven't talked about such worries. Because of the secretiveness of middle schoolers, boys who worry about popularity with girls may not acknowledge their anxieties.

The Intelligence Effect on Popularity

Although fewer kids stated that they were worried about feelings of intelligence and self-confidence, there were definite correlations between these attributes and worries about popularity and appearance. Those who evaluated their intelligence and confidence more highly worried less about being pretty or popular than did those who considered themselves less intelligent and less confident. It may be that feeling popular caused kids to have better self-confidence, and thus kids were less worried about being popular since they already were.

As I traced worries about popularity and appearance from third to eighth grades, I noticed that the pressures for popularity and most appearance issues increased with each grade level. Except for worrying about not being tall enough, which remains constant through all grades, children weren't likely to be as worried about appearance and popularity in third and fourth grade as they were in fifth through eighth grade. As kids get older, their beliefs about what makes them popular multiply their other

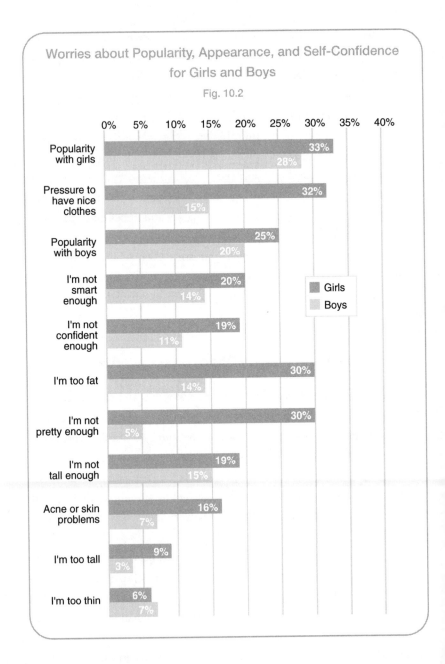

Worries about Popularity, Appearance, and Self-Confidence for Girls and Boys

Fig. 10.2

concerns. For example, girls' popularity with other girls became slightly less important in seventh and eighth grade, when popularity with boys took on greater importance. Because some kids are concerned about popularity with the opposite sex as early as third grade, it's important to invest in the time to teach your kids to cope with popularity stress early on.

What Parents Can Do

In all areas of my survey results, it was apparent that good family relationships have the power to combat adolescent fears and worries. Kids with very good family relationships worried less about all appearance and popularity issues, including being pretty enough, pressure to have nice clothes, popularity with girls, being too fat, and not being tall enough (see Figure 10.3 on page 178). It's gratifying to realize how influential parents can be in relieving some of the angst in middle school youngsters.

Maintaining very good family relationships is the most important key to preventing kids from getting hooked into the popularity and appearance culture. More recommendations for improving these relationships will be given in Chapters 13 and 14, but in this chapter I've included targeted suggestions on how parents can help tweens cope specifically with the popularity and appearance issues.

Talking about Peer Pressure

Peer pressure doesn't just affect kids. Your children may be less defensive when you talk with them if you explain that adults also experience and are affected by peer pressure. Even adults whose friends smoke or drink alcohol are more likely to do the same. Kids often feel independent, but adults and kids alike are sometimes tempted to go along with the crowd. When people change themselves to fit within a group, they're responding to peer pressure. Kids may start cursing, stealing, cheating, spreading rumors, bullying, or calling people names to fit in with a group of kids who are also doing those same things. If their friends gossip, drink, smoke, do drugs, or become sexually active, kids may feel that they have to join in

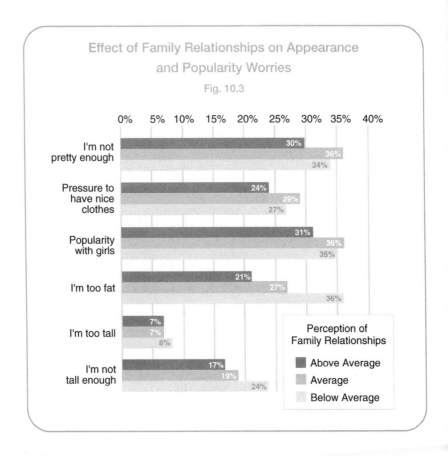

Effect of Family Relationships on Appearance and Popularity Worries

Fig. 10.3

	Above Average	Average	Below Average
I'm not pretty enough	30%	36%	34%
Pressure to have nice clothes	24%	29%	27%
Popularity with girls	31%	36%	35%
I'm too fat	21%	27%	36%
I'm too tall	7%	7%	8%
I'm not tall enough	17%	19%	24%

Perception of Family Relationships

these behaviors to fit in. On the other hand, if their friends frown on these bad habits, they're more likely to frown on them, too. There are actually times when peer pressure can be a good thing!

Being liked and accepted is important to everyone but especially to middle schoolers. If they can find loyal friends who like them and have good values, friends who can influence them in positive ways, then tweens will be more likely to follow a safe and stable path.

To Conform or Not to Conform

Conforming to friends can be fun and harmless or it can cause conflict. Either way, you can search for opportunities to discuss conformity with

Popularity Ends at Grade 12!

Here are some helpful hints about popularity that you may want to share with your own kids. Teaching your children to think about appropriate versus inappropriate or even dangerous conformity is central to the discussion of popularity.

Popularity is a competitive distortion of the concept of friendship. *Popular* is the name given to the kids with the most friends. It has nothing to do with kindness, commonality of interests, sensitivity, or fun. It simply reveres the kids who have managed to compromise enough values so that lots of people like them.

True friendship isn't a competitive activity. It's a valued relationship between persons who exchange feelings, interests, and support. Friendship is an important experience for all kids as well as for all adults.

The pressure to be popular does end at grade 12. After high school graduation, absolutely no one cares about popularity. In college, the use of the word *popular* disappears. Friendships and reasonable social skills remain important, but the geeks, brains, and nerds make it, and hardworking kids succeed, whether they're brilliant or average, fat or thin, tall or short! Many live happily ever after, even if they lacked popularity in high school.

Be personally honest and independent. You don't have to depend on meaningless friendships to develop good interests and talents or to do good work. As you find your own identity, popularity will become less important.

Balance your life with good work, good friends, and good fun. Turn off the popularity value system. Try it. It will be like removing shackles to freedom and self-confidence.

your kids. Here's an example: Your daughter's friends have all agreed to dress in red on Valentine's Day, but she doesn't have a red sweater and begs you to rush out and buy one specifically from the Gap or Abercrombie and Fitch. Now, arranging for your daughter to be included in this fun day may cause some problems, but it can also give you an opportunity to teach her about finances, time management, and creativity.

If your daughter needs an extra sweater anyway, and you have several days to make the purchase, you can probably take her to the mall to buy one. On the other hand, if your daughter needs the sweater by the next day and she has plenty of other sweaters, you may have to offer her some creative alternatives, like wearing an equally festive pink sweater she owns, donning her big brother's red sweatshirt, borrowing a red sweater from her mother or sister, or even wearing a green sweater with a sign on it that says RED just for laughs. This would be a good opportunity for your sense of humor to ease tensions. You can help your daughter to see there's no harm in conforming to the fun, as long as she's flexible enough to consider reasonable alternatives.

You can easily imagine scenarios where your daughter's wish for immediate gratification could lead you and your daughter to a major brouhaha, but helping her to step back and put things into perspective could lead to positive and even funny solutions. The example of dress-up days is relatively simple to handle, but it gives you the opportunity to explain to your kids how important it is to think about appropriate and inappropriate conformity. Discussions about more-serious issues (like using tobacco, alcohol, or drugs, wearing sexy or inappropriate clothes, having strange hairstyles, or getting piercings or tattoos) may cause much greater controversy. I encourage you to talk about the issue of conformity at least by the time your tween enters middle school, whether that be fourth, fifth, sixth, or seventh grade. Of course, if the topic presents itself earlier, don't postpone the discussion. Your most important goal is to teach your child to determine when going along with the crowd is okay, when it's preferable but simply not possible, and finally, when standing independently is absolutely mandatory.

Appearance: A Delicate Balance

I wear baggy pants and baggy shirts. People stereotype me as
a fat person who does drugs, smokes, and has sex all the
time because of what I wear, but I don't do any of that stuff.
My clothes make me look like a punker or rapper, but I'm
not. It's just what I like to wear.

8th-grade girl

While it's true that people are much more than their looks, it's also important for kids to understand that appearance does make a difference in how adults and kids alike evaluate them. When kids enter any new environment, their dress, makeup, cleanliness, and piercings (or lack thereof), communicate their values to observers. While the eighth-grade girl quoted above prided herself on dressing like a punker or druggie, she may have deterred kids with her values and attracted other kids who may have assumed she did drugs or was ready to have casual sex. Sexually provocative styles will attract those who are searching for early sexual relations. Dressing like a druggie will bring druggies around. Even though kids say that style doesn't matter, you should be aware that clothes, makeup, hairstyles, and piercings may make a difference to other kids—your tweens' potential friends.

Parents and middle schoolers argue about clothes, and many of these battles can be quite unnecessary. Here are some simple guidelines to help you and your kids reach a reasonable compromise.

Be sure your tweens respect their school dress code. Ignoring your children's inappropriate clothes or openly supporting your kids' determination to dress counter to the school code will be viewed by your kids as permission to defy school authority. Supporting their opposition can generalize to disrespect for other authorities as well, including you.

Give your kids appropriate style guidelines that fit with your own personal values. Hear and be open to what your kids are thinking and worrying about and take time to consider their perspectives. Avoid being too rigid, but be firm in your final guidelines. Your standards can be the same or different for school and casual wear, but that depends on your family values. If parents' opinions differ, you should compromise but be united in your message to your kids.

Set reasonable price limitations within your budget. Saving kids' earnings or using gift money can help them meet the difference if certain clothes exceed your price. Teach them to watch for sales and buy at bargain prices. Parents should provide the final word for the clothing styles middle schoolers are allowed to buy, regardless of the source of their money.

Allow freedom within your guidelines for your kids to choose styles and color combinations for what they wear to school. Don't get hung up on controlling exactly what they wear, and don't assume their daily appearance is a judgment of your parenting. It's okay to back off a little, but not entirely.

The Right Clothes, the Right Labels

Each generation of educators and parents copes with the dilemma of determining the appropriateness of kids' clothes for school, dress-up, casual, and beachwear. Fashions keep changing, so that tight, loose, short, long, flared, or straight styles or exposed shoulders and navels seem to vacillate between generations. While there are always variations, the current fashion of spaghetti straps, bared navels, and drooping pants accompanies the earlier interest in sexuality displayed by kids. Thus, the guidelines and arguments may also begin earlier.

Identifying status by brand labels in clothes is very prevalent in middle schools today. Many kids will push parents for the latest fashions, but I've noticed some parents pressing kids to be fashionable, too. My focus group students explained that students are branded as *popular, rich,* or *poor* based on their clothing labels—a topic that you must discuss with your tween. It's reasonable for your kids to choose specific brand names of clothes because they fit well, are styled to their preference, or offer dependable quality, but buying clothes just because of how a label is interpreted by peers is something I caution against. There's no reason not to buy clothes of high quality for your kids, but their tastes or preferred labels may exceed your budget. In this case, kids can learn to save their money toward a new outfit or wait until the store has a sale for a cheaper purchase. Again, discussing with your kids the pressure to have brand names can help them see the foolishness of conforming to achieve status.

Sometimes, however, parents wish their children would fit in. There could be many reasons why some kids are determined to dress very differently from others. Some kids may want to define themselves as fashion leaders or as creative people. Others may be using fashion to say, "I refuse to conform." Some of those who verbalize their wish not to conform are demonstrating their independence, but others may only be masking their feelings of inadequacy. They may not believe they're capable of dressing fashionably because either they don't know how or they can't afford the clothes that popular kids wear.

If you're unhappy about the inappropriate styles your kids are wearing, try to determine what they're really feeling or saying by their choices. Remember that they may believe what they're saying, but they may not be in touch with what they're actually feeling. Competition is almost always part of kids' choices in style. Sometimes they are truly trying to be independent, but more often they may choose their different clothing because they fear if they tried to dress more appropriately, they might feel like a loser compared to other more stylish kids in their peer group. They may say, "It doesn't matter" when they really mean, "I can't do it right because I don't know how/can't afford it/am overweight." If you sense your kids are using sloppy dress as a cover-up for feelings of inadequacy, try encouraging a shopping trip with an older sibling or a favorite aunt, uncle, or grandparent who can give them some tips or suggestions for what looks good on them. Shopping with a well-dressed friend can have positive influences on your child, too. Just make sure to establish cost guidelines and your general rules for clothes. After all, clothes can be returned if your kids make big mistakes.

Hair-Raising Antics

Short, long, curly, straight, or spiked hair probably doesn't make most parents cringe, but extremes like shaved heads, Mohawks, very long hair for boys, or dyed or streaked hair can cause battles. Parents should choose their battles, based on their own personal values, while allowing their kids freedom within those guidelines. Most middle school kids will still accept *no,* as long as their parents have heard their reasons, taken time to consider their requests, and then set boundaries. Here are some principles to consider for setting hairstyle standards for your kids.

Cleanliness. Hairstyles should be such that kids can keep their hair neat and clean with minimal parental assistance. Long hair is always harder to care for.

Safety concerns. Parents' guidelines should protect children from permanently damaging their hair. Strong dyes and permanents should be researched before permission is granted to use them.

Expressing values. If your kids' hairstyles communicate values that you oppose, you need to be clear on your boundaries. For example, while it may be okay with you if your son shaves his head in sympathy for a pal who is undergoing chemotherapy, it wouldn't be okay for him to shave his head only to defy his principal, teacher, or a school dress code.

Glamor Girls

So far, makeup and high heels are issues for girls alone. Market research guides manufacturers in designing makeup and shoes to appeal to girls at an early age. The sooner kids buy grown-up items, the more of these items are able to be sold. The girls in my focus groups defined makeup as a means of attracting popular boys. Makeup is intended to encourage girls to look older than they are, and it does. You'll need to decide at what age your daughter will be allowed to wear makeup, and what kinds are appropriate. You will want to remind her that it may send a message she's not ready for.

If you give your daughter permission to wear makeup and she puts on too much, Mom or an older sister may want to offer her some tips. You could also arrange a special outing to a salon or department store for a demonstration on proper application for tweens. The price of wearing makeup is also learning how to remove it, which needs to be a faithful practice so that girls' complexions aren't marred by strong chemicals.

If you don't feel that your daughter is old enough to wear makeup yet, talk it over with her other parent and be united and firm with your joint decision. You'll have to set and follow through on consequences for defiance, so think carefully before you set this limit.

Shoe manufacturers have discovered that many kids worry about not being tall enough. Shoe stores are now selling chunky, high-heeled shoes for children as young as kindergarten-age. Seeing little girls hobbling and stumbling around in their dress-up clothes and high heels seems strange to me, but parents are buying them. Many parents won't have much choice, since shoe stores carry so many styles of high heels. I haven't seen research on the harm high heels may hold for children, but you and your daughters will probably feel pressured by the style standards unless you take a firm position. Again, you may not choose this battle, but it's one more area where tweens are encouraged to act or look older too soon.

Piercings and Tattoos

It's illegal in most states for kids to get piercings or tattoos without adult permission, so kids may push you mercilessly for permission or discover a piercing or tattoo artist who will ignore the law. Piercings and tattoos communicate a person's values. Pierced ears don't send the same sexual messages as pierced tongues or navels, and the latter are more prone to infection. While some parents pierce girls' ears when they're very young, other parents consider this to be more appropriate for the teen years. One piercing may suffice for some kids, while others may push for multiple. Be clear about your values on this issue. Piercing tongues and navels is often a message of rebellion, and again, parents need to be clear and united about granting or withholding permission. It's all right for parents to say *no* firmly and together, but if you do, mean it and don't be a pushover.

Kids will respect your authority if you're firm and provide them with a few reasons.

Tattoos also give messages of an alternative peer group. I recommend that parents stay firm about this choice being an adult decision, one that kids can make only when they live on their own and pay their own way. Because of a tattoo's permanency, your kids may put you in a difficult position if they defy you, so think ahead about the consequences you'll apply if they do get a tattoo. For example, a consequence could be loss of privileges to use their DVD player, CDs, or computer. Hopefully, your threats will be enough to prevent all but the most rebellious tweens. Kids in my focus groups reported that threats like the one below only cause anger and sometimes tempt kids to defy their parents.

> *My dad and I were in the mall and we went to Hot Topic. There was this dude with 15 piercings. My dad said, "If you ever get that kind of crap hardware on your face, I'll beat the shit out of you."*
>
> *8th-grade boy*

Blemish Battles

In the appearance-driven culture of middle school, acne is an especially difficult scourge for kids to cope with. Unlike the other appearance issues I've discussed, having acne isn't a choice any child would make, but it surely makes kids feel uncomfortably different. A child's acne may feel like a double whammy to a parent who struggled with a similar problem in his or her own adolescence. If you did, however, this may be an instance where saying, "When I was a kid . . ." may actually provide helpful reassurance to your middle schooler. She'll be able to see that you no longer struggle with pimples, so it may give her the needed hope that she won't be permanently defaced. Emphasizing to your tweens that they have personality, talents, and interests and that their acne will soon disappear will hopefully sustain them during this temporarily uncomfortable time.

You may be able to reassure a child who has only occasional pimples to be patient, permitting time and maturity to assist in clearing her skin. Some kids may need more than just your reassurance, though. Extreme acne inevitably requires treatment. Taking tweens to an understanding dermatologist can give them access to new medications that are helpful for controlling acne. Antibiotics, Accutane, and birth control pills (for girls) are helpful for clearing skin, but certain prescriptions may have mild or serious side effects that need to be carefully discussed with the dermatologist. Being sensitive to your tween's feelings, but not overreacting, will provide the support he needs in order to value himself despite having a facial blemish from time to time.

When Your Kids Are Popular with the Wrong Crowd

One boy in my school got his ears pierced. His friends thought he was cool, so they got their ears pierced, too. Other people thought they were weird, so they formed their own group.

5th-grade boy

There seems to be nothing more difficult for achievement-oriented parents to tolerate than seeing their kids bond with a negative peer group. Students who don't value school are often antiparents and pro-alcohol, tobacco, drugs, and casual sex and thrive on irreverent and often obnoxious music. Your kids will probably proclaim that they are good and loyal friends or that they're much nicer and less shallow than the "preppies" and "jocks." These negative peers may indeed be kinder to your children than some other kids you'd prefer for them to befriend. Your kids may become secretive, say that you're controlling, and protest that you have no right to say with whom they can be friends.

Below are preventive strategies that can work well for encouraging your kids to avoid negative peers.

Don't pressure kids to make friends. Many of the antischool kids I've worked with are lonely, attention seeking, and sometimes aggressive as elementary-age children. Parents and teachers are anxious about their kids' lack of friends, even when they do have a few. Parents and teachers often put pressure on them to make friends, and the kids connect having a large group of close friends with healthy adjustment. They feel that adults are disappointed in them when they don't have friends, and by middle school, they become so anxious about making friends that they're willing to do almost anything to be included in any group that validates them. They develop a deep resentment toward the bright, achieving, or athletic kids who haven't accepted them, and they share that resentment in order to build solidarity with another group. In some ways, they believe that "good kids" are bad, because the "bad kids" are loyal to each other, although they may appear tough or mean to outsiders.

When your kids are a little lonely, it's important to label it as *independence* even though you realize it isn't easy for them. In that way, you avoid putting too much pressure on them to make friends and become popular. Use this time to help them learn skills and develop interests that will enable them to share activities with others. For example, learning to play chess will encourage them to play with other kids, developing an interest in music or art will give them a passion to share with other positive young people who also enjoy those activities, or playing soccer or taking gymnastics classes will make them feel like part of a team. Once they have friends who share their interests, they will be less likely to feel pressured to unite with negative kids.

Avoid conspiratorial relationships. Rebellious adolescents are often overempowered by parents who are divided. A mother who allies with her child against the dad, or a father who allies with a child against the mom, teaches a child that relationships become closer and more intimate when two people share a common enemy. Learning to feel close to a person only when there's a common enemy can become a very negative but intense habit, which transfers naturally to finding a peer group or even a boy- or girlfriend who is against school or parents.

This alliance-against-an-enemy relationship with a parent becomes an even greater risk during or after a divorce. Mothers who have been rejected by their husbands can be especially vulnerable to sharing intimate details about the husband's behavior. Although at first it seems that kids understand the situation and value the intimate sharing, this too-intimate practice almost always backfires. Divorce is no time to assume that children are mature enough to be your counselors or confidantes. Not only does this place kids in an impossible dilemma, but it also teaches them to disrespect and rebel against their other parent, which will in turn cause the other parent to teach them disrespect for you. You're giving up your adult responsibility when your kids may require it most.

Help kids adjust to a move. Another important prevention scenario takes place after a move to a new community. I recommend having your child paired with other kids initially when moving to a new school. The kids with whom she's paired could make her feel more comfortable, as well as include her in a positive group. The selection of those new friends should be made carefully. You can probably do that most diplomatically if you share with the teacher or counselor your child's positive interests. If you do this, it's more likely that your child and those with whom she's paired will have activities or interests in common.

Sometimes teachers pair negative or needy kids with new students in the hopes of helping them. Caution your child that finding good friends takes time. Be reassuring that there's no need to hurry it along, and that you're certain that eventually he'll find good friends. Seeking popularity encourages the quest for status and quantity of friends, which may or may not turn out to be a good thing, depending on the values of the popular peer group in the school.

What if your child has already been influenced by a negative peer group? The solutions below may help when you need positive intervention.

Change schools or teams. There are several possibilities for helping your kids ditch negative peer groups. Sometimes changing schools or teams can be effective. This has proven to be extremely powerful for some kids who have been clients at my Family Achievement Clinic. Most middle schools use a team approach with between two and four teams in a school. Talk to your child's school counselor about the possibility of changing to a different team to get him away from negative peers. This may help your child make new friends, particularly if he has at least one positive friend in a new team. Changing schools or teams works most effectively when negative relationships are just beginning, before your child is overly engaged with the group. It also works best if the negative group doesn't live in your neighborhood.

Prohibit friendships. Sending a clear message to your child that you wish he not befriend a particular individual or group may make a difference for middle schoolers. You'll need to justify the prohibition by explaining that the other kids' behavior is unacceptable, and you'll permit them to be friends outside of school only if you see a change in the other kids. When both parents agree on that philosophy, your child will likely accept it. When both parents don't agree, don't waste your time prohibiting the friendship. This is an important communication that both parents should talk through carefully.

Develop new interests. The most positive technique for removing kids from a negative peer group is to get them involved in positive peer experiences, such as fun enrichment programs, special-interest groups, drama, music, sports, Scouts, religious groups, summer programs, camps, or youth travel programs. They may not want to join without their friends, so introducing them to someone who's already part of a group may encourage them. A teacher or group leader may help to facilitate new friendships.

Enter contests. Encourage your child to enter contests or activities in which he has a chance of winning or receiving an important part. Don't hesitate to talk to a coach or teacher privately about your efforts to reverse your child's negativism. Winning kids are often excluded from peer groups that are negative about school. Winning a speech, music, art, or sports contest often gives status to students and causes them to appear more interesting to positive students. Sometimes a victory is enough to separate a tween from a negative peer group.

Plan an exciting family trip. A family trip is also an option for distracting your wayward child from negativity. Time away from peers in an entirely new environment can channel your child's independence. One-on-one trips with a parent may be effective in reducing tension and enhancing family closeness. A trip with only one parent and one tween may be more productive than if the whole family is present, because the tween will be freed from sibling rivalry issues.

If you introduce any of these courses of action to your children, don't expect them to like it. These options shouldn't be suggested as choices, or your kids surely won't choose them. You can, however, permit or even encourage them to make choices among the options. For example, they can choose between a summer writing or music program, which will hopefully encourage new and positive interests and friendships.

While all of these possibilities can develop good relationships and are applicable for all kids, the next chapter will sensitize you to the special social struggles for overweight kids.

CHAPTER 11

TWEEN WEIGHT PROBLEMS

If you're overweight and not good at sports, you can't be popular.

7th-grade boy

Some girls think they're fat, and they're not fat at all. Half the girls are a little bit anorexic.

7th-grade boy

I play football, but I don't really like it. I'm not that aggressive.

Overweight 8th-grade boy

I kind of like someone; she's really nice. I met her last year. People said, "Oh, she's fat," or "Oh, she's ugly, you shouldn't like her." I don't care if she's fat because she's really nice to me. I don't really care if girls are pretty or not. I just look at people's personalities.

8th-grade boy

EVERY FILM AND BOOK ABOUT adolescent development that is directed toward kids emphasizes the importance of accepting individual differences in weight, height, and appearance. But despite those omnipresent messages, my survey proved that many tweens don't accept or even tolerate kids who are "different," especially when kids are overweight.

Kids' Worries about Being Overweight

Kids are either in or out, and fat kids can't be in.

6th-grade boy

Because weight issues are quite different for girls than they are for boys, most of my data on weight is sorted by gender. Figure 11.1 shows clearly the differential worry between girls and boys about being too fat. While almost the same percentage of third-grade boys and girls worried about being too fat, the percentage of girls increased by grade level from 14 percent in third grade to a whopping 39 percent by eighth grade. The percentage of boys who worried about being too fat stayed fairly constant in all grades, ranging between 11 percent and 18 percent. If you look at Figure

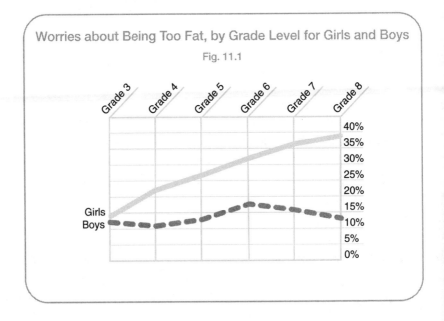

Worries about Being Too Fat, by Grade Level for Girls and Boys

Fig. 11.1

11.1, you'll see that girls' worries doubled those of boys in grades four and five, and by eighth grade, girls' concerns were triple that of boys'. It's evident that girls are particularly susceptible to the fear of being overweight.

A World Record

In a study of overweight conducted in 15 countries, the United States had the dubious honor of being ranked first in its prevalence of adolescents who were overweight and obese.[1] The rate of obesity has tripled for our children since 1970 and is accompanied by more than just the social stigma that excludes popularity.[2] The epidemic proportions of overweight kids project major public health problems; adolescent overweight typically leads to adult overweight or obesity, which increases the risk for heart disease, diabetes, stroke, cancer, and other very serious diseases.

Because of the psychological trauma caused by being bullied, shunned, or abused by children and adults, there's little likelihood that overweight children will be able to take personal control of their lives to change their poor eating and exercise habits. Furthermore, many suffer lifelong emotional scars that are almost never completely eradicated. In order to help children improve their health and cope with their overweight, parents and other caring adults will need to coach them toward finding their strengths and believing in themselves, despite a peer culture that treats them cruelly.

The kids in my focus groups were particularly malicious toward overweight girls. Although very underweight boys were also ridiculed, very underweight girls were well accepted. Here's what some kids in my focus groups had to say about their overweight peers.

Fat girls try to wear tight shirts, and the fat rolls hang out. They look nasty. They want to be like the good-looking girls, and they can't look good. They say, "We know you want us, but don't touch," and who wants to touch them? They're ugly.

The focus groups weren't quite as cruel when they described overweight boys, but they still laughed plenty at them.

Fat kids get teased most in gym [laughter]. Even the coaches and gym teachers make fun of them. They're so clumsy; you'd better stay away from them. If they fall, you'll get smooshed just like a pancake [more laughter].

The adolescent girls in my focus groups were more sensitive with their descriptions of overweight peers, but they clearly acknowledged that overweight boys had problems, as illustrated by the story of Thomas described by seventh-grader Angelee below. Angelee showed some sensitivity to Thomas's feelings, but the girls could also be insensitive.

The coach had the boys playing basketball—skins and shirts. Thomas, my good friend, was on the skins team. He has big breasts, like a girl, and when he started running with the ball, his breasts bounced up and down. His face turned red, and he put his arms over his chest to cover himself. All the kids were talking about Thomas's breasts. Then the coach noticed and told him to put his shirt on, but I know Thomas will never forget what happened that day.

Underweight Is Different for Girls Than Boys

Children's perceptions of their weight dramatically affect them. Overweight girls worried about almost everything in greater percentages than overweight boys (Figures 11.2, next page, and 11.3 on page 198). Being very underweight rarely caused major problems for girls. The very underweight girls weren't much different than average-weight girls with respect to most worries. There were only two areas where very thin girls worried significantly more than average-weight girls: They worried more about being bullied and that their teachers didn't understand them. Even in these two areas, the very overweight girls' worries far surpassed the others.

The effects on boys from being very underweight were in some ways as extreme as the effects of being very overweight. Very overweight and very underweight boys worried almost equally about self-confidence and loneliness, and more so than average-weight boys

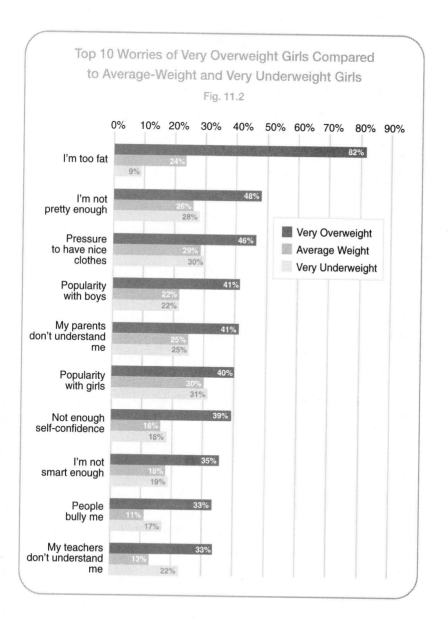

Top 10 Worries of Very Overweight Girls Compared to Average-Weight and Very Underweight Girls

Fig. 11.2

■ Very Overweight
▨ Average Weight
▨ Very Underweight

- I'm too fat: 82% / 24% / 9%
- I'm not pretty enough: 48% / 26% / 28%
- Pressure to have nice clothes: 46% / 29% / 30%
- Popularity with boys: 41% / 22% / 22%
- My parents don't understand me: 41% / 25% / 25%
- Popularity with girls: 40% / 30% / 31%
- Not enough self-confidence: 39% / 16% / 18%
- I'm not smart enough: 35% / 18% / 19%
- People bully me: 33% / 11% / 17%
- My teachers don't understand me: 33% / 13% / 22%

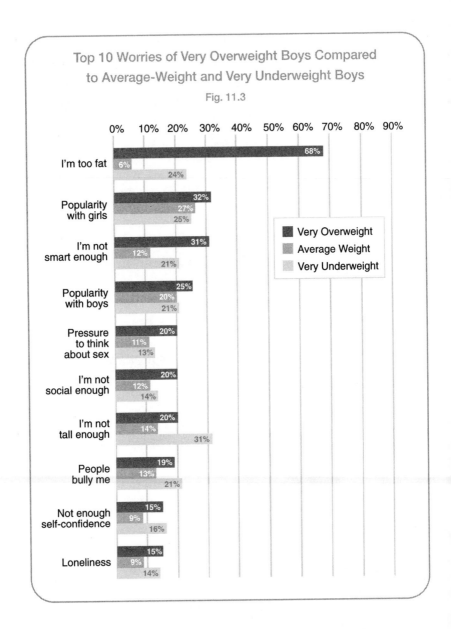

Top 10 Worries of Very Overweight Boys Compared to Average-Weight and Very Underweight Boys

Fig. 11.3

Legend:
- Very Overweight
- Average Weight
- Very Underweight

Worry	Very Overweight	Average Weight	Very Underweight
I'm too fat	68%	6%	24%
Popularity with girls	32%	27%	25%
I'm not smart enough	31%	12%	21%
Popularity with boys	25%	20%	21%
Pressure to think about sex	20%	11%	13%
I'm not social enough	20%	12%	14%
I'm not tall enough	20%	14%	31%
People bully me	19%	13%	21%
Not enough self-confidence	15%	9%	16%
Loneliness	15%	9%	14%

(Figure 11.3). Both groups of boys worried about not being smart enough. Overweight girls worried more about being bullied than overweight boys did, but among the boys, it was those who are underweight who worried the most about bullying. Very underweight boys whom

I've worked with at my clinic have shared their desires to be taller, stronger, and bigger in general. Boys often lag behind girls in growth during middle school, which makes size a big concern—especially for underweight boys. They are often the last group among their classmates to reach sexual development, and they often have the greatest difficulty fitting in with their peers.

How Weight Affects Self-Descriptions

Fat kids are called ugly! Small is the perfect size.

5th-grade girl

Weight had a dramatic impact on kids' self-descriptions, with overweight generally having a negative effect. Again, there were differences between the boys and girls.

Girls' Self-Descriptions

Very overweight girls *always* described themselves more negatively compared to average-weight girls. They were much less likely to describe themselves as athletic, beautiful, cool, confident, creative, fashion leaders, gifted, good little girls, happy, hard workers, kind, leaders, popular, secure, smart, sweet, or talented. Overweight girls were much more likely to describe themselves as bossy, different, fearful, followers, lazy, lonely, mean, sad, self-critical, unhappy, and wimpy. With such negative self-images, it's no wonder they consoled themselves with food.

Thinness is so valued by girls that the very underweight girls who participated in my survey often had better self-images than even the average-weight girls. They were more likely to consider themselves athletic, beautiful, cool, fashion leaders, gifted, good little girls, happy, hard workers, popular, smart, sweet, and talented. They were less likely to consider themselves followers or describe themselves as self-critical.

The reverence for thinness pressures girls to be as skinny as possible. It also explains the disproportionately large number of girls who develop dangerous eating disorders like anorexia or bulimia.

Boys' Self-Descriptions

Very overweight boys also had negative self-descriptions. They were less likely to consider themselves athletic, cool, confident, gifted, happy, hard workers, popular, smart, or talented, and more likely to consider themselves bossy, chatterboxes, different, emotional, fearful, followers, immature, lazy, lonely, nerdy, rebellious, sad, self-critical, troublemakers, unhappy, and wimpy. There was one positive exception; more overweight boys described themselves as leaders than average-weight boys. Apparently their larger physical size afforded them the sense of power to lead others.

Very underweight boys didn't describe themselves quite as negatively as very overweight boys, but their self-concepts definitely suffered in comparison to average-weight boys. Very underweight boys were less likely to think of themselves as athletic, cool, confident, happy, hard workers, leaders, popular, smart, and talented, and more likely to describe themselves as different, emotional, fearful, followers, immature, lazy, lonely, nerdy, sad, self-critical, unhappy, and wimpy. While their lot may not be quite as distressing as that of overweight kids, it's certainly worse than that of average-weight girls and boys and much worse than that of very underweight girls. Very underweight boys probably feel bad about themselves because their immaturity is often a poor fit with their peers.

Weight Effects on Self-Confidence and Belief in Intelligence

The boys are mean to the girls who aren't skinny, don't have perfect figures, and don't wear tons of makeup. Those girls can't be popular.

6th-grade girl

Children's perceptions of their weight during their middle school years impacted both their self-confidence and their perceptions of their intelligence. By comparing the boys and the girls, we again see some important differences. For girls, being very overweight dramatically lessened their general self-confidence (48 percent reported having very good self-confidence, compared with 72 percent of average-weight girls), but underweight girls had the exact same rate of self-confidence as average-weight girls. On the other hand, boys who were very overweight (58 percent) or very underweight (63 percent) were both adversely affected; their self-confidence was significantly lower than that of average-weight boys (79 percent).

The relationship of weight to general self-confidence is slightly different than it is for perceptions of intelligence. Fewer overweight and underweight kids, whether they were boys or girls, considered themselves to be of above-average intelligence. Overweight boys suffered the most in this particular instance. Only 47 percent of overweight boys thought they were above average in intelligence, compared with 69 percent of average-weight boys.

In my focus groups, overweight kids were more reserved and less confident when describing their intelligence. Adults that I interviewed who were overweight as children provided insights as to the adverse effects of being overweight on their perceptions of their intelligence. Darlene, an adult interviewee, explains below.

> I didn't believe anything good about myself, so I couldn't believe I was smart. I felt like a blob. I had terrible grades. I didn't believe in myself, so I didn't try hard. My attitude was "Why bother?" When I was in eighth grade, they gave us IQ and achievement tests to place us in high school. My dad got the report and he said, "Your teacher said you have the second-highest IQ in the class." I was floored. It was the first time I realized I might be really smart.

Kids and Activity

Kids' passive activities, like watching TV and using the computer, certainly contribute toward being overweight. But what most parents don't consider is the idea that their kids' sad emotional lives may lead them to the solace of a screen. Very overweight children from my survey spent much more time watching television, playing computer games, sending e-mail, and surfing the Internet than either average-weight or very under-weight kids. Except for sending e-mail (a favorite among girls), boys spent the most time on passive activities. Very overweight boys spent an average of 4.1 hours a day watching television.

Furthermore, my study found that average-weight girls and boys participated in more-active extracurriculars like sports, hiking, camping, and dance, while overweight kids were more likely to choose less physically active interests like art, choir, and piano. There was one exception. Average-weight girls did more reading, a passive activity, than very overweight girls. That may be because they felt more intelligent, which in turn linked to a love of reading. The suffering that overweight adolescent girls experience has an incredibly adverse impact on most of their activities during the middle school years.

Weighty Family Issues

I'm not allowed to eat much junk food. I can only have 15 chips at a time. I still have Halloween candy left over! I can only have two chocolates a day, or one piece of hard candy a day. My mom makes a lot of good dinners for me, but I don't have that great of snacks.

5th-grade girl

Weight makes a difference in middle school children's relationships with their families (Figures 11.4 and 11.5). Some parents may be concerned about their kids' appearances, and how this affects peer relationships. Still others are worried about health problems for their overweight kids. Regardless of parents' motivation, it's apparent that weight makes a difference in how kids describe their family relationships.

Battles over eating too much or too little often permeate family meals, and these battles can worsen the tween/parent relationship that is already such a challenge. When kids don't feel good about themselves, parents easily become the whipping posts for their tense emotions. Furthermore, parents who themselves struggled with weight often identify with their children's problems, and parents' resultant anxiety can interfere with their family relationships.

The good news is that improving family relationships can help children to healthfully cope with their weight issues, and coping healthfully

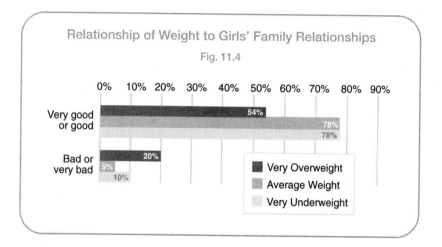

Relationship of Weight to Girls' Family Relationships

Fig. 11.4

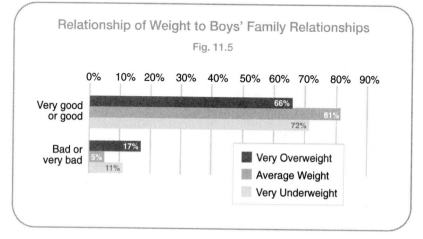

Relationship of Weight to Boys' Family Relationships

Fig. 11.5

with weight problems may in turn have the effect of improving family relationships.

The Weight/Optimism Link

Optimism about the future has long been tied to resilience and success. A positive "I can" attitude was characteristic of the successful women I studied for my book *See Jane Win*. The results of my survey of middle school kids showed that average-weight girls were likely to be optimistic about their futures. That optimism may be a reflection of peer and family acceptance.

While girls and boys responded similarly when asked about their expectations of happiness for their futures, a much greater percentage of girls in all three weight categories were also worried or afraid about their futures. At a time when girls have caught up with boys in so many areas of competence, more of them continue to worry as early as the middle school years that their futures aren't as assured as are boys' futures.

What Parents Can Do to Help

There is much that parents can do to help their overweight children. I interviewed healthy, average-weight adults who were overweight as kids, and they reported two major commonalities:

1. A mentor: Someone believed in them and gave them enough confidence to take control of their weight.

2. A turning point: Some event in their lives caused them to recognize their weight problem.

The turning point for these healthy adults could have been positive or negative. Not making the cheerleading squad or being teased by a boy about their weight were some of the negative stories. But others had positive stories, like having a basketball coach convince them to eat healthier for improvement in athletic ability. Often a parent, teacher, or other adult can form an alliance with an overweight child and give him the confidence to change his unhealthy lifestyle for the sake of his future. Eighth-grader Alyssa told me about a teacher who made a difference in her life.

Ever since I was a little kid, I was fat, and that made me feel different from other kids. Kids left me out of their groups. I had absolutely no one to play with on the playground—not a single friend. On Valentine's Day, when other kids got valentines saying "I love you" or "Be mine," my valentine had an elephant on it. Some love! I felt like an elephant. A wall kept going up, higher and higher, separating me from everyone. I felt imprisoned until this year. This year my teacher liked me. She helped me find my talents. She told me I was good at writing, math, and music and that I had a good personality. Her confidence in me made me feel different, but in a good way. I started making friends and felt smart and better about myself. Now I think the wall is tumbling down, and I have new hope for my future.

In my book *Rescuing the Emotional Lives of Overweight Children*, I developed the Six-Step Healthy Rescue Plan, which I have summarized below. The principles of the rescue plan involve providing unconditional nurturance for children, setting clear and reasonable boundaries, promoting honesty, and being a role model for healthy living. These basic principles of good parenting also serve to guide children to better health and healthier weights.

The Six-Step Healthy Rescue Plan

Step 1: Be a coach instead of a judge. Coaches are enthusiastic and positive. They're in alliance with the kids they guide, and kids feel that coaches believe in them and are on their side. On the other hand, judges are like the "Food Police." They notice what kids do wrong but hardly ever recognize kids' progress, causing kids to feel angry and rebellious—even if the messages about eating and exercise are appropriate.

Step 2: Go for the goal. Help kids set realistic short-term goals so that they can experience small successes and maintain hope. Emphasize healthy eating and exercise, rather than fad diets with unrealistic goals.

Step 3: Recruit additional support. Other family members can be supportive if you talk to them privately about how they can help. You also may be able to find adolescent healthy eating groups in your community or schools.

Step 4: Design a nutritional plan. Your family physician or a registered dietitian can help with a realistic nutritional plan. Your kids are more likely to be willing to listen to information from an outside expert than from their parents.

Step 5: Organize an exercise effort. Family exercise is good for all, and parent participation encourages kids. Be sure to set limits for screen time and commit to exercising an hour a day, as recommended in government guidelines.

Step 6: Celebrate strengths. Kids take charge of their weight more easily if they feel good about their lives. Discovering your children's strengths and interests and encouraging an active and interesting lifestyle helps them to build self-esteem. There are many activities for them to try, but they'll need you to believe in them so they can be brave enough to begin.

Caring Adults Can Activate Schools and Communities

Health can become a community priority. You can ask your favorite restaurants, even fast-food franchises, to put fruits and vegetables on their children's menus and cut down on the quantity of fries and pasta. Encourage your school district to provide more physical education classes, particularly centered on lifetime sports like jogging, tennis, golf, dancing, and swimming. You can also lobby to get soft drink and candy vending machines replaced with healthy snack machines that include milk, string cheese, fruits, and veggies among their offerings.

Suggest that your recreation departments and community groups (like the YMCA or YWCA) provide noncompetitive exercise and nutrition classes for adolescents. If kids connect fun with learning about nutrition, eating right, and exercise, being healthy can be cool. You can also encourage your school to sponsor antibullying programs to sensitize kids toward individual differences and provide safe havens and friendship for kids who are overweight.

What Parents Can Do for Underweight Kids

When late-maturing underweight kids are healthy kids, they may only need the reassurance from parents that they'll grow larger with maturity. Encouraging their physical activity can keep them strong and confident about their bodies. While they're less likely to be basketball or football players because of their size, being small shouldn't prevent them from swimming, running track, bicycling, or playing tennis to develop healthy stamina and strength. On the other hand, if they're underweight because they have eating disorders or troubling eating habits, they'll require professional treatment. Your family physician can help you determine if your child has an eating disorder and can refer you to an eating disorder specialist.

CHAPTER 12

ACHIEVEMENT OR UNDERACHIEVEMENT

*Some kids get the worst grades—Ds and Fs—and they don't
care. They're proud of bad grades and think they're cool.*

7th-grade girl

*When we have 2 hours of homework, smart kids spend 4
hours perfecting theirs. It makes me angry that they don't do
anything but their homework, so they get better grades.
They think they're better than you because they're smarter. If
you know someone who's smart and you aren't as smart as
them, they shove it in your face.*

8th-grade girl

*Sometimes you can be hot and still get good grades, but usu-
ally if you get good grades, you're a loser.*

8th-grade boy

*This one kid's a bookworm, and he just doesn't "get it"
socially. Kids don't tease him, but they're not nice to him
either.*

6th-grade girl

I get straight A's, but I like having fun and I don't show that I'm a straight A student.

6th-grade boy

MOTIVATION MAKES MORE OF A DIFFERENCE than IQ in kids' school success. Children who are stimulated to achieve—almost regardless of their abilities—can be successful students. However, there are many kids whose parents would like to light a fire under them so they work harder and achieve in school. These children are typically known as underachievers.

School Success Pays Off for the Rest of Life

The reason my mom put me in therapy is because I'm bright and I wasn't getting good grades. She said I took a test in third grade and was above average, but schoolwork's not that easy for me. My mom threatens me and says she's going to whup me if I don't improve.

7th-grade boy

School success increases the chances of achieving life success. Average adult salaries actually increase with advancement of degrees earned. While higher salaries aren't the only measure of happiness, it's true that most people prefer prosperity to poverty. While money alone can't make you happy, those strapped with economic woes would agree that they'd be happier if they made a better living. Most parents hope—at a minimum—that their children will grow up to be able to support themselves. They also want their kids to enjoy their future careers and even acquire social status, if possible. But for the majority of middle school parents, and for the kids themselves, future careers are a far-off concern.

For the present, parents are pleased if their tweens do their homework, enjoy school, and work to the best of their abilities. Some parents feel their kids are working to their abilities only if they earn A's, while other parents will accept Bs and Cs, but parents are never happy when their kids bring home Ds and Fs. Middle schoolers earn these low grades only if they don't study or complete their homework. Because you as parents aren't always able to determine your children's abilities, you can consider them successful achievers if they:

- Do homework regularly
- Study for tests
- Enjoy and are interested in learning
- Find schoolwork reasonably challenging (not too easy or too difficult)
- Feel fairly intelligent

The Critical Value of Feeling Smart

My friends call me a geek and "smarty pants." One of my friends is a little jealous. I take it as a compliment.

8th-grade girl

Kids compare themselves to siblings, classmates, and friends—whether or not their parents do. Although they don't have to feel like they're *the* smartest to feel good about themselves, my study showed that if kids felt they had above-average intelligence, they also felt better about many of their other qualities. For example, compared to kids who viewed themselves as having average or below-average intelligence, kids who believed they had above-average intelligence worried less about almost everything (see Figure 12.1 on page 212). Even appearance issues, like not feeling pretty enough or being too fat, seemed to cause less worry for kids who felt intelligent.

Furthermore, kids who described their intelligence as above average were more likely to describe themselves with good characteristics than bad. Kids who described themselves as having above-average intelligence were more likely to think they were smart, talented, athletic, happy, creative, kind, funny, gifted, hard workers, confident, special, independent, leaders, courageous, popular, good, brainy, adultlike, sensitive, bookworms, modest, persistent, and secure. These kids also considered themselves perfectionistic and self-critical, which aren't good characteristics, but are common among bright kids.

Not only were kids with above-average intelligence more likely to select positive characteristics to describe themselves, they were also less likely than those of below-average intelligence to consider themselves

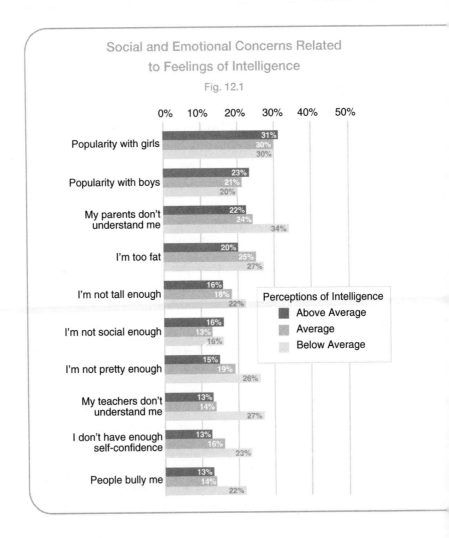

Social and Emotional Concerns Related
to Feelings of Intelligence

Fig. 12.1

unhappy, mean, wimpy, sad, fearful, immature, lonely, bossy, rebellious, troublemakers, lazy, and chatterboxes. You can see by these comparisons how imperative it is for kids to maintain feelings of intelligence, and how devastating it is for them to feel dumb. Children will feel smarter if they learn to be achievers in school, but ironically, peer pressure in middle school confuses kids on how to define *intelligent*.

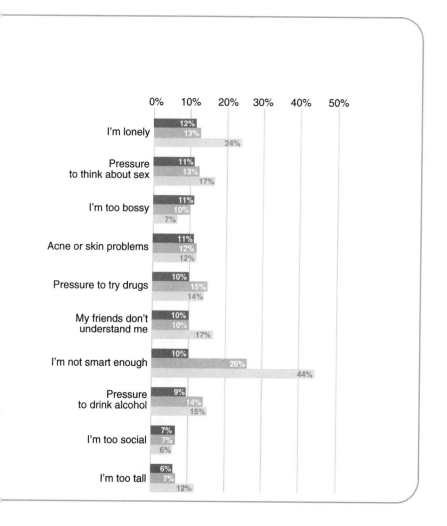

Classroom Environments Can Foster Underachievement

When teachers hand out report cards and you smile, and a
bully knows you got good grades, he'll bully you around.

6th-grade boy

Classroom environments make a difference for kids as well. An underlying characteristic revealed in most studies of underachievement is a lack of personal locus of control.[1] That is, underachievers don't internalize the relationship between effort and outcome, process and product. They'll say, "The teacher gave me that grade," "I got lucky," or "I must be dumb" rather than "I studied hard and earned that grade" or "The test was harder than I expected, so I'll prepare better next time."

Illustrated in Figure 12.2 are the relationships between efforts and outcomes. The figure shows how the appropriate relationship will support your children's achievement and motivation and help them to define intelligence. Quadrant 1 illustrates the appropriate relationship that

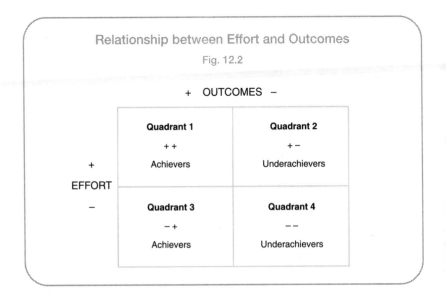

Relationship between Effort and Outcomes

Fig. 12.2

	+ OUTCOMES −	
+ EFFORT	**Quadrant 1** + + Achievers	**Quadrant 2** + − Underachievers
−	**Quadrant 3** − + Achievers	**Quadrant 4** − − Underachievers

Rimm's Laws

1. Children are more likely to be achievers if their parents join together to give the same clear and positive message about school effort and expectations.

2. Children can learn appropriate behaviors more easily if they have an effective model to imitate.

3. Communication about a child between adults (referential speaking) within the child's hearing dramatically affects children's behaviors and self-perceptions.

4. Overreaction by parents to children's successes and failures leads them to feel either intense pressure to succeed or despair and discouragement in dealing with failure.

5. Children feel more tension when they are worrying about their work than when they are doing that work.

6. Children develop self-confidence through struggle.

7. Deprivation and excess frequently exhibit the same symptoms.

8. Children develop confidence and an internal sense of control if power is given to them in gradually increasing increments as they show maturity and responsibility.

9. Children become oppositional if one adult allies with them against a parent or a teacher, making them more powerful than an adult.

10. Adults should avoid confrontations with children unless they are sure they can control the outcomes.

11. Children will become achievers only if they learn to function in competition.

12. Children will continue to achieve if they usually see the relationship between the learning process and its outcomes.

fosters an achievement orientation. Quadrants 2, 3, and 4 show unbalanced relationships, which destroy the relationship between efforts and outcomes and initiate defensive and avoidance patterns, which in turn foster underachievement and confused definitions of intelligence. As parents, you'll want to ensure that your kids are in a school environment that fosters the relationship in Quadrant 1 and that most of their schoolwork is neither too easy nor too difficult.

Quadrant 1 represents achievement. Kids in this quadrant might feel bright and creative, and they will feel that their parents and teachers approve of them. They're motivated to earn good grades and approval from adults and friends, but they also feel a sense of intrinsic and extrinsic satisfaction with their accomplishments. They set realistically high goals and demonstrate appropriate effort because they have learned to work hard. They understand perseverance. These children achieve as long as they *usually* continue to see the relationship between process and outcome (see "Rimm's Laws" on page 215), and as long as they don't cave in to negative peer pressure.

Quadrant 2 represents underachievers whose efforts begin appropriately but whose goals are set either too low or too high. Children with goals set too low have internalized a message from parents or from peers that being "too smart" is not as important as being popular. They don't want to be "geeks" or "nerds" because intellectual accomplishment is valued less than beauty, athletic prowess, or popularity. If goals are set too low, kids halt appropriate efforts because it's easy to achieve lower outcomes.

The "too high" goals or outcomes may come in a highly competitive school environment where, despite a child's intelligence and good study skills, good grades don't feel attainable. If parents set expectations or goals beyond children's abilities—and of course some do—this too will have an impact. Also, children who have learning disabilities may have a Quadrant 2 experience because even if they work hard, achieving positive outcomes may feel impossible. Quadrant 2's unrealistic goals can make kids feel "dumb," even if they are reasonably intelligent.

Quadrant 3 illustrates what causes underachievement when the achievement process isn't learned appropriately. That is, parents, children, and schools value good grades and school performance. Grades initially reflect excellent performance. Kids begin by feeling positive about school, but they're not sufficiently challenged. They learn that achievement is easy, that success is readily attainable, and that learning and study are effortless. Occasionally, they may comment about boredom or the lack of challenges, but, as long as grades continue to be high, they exhibit no problem behaviors, and few parents complain because their kids seem happy and successful.

In middle school, however, the curriculum becomes more challenging. Some kids learn more appropriate study habits. Others worry that they're not as smart as they'd like to be, and they invent or discover a whole group of rituals and excuses that prevent them from making further effort. They worry about their changed self-images. Many of these students have said, "If you're smart, schoolwork should be easy." These students change their attitudes only when parents and teachers gradually persuade them to work harder, showing them that they are, indeed, capable students—as long as they put forth the effort.

Quadrant 4 represents an advanced stage of underachievement. It results after the children described in Quadrants 2 or 3 have underachieved for a period of time. Quadrant 4 underachievement (which often begins in middle school) takes place when children have given up on reasonable goal-setting because their efforts and skills have had extreme deficiencies for a long time. Teachers and parents begin to doubt these kids' abilities. Parents recall that their children were achievers in the past, but they are often willing to settle for their children's barely passing grades. Kids groan about assignments that are too difficult or boring because they haven't learned to put forth effort.

Quadrant 4 underachievement can be difficult to reverse and sometimes requires therapeutic help. Hopefully, you as parents can prevent your kids from reaching Quadrant 4 by correcting problems in Quadrants 2 or 3. Identifying learning disabilities and asking for an appropriately challenging curriculum are important steps in parent advocacy. In discussing changes in your children's curriculum with their teachers, share your perceptions of your children's skills, but be sure to listen carefully to teachers' perceptions of their performance as well.[2]

Peer Pressure

I hate 'em. Those smart kids get on your nerves. They're just so perfect, like they've never made a mistake on anything or turned in homework late.

8th-grade boy

Kids in elementary school typically strive to please their parents and teachers by achieving good grades. In the past, adolescence brought with it peer pressure to fit in, and because most kids can't get all A's, "fitting in" meant being a B student without too much effort. Those who could earn A's but earned only Bs or Cs were considered underachievers by their parents and teachers. Because they underachieved only to a small extent, maturity and the desire to get scholarships or entrance to college was usually enough to reverse underachievement in high school.

Today, however, it's a different story. Many teachers I've talked to agree that the problem of underachievement has become more widespread and more extreme for kids who are in middle school today. As early as fourth and fifth grade, students in my focus groups said they resented kids who got all A's, worked too hard, and did schoolwork perfectly.

Not only does peer-pressured underachievement seem to start earlier than it used to, it also seems to be more extreme. Students who think it's cool not to do homework now earn Ds and Fs rather than just Bs and Cs. These extreme grades are alarming to parents and may cause kids to gradually lose confidence in their intelligence. In one kid's words, "I've dug a hole, and I'm no longer sure I can work my way out of it."

The irony of underachievement is that kids often begin underachieving to prove to themselves that they're smart without effort, but they end by losing confidence in their intelligence. Kids think that they'll have a better chance of being accepted by other kids if they show that they can get good grades without effort. On the other hand, studying too hard, carrying too many books, or using advanced vocabulary turns off mainstream peers. When these kids' Bs and Cs drop to Ds and Fs, they don't think they can turn their grades around. They either give up and feel like losers, or pretend they don't care and act like it's cool to fail.

An Epidemic of Underachievement

Although some kids begin underachieving in elementary school, the number of underachievers expands dramatically in middle school. A number of factors combine to make middle schools hatching grounds for underachievement: kids' stress about intelligence and self-image, peer pressure for kids to achieve without trying, a more challenging middle school curriculum, the typically larger size of schools, and the competitiveness of adolescents.

Parents recognize the symptoms of underachievement, but many are not sure how to reverse the pattern. Just one of my segments on NBC TV's *Today* show about bright, underachieving children generated more than 20,000 phone calls and more than 5,000 letters from distressed parents.

There is neither a gene nor a neurological or biological explanation for underachievement. You can't blame the school for your child's underachievement—there are probably many other children with similar abilities who achieve well in the very same school. It's important for parents to remember that underachievers *learn* to underachieve. And because the behavior is learned rather than inherited, parents and teachers can reteach underachieving children to achieve.

Recognizing Underachievers

Underachievers usually begin as bright and often very verbal preschoolers, but at some point (typically in middle school) their enthusiasm for learning and their satisfactory school performance changes—gradually for some, suddenly and dramatically for others.

Underachievers become disorganized. They dawdle. They forget homework, lose assignments, and misplace books. They daydream, don't listen, look out the window, or talk too much to other kids. They have poor study skills, or none at all. They believe they've studied if they briefly read the material while lying on their beds, watching TV. Some are slow and perfectionistic and say that if they finish their work, it'll probably be wrong anyway. Others complete their assignments quickly but are much more concerned about finishing than about doing quality work. Their papers have so many careless errors that one wonders if they gave any thought to the assignments at all. It seems that their goal is only to finish their homework before the end of the school day so they don't have to take any home.

Some underachieving children are lonely and withdrawn. They don't seem to want any friends. They may cry, whine, and complain, or they may be teased and tormented by their peers. Others are bossy and lose their tempers easily. Some are aggressive and may start playground fights. If underachievers show any interest in school, it's usually related to their social life or sports. They may select one subject or teacher they like, but in general, they think school is "boring."

Underachievers are unconsciously manipulative. They may overtly attempt to manipulate parent against parent, teacher against parent, parent against teacher, or friend against friend. Covertly, they may manipulate parents to do their homework for them. They may convince their teachers to postpone deadlines or give them assistance or less challenging assignments. Sometimes they complain that schoolwork is too easy and use this as an excuse for not wasting their time. Other times they claim their teachers expect too much work.

Types of Underachievers

Underachievers come in many varieties, and although they're truly individuals, they often fit into two categories. In real life, the prototypes are not pure in any one child; they're blended.

Dependent underachievers manipulate adults to do more for them than they need done. They communicate with tears and body language that proclaim their helplessness. Adults intuitively respond by doing too much for them. Unfortunately, the more adults do for them, the less the kids learn to do for themselves, adding to kids' feelings of helplessness.

Intuitively, it feels appropriate to help dependent kids who are looking for direction, but parents should beware of encouraging their kids' overdependence. Parents must support dependent kids, insisting on small steps of independence and complimenting small efforts. Although they may teach their children strategies and techniques for achievement, they must avoid being sucked into doing too much for these kids or sitting at their sides during homework time.

Dominant underachievers are overempowered kids who argue and protest that their schoolwork is boring or their teachers are unfair. They provoke parents and teachers, who become angry and lose control. The kids then cite the adults' anger as the cause of their problems, avoiding responsibility by blaming the adults who try to help them.

It may feel natural to argue with and overpunish dominant kids who are determined to push all the limits you set, but this strategy is rarely effective. Parents will have to hear kids out, form an alliance with them, negotiate agreements, document the terms in writing, and then hold kids firmly to their agreements without overreacting or overpunishing. Parents should reiterate their trust in their kids' promises to follow through in completing their work. It's not easy to stick with these approaches, but these responses together with the Six-Step Trifocal model (presented later in the chapter) are effective for reversing underachievement for many dominant children.

What's Really Happening? The Dynamics of Underachievement

Underneath the poor study habits, weak skills, disorganization, and defenses, underachieving kids feel a loss of personal control over their educational success. They don't really believe that they can attain their goals—even if they work harder. They may readily acknowledge that their lack of effort is the cause of the problem. Effort, they think, might make a small difference, but small differences aren't enough and not worth their time. They're too busy, they say. They want to be millionaires, professional athletes, rock stars, winners of the *American Idol* contest, Olympic gymnasts, or inventors of computer games. They have magical dreams about how they will arrive at these unrealistic goals with very little work.

Kids can't build confidence by accomplishing only easy tasks. It's when kids accept the risk of struggle, and they find they can accomplish what they thought was impossible, that they begin to build self-confidence. It's from actual achievement that one develops motivation to achieve further. Underachievers have denied themselves the opportunity to build confidence. They direct their energies toward avoiding responsibilities and therefore don't understand the relationship between process and outcome, between effort and achievement.

Competition and Underachievement

Underachievers are typically highly competitive, though they rarely admit it, even to themselves. Though they aspire to be winners, they're typically poor losers. If they don't believe they can win, they may quit before they begin, or they may select only the activities in which they're certain of victory. These competitive kids haven't learned to handle defeat.

It's not possible for kids to be productive in society or school until they learn to cope with competition. All kids should have winning experiences, but it's important for kids to learn and understand that winning or losing is always temporary. When parents and teachers attempt to create home and school environments in which children can always succeed, the kids suffer. All kids need to have some losing experiences. Kids who can lose without feeling like losers discover the key to positive growth. As parents and educators, our goal shouldn't be to provide schools without failure. Instead, we should try to shape schools without kids who feel like failures. Kids who learn to both win and lose become resilient, and resilience leads to school and lifelong achievement.

Middle schoolers who claim they don't care about grades can be motivated to learn and achieve by parents and teachers who understand the underlying causes of their problems. Underachievers can master the skills that will enable them to cope with competition in our society and, therefore, can be free to experience the joys of self-motivated learning and accomplishment.

Reversing Underachievement in Six Steps

The Trifocal Model in Figure 12.3 has been used by psychologists and educators for 25 years for reversing underachievement. The Trifocal Model focuses on the child *and* on the home and school environments. At the Family Achievement Clinic, our psychologists have found an 80 percent

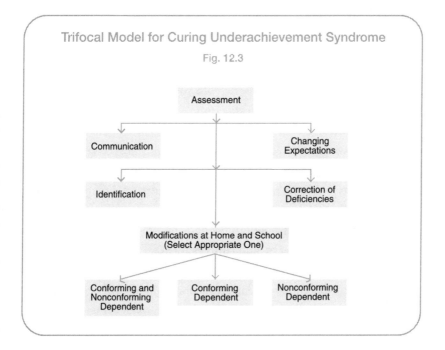

Trifocal Model for Curing Underachievement Syndrome

Fig. 12.3

success rate in reversing underachievement when implementing this model. I'll briefly describe the six steps of the model, but if your kids are underachievers, you'll want to consult my book *Why Bright Kids Get Poor Grades* for a more thorough explanation.

Step 1: Assessment. School or clinical psychologists can test your child to help determine her approximate ability and achievement level. Teachers can also inform you of what skills are not sufficiently developed. To determine if your child is dependent or dominant, observe your child's approach to coping with school responsibilities. You'll recall from my earlier descriptions that dependent children request more help from parents and teachers than they actually need, and they often feel and act helpless. Dominant children argue and compete with parents and teachers and oppose the learning process unless assignments are offered the way they prefer to complete them. Some kids are both—dependent and helpless sometimes, and dominant and argumentative other times.

Step 2: Communication. Communicating with your child's teachers about your concerns, listening carefully to what teachers identify as problems, and setting up accountability notes or e-mails between school and home can help you to keep tabs on what your child is accomplishing in school. (Chapter 13 includes further suggestions for communicating with teachers.) Communicating regularly with your child's teachers will permit you to encourage your child to stay on top of homework and allow you to develop contracts with him about work completion. You can develop reasonable rewards for weeks when all assignments are completed and set punishments (like a loss of weekend privileges) for incomplete work. Accountability needs to take place weekly at first in order for it to be effective.

Step 3: Changing expectations. Underachieving children's habits have led parents, teachers, peers, and siblings to expect low levels of performance from them. Even children's expectations of themselves often don't match their true potential. Parents, teachers, and kids will need to change their expectations to match new and realistic levels of achievement.

Changing adult expectations can help kids to develop realistic expectations for themselves. Learning to be patient in the process of reversing underachievement will be important for everyone involved. Kids rarely succeed immediately, but with time they'll build confidence and a work ethic that will help sustain realistic expectations.

Step 4: Role model identification. Children learn appropriate behaviors more easily when they have effective models to imitate. When underachievers spontaneously reverse patterns of underachievement, they frequently cite important people who were pivotal in their change of direction. These adults are the models with whom they identified and from whom they adopted adjustment patterns, work habits, studying practices, and general life philosophies and career goals.

Kids often see their parents as role models. It's important that parents' achievement orientation is visible to their kids, because kids can copy only what they see. I've included more in Chapter 14 on how parents can become role models for achievement.

Teachers and other adults can also be good role models for kids. Parents can encourage their kids to learn from effective role models in their environments. You will recall from Chapter 7 that many kids look to media celebrities for role models. Some of these role models can be positive, but unfortunately they don't necessarily inspire children to work hard in school. Some may do the opposite and model an easy-way-out work ethic.

Step 5: Correction of deficiencies. Discovering and adjusting to learning disabilities, teaching kids to cope with anxieties related to schoolwork, and arranging for goal-directed tutoring are all helpful for correcting a child's deficiencies. Parents should feel free to ask for assistance in determining how schools can help children cope with learning differences. I'll also discuss learning disabilities and emotional disorders in Chapter 13.

Step 6: Modifications at home and school. In order to help underachievers learn to achieve, parents must work toward modifications at both home and school. I'll discuss strategies in Chapter 13 and show parents how to teach a work ethic, guide children toward handling competition, improve organizational skills, and encourage good study habits. Helping children to develop their strengths and interests as well as guiding them to use those strengths to correct problem areas will be helpful.

Other strategies for encouraging achievement are included in Chapter 14. General, good parenting is most critical for fostering achievement, and this will be discussed further in Chapters 13 and 14.

PARENTING
TWEENS

CHAPTER 13

PARENTING FOR ACHIEVEMENT

If I get anything less than an A, I get in trouble. We're building a house and my parents are all stressed out, so they take it out on me. It's not so much the grades but the house that gets them mad about the grades.

5th-grade boy

Kids today are much nicer to special education kids than they were when I was growing up.

Father of a blind 7th-grade girl

There's this one person I know who's under a lot of pressure. She has to get straight A's, and if she doesn't, or if she has late homework, her parents get really mad at her. Then she's mean and takes it out on other kids.

6th-grade girl

If you get a bad grade, parents shouldn't get mad if you tried your best. If you didn't care or weren't trying, parents should talk to you about it.

6th-grade boy

In my class, we have two people in fifth grade, but they're in sixth-grade math. People are jealous and say, "You're just so smart." They try to beat them up and they just don't say anything, so the jealous person gets mad and hurts them.

5th-grade boy

PARENTS CAN DO MUCH TO HELP their children achieve while they're coping with peer pressures in middle school. For many years, I've answered parents' questions and given advice on national public radio, on television, and in my syndicated newspaper column. I've also presented hundreds of parent and teacher workshops on facilitating kids' achievement at home and school. The techniques in this chapter, which I also share with parents who come to my Family Achievement Clinic, can help you prevent your own children's underachievement.

Setting High Expectations without Pressure

We know that when kids feel smart, they feel better about themselves. Therefore, it's important for parents to value their kids' intelligence. If you don't believe in your kids' abilities to learn, they won't trust themselves. In communicating your belief in their capabilities, it's important to get them to understand that you believe they're smart, but you don't necessarily expect them to be the smartest. If this is not made clear, you kids may assume that you'll be disappointed with anything less than straight A's, which puts them under a lot of pressure.

Many children I see at my clinic tell me that they think their parents expect them to get all A's, even when their parents tell me differently. Sometimes parents will tell a child who isn't working hard enough, "If you only did your work, you'd get A's." Parents think they're giving their kids a vote of confidence, but in actuality, kids feel pressured to achieve goals that seem impossible to reach. If they don't get all A's, they may think their parents won't believe they've worked hard and will criticize their lack of effort.

It's important to emphasize to your kids that you expect them to complete all assignments to the best of their abilities, but you understand there will be times when they make mistakes or don't comprehend everything. If kids internalize too much pressure and feel unable to accomplish what they, their parents, or their teachers anticipate, they become anxious or angry. If you stress the importance of a work ethic, your kids will benefit for the rest of their lives.

Imparting a Work Ethic

Kids will continue to feel smart in school if they develop a work ethic. Bright children in younger grades can often feel smart with little effort because the curriculum is relatively easy, but as they encounter more challenging studies in middle school, their confidence will dissipate if they don't learn to work hard. Pairing intelligence with hard work will ensure that children continue to feel smart. It's good to tell your kids that the harder they work, the smarter they become, and the smarter they are, the harder they'll work.

Teaching your children a work ethic for schoolwork as well as other kinds of work will make a big difference in their confidence, intelligence, and overall self-esteem. Here are some strategies that can help.

Praise kids as hard workers when you observe them making strong efforts. Their efforts may be in schoolwork, housework or chores, yard work, or volunteering in the community. Praising them with compliments like "You persevere," "You're not a quitter," "You make a difference," "I can count on you," or "You accomplish so much" will make your children value their hard-working capabilities.

Refer to your children's positive efforts in referential talk with other adults. Parents seem even more believable to children when children hear them talking to other adults. Kids never fail to listen when they hear you talking about them. Saying, "She's such a great help," "He's so responsible," "She accomplishes so much," or "He doesn't quit" to other adults will boost your children's confidence.

Work in a one-on-one partnership with your child. Whether it's setting a table, making a bed, painting a room, constructing a birdhouse, or working on an important school project, adult-child bonding during projects can make children realize that work is important and that they can be effective workers. Kids love the one-on-one attention they receive while working with parents, and parents become positive models for work in partnerships.

Take breaks with your child during projects. Include healthy snacks and drinks, talking, and especially laughing together. Breaks provide balance and will help your child recognize the total satisfaction that comes with work.

Don't compare siblings negatively by telling one that he or she doesn't work as hard as the other. That will only increase sibling rivalry and cause one child to feel like the shirker, while the other feels like the worker.

Kids' First Jobs Can Help Build a Work Ethic

Middle school kids aren't old enough to be formally employed, but they are at an age where they're likely to take on their first side jobs for neighbors, friends, or their own families. Mowing lawns, washing cars, weeding gardens, caring for younger children as mothers' helpers, scrubbing floors, or doing laundry will all teach kids a positive work ethic. You can help ensure these first jobs are good learning experiences by patiently insisting that your children perform tasks in a timely and satisfactory manner. They will need "training" from their friendly employers on how to fold laundry neatly, mow even the difficult to reach places, or play gently with the children they're babysitting. Learning to accept criticism as well as appreciation and payment from their "bosses" are elements of a work ethic that can generalize to motivation in school now and in their careers later.

Talking with Teachers

Monitoring kids' progress and communicating with parents may seem like the school's responsibility. Obviously, such communication is partially a school's task, but it's important to remember that the adult-child ratio is much greater at school than it is in your own home. Therefore, despite the best intentions, there's a risk that your kid's school may not alert you to problems. The cliché "falling through the cracks" aptly describes what easily happens to those kids whose parents don't take an *active* and *orderly* approach to talking with their teachers.

I emphasize *orderly* here because sporadic overreaction when a problem occurs may seem like communication, but it's not very effective. Parents frequently feel threatened by teachers and vice versa, so both may tend to wait for an emergency before starting a dialogue. Certainly, emergency conferences are sometimes necessary, but steady, persistent efforts to stay in touch with teachers are far more helpful. Parent-teacher conferences have a purpose, and parents (both of them, if possible) ought to attend. However, if you suspect even minor school problems, one or two conferences a year probably won't be enough.

Four to six weeks into the school year is an appropriate time to call your children's teachers if, for example, your kids tend not to complete assignments or have problems getting along with other kids. By 6 weeks, the "fresh beginning" is wearing thin, and kids may be resuming some bad habits of previous years. On the other hand, they won't be so far behind that they can't catch up.

An early call to teachers is also appropriate if your kids' comments about school cause you to suspect problems. Explain to their teachers that you're concerned and you wonder if they've noticed any problems at school. If the teachers haven't observed any problems but you're still concerned, you might then specify the former problem areas or difficulties your kids have experienced.

If things are going well and your kids don't have problems, you need only to thank their teachers and ask to be notified if anything changes. If the teachers do indicate concerns, offer to meet at their convenience. Most teachers will appreciate your interest, and it can be the beginning of a good teacher-parent relationship, which is important for keeping your kids interested and achieving in school.

While personal communication is most effective, you may find that teachers are willing to use e-mail or notes to maintain ongoing, regular communication with you about your child, especially if your child needs additional teacher-parent accountability and support.

Developing Children's Interests

School will always be more interesting to your kids if you become involved in their learning. Teachers often designate some projects that they'd like kids to work on together with their parents, so you should be sure to ask your children's teachers if there are any such projects planned. Even without parent-child projects, you can get involved and help your kids to extend and enrich their learning. For example, if they're studying the Renaissance, take them to an art museum or concert to learn about art or music of that period. Hands-on activities help children remember what they've learned. Encourage family science or social studies projects that teach them how to go beyond what's expected. Teachers notice kids who submit special projects, and the recognition motivates kids to love learning.

There is one precaution. Although it's important to be interested in your children's learning and to invest time in expanding their enrichment activities, it's crucial that you don't do so much of the work that you overshadow their own work. This will steal their self-confidence. A perfect A+ that you earned, rather than your children, may cause grave problems for your kids later on. Charlotte Otto, senior vice president at Procter and Gamble, shared her story with me during my research on successful women. In this case, well-meaning and loving parents probably did a little too much for their daughter.

> My parents concentrated all their efforts on me. If I had a school project, we all did it. For example, in anticipation of California history, we went to most of the California missions the summer before. Then we made one of the missions out of salt, flour, and cardboard. We always tried to do something

distinctive, above and beyond, that set me apart from others. It was unsatisfying for me to be ordinary. Yet sometimes I had difficulty separating out what I contributed from what my parents did.

I see now that I lacked confidence growing up. I had a real fear that I couldn't be perfect. I lived in constant fear of failure and of disappointing my parents. I had a nagging doubt that if Mom and Dad weren't there, I couldn't be successful on my own. That seed of doubt was there for a long time. My parents filled me with affirmation, but I felt too dependent on their affirmation.

Encouraging Kids to Feel Smart by Reading

Many of the successful women in my *See Jane Win* study attributed their feelings of intelligence to their extensive reading. Frequent reading likely contributes to children's measured intelligence as well, since it increases vocabulary and knowledge. In my survey of middle school kids, tweens who felt intelligent were more likely to read a lot, and those who read a lot were more likely to feel highly intelligent. Of those who considered themselves to have far above-average intelligence, 45 percent described themselves as reading a lot, compared with only 12 percent of those who considered their intelligence to be far below-average. Encouraging your kids' interest in reading can make a great difference for their intellectual self-confidence. "Tips to Encourage Readers" on page 236 includes tips on how you can encourage your kids to read. The Appendix also includes Web sites with recommended reading for middle schoolers.

Helping Kids Learn to Compete

The ability to function in competition is central to achievement. Under-achievers haven't learned the techniques of healthy competition and may be overly competitive, although it may not be readily apparent. While

Tips to Encourage Readers

- Continue family reading through the tween years. Reading together aloud or silently creates an atmosphere in which kids are likely to love books.
- Permit tweens to stay up half an hour later at night if they're reading to themselves in bed. (Kids don't usually like to sleep; it's adults who do!)
- Encourage kids to read whatever they enjoy. Don't insist they read grade-level material. Comics, cartoons, sports magazines, easy-reading material, and books read multiple times are all good for building reading confidence.
- Model reading by keeping a book or magazine around that your tweens see you enjoying.
- Regularly visit libraries with your kids. Wander through them as part of your travels.
- When shopping, stop by bookstores and browse and purchase books.
- Encourage your kids to join library or classroom contests that reward reading.
- Provide your kids with lists of interesting books they might enjoy.

they may win happily, they don't know how to recover from losses. They lose their tempers, sulk, quit, or don't take the risk of playing unless they're certain of winning. Parents should teach their kids how to cope with a competitive lifestyle because it will help them in school and in their futures.

Children who are success-oriented achievers view their failures and losses as learning experiences.[1] When failure occurs, they identify the problems, remedy the deficiencies, reset their goals, and grow from the experience. Failure is only a temporary setback, and they learn to attribute their failure to lack of effort, the unusual difficulty of a task, or perhaps the extraordinary skill of other competitors. As coping strategies, they may laugh at their errors, be determined to work harder, or redesign their achievement goals. Most important, they see themselves as falling short of a goal, not falling short as people. Achieving children are *optimistic* and *resilient*.

To help your kids cope with losses, you as parents should first examine your own competitive style; your children may have learned maladaptive responses to failure from watching you. For example, you or your partner may show an attitude of quitting too quickly if a problem gets difficult, of avoiding competition unless you can win, or of habitually blaming others for your own shortcomings or lack of effort. Adjusting your own attitudes and expectations may be the first step in helping your kids if they too avoid competition.

Kids can be taught to identify creative responses for their losses or failures. For example, they should recognize that normal people—even very talented ones—can't be number one in everything, but that every person has areas in which he or she is talented. Kids shouldn't feel insecure or threatened by an occasional setback, nor should they receive too much sympathy. If your kids experience a loss, discussing it may need to wait until after their emotional tension has subsided. You can't expect rational perception or logical thinking immediately following an upsetting defeat. A dialogue, rather than a lecture, will be more effective for helping children understand that they can't always win, disappointment doesn't mean they're failures, this particular experience simply wasn't as successful as they had hoped it would be, everyone would like to be smarter than they are, and especially, the main goal is to play the learning game at their best performance level, regardless of their competitive ranking. Effort, attitude, optimism, and interest count.

Cooperation in and out of Competition

Although kids must learn to function in competition and, especially, to emerge from failures and losses, they should also become involved in noncompetitive activities that are intrinsically reinforcing—interests that they enjoy for personal and not competitive satisfaction. Some fun non-competitive activities for middle schoolers can include art, music or drama classes, bicycling, jogging, inline skating, canoeing, hiking, or camping, or collecting stamps, coins, or models. If all the activities children participate in are tied to recognition or competition, they may be unprepared for relaxation, fun, developing new and noncompetitive interests, or socializing. Kids who haven't learned to enjoy noncompetitive activities may feel bored or depressed when they're not accomplishing something or moving toward a goal.

Highly competitive kids can sometimes find it difficult to participate in cooperative activities where they don't receive individual recognition for winning. There are at least as many collaborative opportunities in careers as there are competitive ones, so kids need to learn both approaches. Planning a dramatic presentation with others, working on a group science or social studies project with pals, or being part of a creative problem-solving team all help kids understand the fun, creativity, and satisfaction of sharing in a successful project. Cooperative projects require kids to resolve conflicts with other kids and force them to share the spotlight with peers. There are times when you should encourage your kids' independence, but in doing so, be sure to let them know that there's also great value in collaboration.

Modeling Organizational Skills

Middle schoolers who flounder in school typically have problems with organization. For some, their disorganization shows itself in messy desks, messy papers, and messy rooms. Others seem unable to manage their time, and they hand in assignments late or not at all. Middle school kids may have heightened disorganization problems because this is the first time they're called upon to organize so many different elements of their school days. They have more teachers, classrooms, books, assignments, and extracurricular activities than they had in elementary school. No wonder they have a hard time keeping it all straight.

Parents' Trickle-Down Effect

Two parenting styles seem to foster disorganization patterns in kids. One kind advocates a disorganized lifestyle. These parents often see disorganization as synonymous with freedom and creativity and assert openly that they themselves prefer a disorganized lifestyle. Thus, their children emulate them and simply never learn organizational techniques. Disorganization feels natural, right, and creative, and remains for the whole family a preferred approach to daily life. Extreme disorganization will, however, make it impossible for children to achieve in school.

The second parenting style is common and more difficult to identify. In this family situation, one parent uses disorganization as a passive-aggressive power play in a sometimes oppositional marriage. Typically one parent is a perfectionist, or at least very structured. The second parent, who claims to feel controlled by the first, can't assertively deal with the problem, so this parent uses passive-aggressive strategies such as forgetting things, not preparing things on time, not accomplishing requested tasks, and ignoring responsibilities to cope with anger because he or she feels controlled. Kids may emulate the passive-aggressive parent in opposing or ignoring the more demanding, structured parent. Disorganization in their schoolwork becomes a powerful weapon for these kids. Here's an example from my clinic that may sound familiar.

Dr. Sylvia: Mike, who do you think you're most the same as, your mom or your dad?

Mike: (without hesitation) My dad.

Dr. Sylvia: How are you the same as your dad?

Mike: When my mom calls my dad to do something around the house, he doesn't answer, and when my mom calls me to do my homework, I don't answer either.

Living with a small amount of chaos or tolerance of ambiguity seems healthy and may contribute to creativity and a noncompulsive lifestyle, just as extreme rigidity and perfectionism are likely to interfere with school and life achievement. Reasonable organization, however, is necessary for accomplishment, and it appears again that moderation is more effective than extremism. Take the initiative to model and teach reasonable organizational techniques for dealing with home and school responsibilities. Try talking aloud to yourself about your own organization; it will heighten your children's awareness of organizational techniques.

When parents develop a communication system that enhances effective cooperation with household chores and responsibilities, children are more likely to follow through with their parents' requests. It's important for parents to agree on how to organize. Sometimes communication of tasks through notes, checklists, and charts is an approach that works for parents and kids alike.

Elements of Organizational Skills

You may want to reflect on your family's organizational skills by reviewing the components of organization listed below. Once you identify those components that are problematic for you and your kids, you'll be able to concentrate your efforts on the areas that need the most help.

Putting like things together. This concept is basic to organization. Whether kids learn to pair socks, put their library books in a special place on a shelf, organize incomplete homework separate from complete homework, or arrange their favorite CDs together, they're learning an essential first of organization that will help them find what they want when they need it.

Predicting time. Sensitizing kids to how long it takes them to bathe, dress, brush their teeth, or walk to the bus stop will help them to be ready on time for school or activities. Noticing how much time it takes to study for a test or complete a math assignment will help them plan. Making kids time-conscious will permit them to allocate enough preparation time and prevent the daily frenzy that some parents and kids experience when they're always late. You may want to suggest they use timers or stopwatches at first to measure and chart their time.

Scheduling. After kids calculate the time it takes for their daily activities and study, they can prepare a weekly schedule to visually coordinate their activities. Kids can keep their own schedules and add their personal activities to a family schedule that can be posted on a refrigerator or bulletin board. In this way, parents and kids can better manage car pools, taxiing, and duplication of activities. It may take a fair amount of juggling on the parents' part to cope with gymnastics, soccer practice, and music lessons of several children. A schedule helps immensely.

Remembering. Assignment books are great for remembering schoolwork, as long as kids don't forget to use them. Kids like to believe they'll remember their homework or activities without writing them down, but it's often an excuse for forgetting to do something or be somewhere. Kids can invent their own special system for remembering, but they need to prove it's effective if they plan to continue to use it.

Prioritizing. As kids' lives get busier during their middle school years, it's important to join your kids in prioritizing their most important responsibilities. Discussing priorities helps kids learn to evaluate their activities and determine which ones they absolutely must do and those they can accomplish only if time allows.

Eliminating. In the process of prioritizing, parents and kids together may decide that kids simply have to drop a sport or activity. By discussing what should be eliminated, kids can clarify their own values while understanding their parents' perspectives on activities as well. Sometimes, you may have to insist that kids drop an activity, but it's better to make this a joint decision and ask for their thoughts on which activity your kids would like to drop. There may be times when you'll disagree. Listen to your kids' perspectives, but don't hesitate to prevail if you consider their choices harmful.

Reviewing. The process of review helps kids to realize that their decisions aren't permanent and can be revised at a later date. Prioritizing and eliminating will need repetition every few months if schedules become too hectic again. Kids can add activities they've dropped or drop some they've added as they learn to evaluate their daily lives and interests regularly. Reviewing can also include looking over tests, papers, or homework before handing them in to check for careless errors.

Establishing good habits. Study, chores, and organization become much more automatic and less frustrating if kids develop good habits. School and chores are work done with ease when they're habitual. It's also important to avoid bad habits, because they too can become automatic. Bad habits like skipping breakfast, arguing daily, not brushing their teeth, or procrastinating about homework cause great problems for kids.

Maintaining flexibility. One quotation I enjoy sharing is, "Habits are the best of servants, and the worst of masters." It's true that good habits can foster efficiency, but it's just as true that kids who are mastered by inflexible habits lose opportunities for creativity, spontaneity, and fun. Intentionally teaching kids to make exceptions to their schedules can prepare them to be ready for change and flexibility and can enhance their lives without destroying their organization and efficiency.

Structuring Study Time

For students who lack organizational skills, homework and study habits should be structured. The tools for such structuring should be familiar to most parents. Insist from the start that studying be done in a quiet place, alone, and at a desk or table—no siblings or parents, and no television, video games, or music until the work is complete. If your children are achieving well, quiet music is permissible, but studying in front of a TV is *never* a good idea. Research proves that TV interferes with study even for motivated students. Reading school assignments on the floor or bed isn't effective either, although these positions are fine for pleasure reading. Reclining positions aren't conducive to intense concentration, despite your children's arguments that they prefer such comfort.

There should usually be a break immediately after school for kids to have a snack and some physical and social activity. Kids usually want to use this break to watch TV. However, TV will put them into a passive mode, and they're unlikely to want to shut it off to study. Moving your kids from television to study may involve a massive power struggle. It's better to insist that TV and computer games follow study and homework. Your kids will probably complain that they need to relax after school. Exercise is both relaxing and energizing, and it's more appropriate after a day of sitting at a desk. Certainly, having time to chat or clown around is appropriate for after school—but save the screen time for later.

When you're determining the right time for study, keep in mind that not only should there be an opportunity for an active break after school, but there should be something to look forward to after study. If possible, at least part of your kids' study time should take place prior to the evening meal, leaving time after study for play or family television. Kids often tire after dinner; if their study time is set late in the evening, they aren't likely to be as efficient and there won't be time after study for play. When study time is late, children often sit at their desks daydreaming or half-dozing. With only bedtime to follow, they aren't motivated toward efficiency. Kids may use their homework as an excuse to stay up later if their study time is just prior to bedtime. For some reason unknown to adults, few kids enjoy going to sleep. They often look for ways to stay up as long as grown-ups do.

Having a designated study place is equally important for providing an atmosphere in which kids can learn efficiently. A desk in a kid's own room with a Student at Work sign posted on the door is ideal. If kids share a room with siblings, there are other good alternatives. The kitchen, dining room, and basement are reasonable places for study, as long as no one else is in the same room and it's out of listening and viewing range of the TV.

Studying together as a family or studying at the library may also be acceptable alternatives. Occasionally, I recommend that a parent and child work together at a table, each doing his or her own work, but parents need to be cautious that kids don't get into a habit of asking for more help than they require.

Children who prefer studying in the dining room with siblings, or those who prefer background noise, often explain that they can't concentrate or study at a desk. I point out that they have been conditioned to relax when they are socializing with family members or watching TV; therefore, under such conditions it's easier to relax, but it's more difficult for them to concentrate on studying. When children assert that they study better while lying on their beds, I ask them what they associate their beds with. Their response is usually sleep, relaxation, or rest. They're conditioned to rest or fall asleep when lying on their beds. I point out that their conditioning for sleep doesn't encourage their active involvement in study. Children are reporting only their comfort levels, not their efficiency.

Furthermore, I remind kids that music and social conversation aren't usually permitted by either high school teachers or college professors while taking exams, and I've never heard of SATs or ACTs being given with background music. I ask kids to condition themselves to sit in an upright position so they can be actively involved with their material, have good light, take good notes, and concentrate on their work until it becomes a habit. I point out to them that adults who were good students in college often went to a study room or a table in the library, or a quiet place where everyone was studying and there wasn't any socializing.

Sometimes it's difficult to convince kids to accept an appropriate time and place for study. You should be firm and insist they try it consistently for at least 2 weeks. Once an appropriate study place and time becomes habitual, you'll find you no longer have to nag your kids. They'll automatically go to their desks in their rooms to do their homework, and their concentration and efficiency will improve. Parents with whom I've worked reported that their home atmosphere improved when the whole family changed their study habits. If you insist on organized study, your kids will develop habits that help them learn.

A Destructive Dependency

I'd like to emphasize again that under no circumstances should middle school kids expect a parent to sit next to them regularly at homework time. Don't let your kids convince you that they can't work without you.

Your attention should be directed to their *completed* assignments. On the other hand, it's reasonable for you to give your kids occasional help or explanations. These should be brief and given only after they've tried understanding the work on their own. If they've studied the material first, you can quiz them or give them a trial test. If their performance is poor, they should return to their desks for more independent study. You can't be expected to study for your kids; you can, however, recommend or teach study strategies.

Help your children understand the extent of effort that's needed to earn good grades. Kids often believe they're working hard when they aren't. Teach them to test themselves after they've studied to see what they remember. Review with them after they're done to be sure they're doing quality work. Explain that doing their best truly means being fully involved with their materials.

When you introduce these study guidelines to your children, they may debate you. Your directives should be firm and positive. If they achieve well, they may study their own way; if they haven't been successful using their own style, they should change to yours until they improve.

Coping with the Stigma of Labels

Kids at my school have a lot of problems, and they're not smart because they were born with special needs. Kids pick on them and older kids chuck the ball right at them on the playground.

6th-grade boy

ADHD, AD, and LD are a few of the common diagnoses for children's disorders. The "D" at the end of each acronym stands for *disorder* or *disability*. When a child exhibits a certain number of characteristics that are typical of a disorder, a label is used for communication between professionals, for health insurance reimbursement, to explain to parents the reasons for their child's problematic behaviors, and for a child's inclusion in special school programs. To date, there isn't a biological test for any of these disorders, and children may be labeled with a diagnosis whether they have the disorder only mildly or to an extreme. All this can be confusing for parents, who may see a diagnosis to be as clear-cut as a physical illness.

I sometimes find that a diagnosis can cause as many problems as it solves. A diagnosis labels problem behaviors and assumes they are biologically caused, but it also labels your child. Parents and kids alike often believe they're helpless to change the behaviors. Parents may become more accepting of problem behaviors instead of setting appropriate limits, or they may expect schools to excuse their child's inappropriate behaviors because of a disorder. Kids may think they can't do anything about their problems because they have a disorder, and sometimes they even use their label as an excuse for their behavior.

It will be helpful for you to think about what you're saying about your kids within their hearing so you can intentionally guide them to develop their strengths, cope with their disabilities, and avoid unnecessary pressures. What you say about your children can become a self-fulfilling prophecy, encouraging them to either live up or down to the labels they're given.

Explaining Disorders to Your Tweens

Since mental health professionals sometimes label kids quickly, you as parents should be discerning and assertive before you immediately accept a diagnosis for your child. Before consenting to medication or agreeing to your child's placement in a special education program, consult a psychologist who will guide you to behavioral approaches to changing your parenting style.

Only after making adjustments that have been recommended to you should you accept a label or placement for your child. You may even wish to seek a second opinion. When and if you find placement advisable, "Explaining Disorders" offers examples of ways to help your child better understand the disorder he or she is facing. Each explanation has four components listed on page 248.

Explaining Disorders

Attention Deficit-Hyperactivity Disorder (ADHD)

The doctor says you have something called ADHD. That means you sometimes do things without thinking about them, are more active than many other kids, and have trouble paying attention. The medicine the doctor is giving you will help you with all these things, but you'll still need to try your best. If you work hard to concentrate, and you think before you act, it may even be possible that you won't always need medicine, but right now, the medicine can really help you to feel better and be a better student.

Asperger's Disorder (AD)

You seem to have some problems making and getting along with friends. While some of that is just the way you were born, the special program you're in can assist you with learning how to socialize with kids and understand your teachers better. Socializing may always be difficult for you, but with time and practice you'll probably get a lot better at it.

Dyslexia or Reading Disorder/Disability (RD)

You're a smart kid, but reading is harder for you than it is for most kids. That doesn't mean you can't learn, but your teachers will teach you different approaches to reading than the other kids use. Even so, reading may be hard. That's why we want you to listen to tapes of books. Remember, kids learn differently. What's hard for you may be easy for other kids, and what's easy for you may be hard for others. Sometimes learning to read so slowly may make you sad or mad, but don't get discouraged. You're a smart kid, and if you work hard, you'll figure out how to be successful and happy. Just know for sure that we believe in you.

1. Be honest with your child about the disorder.

2. Encourage your child to accept appropriate help from counselors, school programs, or medication.

3. Set expectations for your child to work hard to overcome problems.

4. Be optimistic about your child's ability to cope with the future.

Giftedness—A Different Kind of Label

If you get all A's, the people who didn't get all A's are jealous and call you a nerd. It puts you with the "out" kids.

5th-grade boy

Parents hardly ever object when their kids are labeled as "gifted," nor do the kids themselves. Many schools have programs for gifted children. There are a variety of definitions of giftedness, and schools may provide programs for some types and not others.

If your children are identified for gifted programs, encourage them to accept the challenge of more complex curricula. They may complain that their work is more difficult, but it's important for kids to learn to accept challenge. In the long haul, participation in a gifted program will benefit their education, prepare them for challenging colleges, and enhance their lives.

If your children aren't accepted into gifted programs, it doesn't mean they don't possess talents or gifts. It means only that they have no particular need for special programming or that the school doesn't sponsor a program that meets their specific needs. If you disagree with a school's decision not to include your child in a program, don't hesitate to make an appointment with a teacher, principal, or gifted coordinator to voice your concern and inquire about the criteria used for identifying giftedness. Also, if the school doesn't offer a program that you believe your child needs, discuss program options first at the school and administrative level, and then even at the school board level. Your state association for gifted children can help you find support for your mission. You can also find information on the Web sites of the National Association for Gifted Children or state organizations for gifted children (see Appendix).

Combating Peer Pressure

Whether your child is in a learning disabilities class or a gifted program, she will feel some peer pressure and may even be bullied by others. Notice the comments at the beginning of the chapter from my focus groups. This is an area where you will need to support your children's feelings of difference, honor their independence, and value their intelligence and achievement.

Homeschooling

Many parents now homeschool their children for a variety of reasons. Some hope to prevent their kids from experiencing the negative peer culture that some middle schools provide, some move or travel frequently, and some feel the school's curriculum is either too challenging or not challenging enough. There may be advantages and disadvantages to homeschooling your children. All parents considering homeschooling need to think carefully about whether there are more advantages for their children and whether it is a commitment they can make. Parents' concerns should be discussed with teachers as well as with other homeschooling parents to gain their perspectives. Consider educational, social, moral, and physical issues prior to making a decision. There is considerable regional and national support for homeschool parents and kids. Web sites on homeschooling are included in the Appendix for more information.

CHAPTER 14

PARENTING IN THE MIDDLE OF THE V OF LOVE

Parents now let us get away with a lot of stuff, like talking back. If my parents had talked to their parents the way I talk to mine, they would've gotten their teeth knocked down their throats.

5th-grade girl

We need more freedom; parents are just too overprotective. It isn't fair that we should be bossed around by our parents 24 hours a day, 7 days a week.

6th-grade girl

Parents just aren't involved enough.

8th-grade boy

Parents think that since our generation is worse than theirs, we're going to turn out bad. We're their kids. They raised us right. They taught us what's wrong, what's right, what we should do, what we shouldn't do. Why don't they just let us use what we've learned and let us live our own lives? We

*know we can't break laws, we know we have to follow the
rules; they should let us live in those boundaries.*

7th-grade girl

Some parents are just right.

8th-grade girl

*Parents are overprotective of kids. It's not so bad, 'cuz they
want to make sure that their kids grow up to be nice, re-
spectable adults who are responsible and caring for others.
But we're growing up, and we're at an age where we know
more than they think we know. All parents need to lighten
up. Get off our cases. Leave us alone. We're not stupid. Parents just need to have more confidence in their kids.*

7th-grade girl

*Parents don't give us a chance to exercise the rules and regu-
lations they set down for us. They jump to conclusions too
quickly.*

6th-grade girl

*I can't talk to my mom. She's always too busy. "Hold on, I
gotta go to work," "Hold on, I gotta go to school," "Hold
on, I gotta help so-and-so with their homework," or "I'm
going to the store now." I'm just kind of left behind.*

7th-grade girl

THE PERCEIVED QUALITY OF FAMILY RELATIONSHIPS affected
almost every middle school issue in my study. My study found that tweens
with good family relationships have greater confidence in themselves, feel
more intelligent, and describe themselves with more positive characteristics and fewer negative characteristics. The kids from my survey who had

good family relationships worried less about almost everything, including appearance and popularity issues. They also tended to be more optimistic and far less fearful for their futures. Perhaps most important, surveys by the National Parents' Resources Institute for Drug Education (PRIDE) showed that good family relationships decrease the likelihood that middle school kids will get into high-risk behaviors like smoking, using tobacco, drinking alcohol, and doing drugs.

All of these conclusions stress how important it is for families to maintain positive relationships with their kids, despite the vociferous demands of kids that their parents back off and let them take charge of their own lives. Your leadership as parents is vital, and this chapter will illustrate the most crucial principles of parenting. The first principle refers to appropriate—*but not too much*—empowerment. Most kids in my focus groups complained about wanting more power than their parents were willing to give.

The V of Love

Visualize the letter V as a model for guiding the extent of praise, power, and freedom given to your children. When your children are very young, they begin at the bottom of the V with limited freedom and power and a few choices. As they mature and are able to handle more responsibility, the limiting walls of the V spread out, giving them gradually increasing freedom and power while still providing parental limits. In middle school, your children are in the middle of the V and have more freedom than in their earlier years, but not as much as they'll have in high school. In later adolescence, your children will move to the top of the V, becoming capable of considerably more independent decision-making and judgment. If you open the V gradually, your kids will feel trusted and continue to respect guidance from you and their teachers. They'll be competent and have more confidence for moving out of the V into adult independence and personal decision-making.

Too Much, Too Soon: The Inverted V

In some families, the V of love is reversed to look like this: Λ. Children who start at the base of this figure are given too much freedom, too much praise, too many choices, and indefinite limits. They become accustomed to having power and making decisions before they even have the wisdom to handle their freedom responsibly.

However, as these children move toward middle school, their parents may notice them making poor choices. Tweens may choose not to do homework or study and instead become involved with negative peer groups. Tobacco, alcohol, drugs, and promiscuous sex are serious threats from which their parents try to protect them.

Concerned about the consequences of their tweens' destructive actions, parents reverse their liberal parenting and begin to make demands on their kids. They set limits and take away freedoms. Tweens who had too much control as children now feel relatively overcontrolled by their parents. They believe they know more than their parents and teachers. Their angry statements reflect their feelings of restriction: "My parents are controlling me," "They're overprotective and have too many rules," "They expect me to be perfect," "My parents need to back off," "They used to treat me like an adult and now they treat me like a baby." Kids rebel, feel increasingly angry, or become depressed. Not only do they rebel against their parents and teachers, they rebel against learning and positive activities as well.

Worried parents overpunish and eliminate privileges, resulting in even more anger and rebellion. The oppositional tweens turn formerly happy homes into conflict zones. Neither the parents nor the tweens understand or communicate with each other. Relative to the power and control these tweens once had, they now feel powerless.

Once freedom is given, it isn't easily taken away. The resulting adversarial mode may force both tweens and parents to dig in their heels, causing the loss of a positive home atmosphere that is so valuable in guiding children. Children brought up with the inverted V of Love expend their energy protecting the power they believe they deserve.

Overprotection: The V That Doesn't Open

While some rebellion during the middle school years can be attributed to kids being given freedom too early and then having it taken away, some parents do overprotect their kids and don't give them enough freedom as they mature. When kids think you're overprotective and angrily claim that you're unfair, they may be comparing their current freedom to past freedom, or they may be making comparisons to their peers' freedoms, which make your limits seem childish. Your kids will constantly challenge you to examine your standards, but if you refuse to gradually increase their freedoms and power as they mature, they'll be justifiably angry.

A good way to determine if you are gradually empowering your kids is to take time every few months to think back on what your children were allowed to do at that same time a year ago. Birthdays, holidays, or the beginning of summer or the school year are good times to grant more freedom with matched responsibility. All you have to do is widen the V in small increments to establish trust. Your kids may still complain about your rules and limits, but they'll also admit that they understand the need for them, as did many of the kids in my focus groups.

Spider-Man's Sage Advice

The V-shaped model encourages children to develop their talents, freedom, and power. Gradual developmental empowerment is much smoother and more comfortable for adolescents and parents alike, and it provides an atmosphere in which children can be inspired to learn and to feel good about themselves. Spider-Man, in the movie by the same name, summarized it well: "With great power comes great responsibility." Raising children with the V of love leads to responsible, confident children and to better family relationships.

Money = Power

Although not all forms of power can be bought with money, many can, and advertisers know that children in this generation have more money than ever before. Some companies have hired kids as young as 9 years old to help them define "cool," a description for which other kids will pay top dollar. And since tweens are projected to spend a whopping $41 billion in 2005, marketers are increasingly looking to keep parents out of kids' purchasing decisions by reaching kids directly through TV ads, the Internet, movies, and magazines.

Just as parents of this generation have frequently overempowered their children with too many choices, they have also overempowered them with too much discretionary money. Parents not only give too much money to their kids, but they grant them the freedom to spend it without limits. Advertisers recognize their innocent victims, who have financial power but lack good judgment or responsibility. Parents can make a difference by teaching their children about earning money and spending it judiciously, again with the guidance of the V of Love.

Managing Your Tween's Money: The Three Ws

In teaching your children how to value and handle money, you'll struggle with the issues of allowances, earning money through chores, and even how you permit them to use monetary gifts. Your own value system will, of course, guide you in making final decisions, but keep in mind the goal of teaching your kids about money management. It's important to teach your children the three Ws: the principle of how to *work* and *wait* for the things they *wish* for. Children who learn to delay gratification receive lifelong advantages. Not only will financial guidance help your children learn to delay gratification, but it will prevent the ugly sense of entitlement that frustrates even the most generous parents.

There are many ways for middle school students to earn money, including washing the car, mowing lawns, babysitting, or gardening for neighbors. Be sure not to pay kids for basic chores. Making their beds, setting the table, and cleaning their rooms fit under regular household responsibilities that shouldn't be compensated. If you pay children for all their chores, you'll soon hear them ask for money for everything they do. Payment for extras like vacuuming the house, cleaning the bathroom, or scrubbing the kitchen floor can be optional depending on parents' preferences.

Gradually increasing allowances with age will permit you to continue to emphasize saving, waiting, and spending appropriately. Dividing allowances and earnings into three or four parts often works well. For example, one part can be spent, a second part can be saved for special purchases or gifts for family and friends, and a third part could go to a college fund. Parents can also encourage a fourth part for contributions to a charity.

Reserve Your Veto Power

By the middle school years, preadolescents can devise a great many ways to spend "their" money. It may be time to remind them that it's only partially theirs, and, as their parent, you can determine the limits to their spending. Some music, movies, and videos should still be off-limits, even if kids volunteer to use their own money to buy them. Reserve your right to give the final okay, but remember that kids need to have some freedom to make choices and even to make mistakes.

Even when their money comes from outside sources, your bywords can still remain "freedom within limits." When your kids remind you that they have their *own* money, you might tactfully point out that you don't charge them for rent or food, and as parents, you reserve the final responsibility that goes with occasionally saying no.

Banking On the Future

Monetary gifts from grandparents or other relatives should be carefully discussed with the givers first. They may have specific intentions for their gifts or wish to leave it up to your guidelines. Spending some and saving some continues to make good sense for kids, regardless of age. Saving gifts of money in an education fund sets the expectation of achieving a higher education.

Money and Achievement

What does money management have to do with achievement? Learning about money teaches kids about the concept of delayed gratification, or how to wait and work for what they want. Research tells us that kids who can learn to delay gratification are much more likely to be lifelong achievers. Kids who think they need instant gratification can't wait long enough to work at something. Thus, they're less likely to achieve in school or in life.

Quality Family Relationships

The paradox of family relationships during the middle school years is that although kids in all my focus groups demanded that parents back off, my survey results showed that middle schoolers mainly described their family relationships as positive. Only a small percentage of kids (7 percent) described their family relationships as *a little bad* or *very bad*. As was expected, positive descriptions of family life declined slightly as children matured and pushed for more independence. In third grade, 64 percent of children described their relationships positively, but by eighth grade that percentage dropped to 43 percent, and the *somewhat good, average,* and *a little bad* categories all increased for eighth-graders.

Although kids vocalized complaints about parental control, they assumed that their minor battles with their parents were normal and didn't interfere with their happy family relationships. This should reassure parents that middle schoolers expect and accept guidance from adults. Clearly, this means that when your kids roll their eyes at you in apparent protest, they hear your message anyway—so don't back off too much. They need you.

The Crucial Principle of United Parenting

My dad is mostly easier than my mom because he doesn't get so mad when I do nothing. But if Mom tells me I can't do something, I won't ask my dad. My parents taught me when one says no, never ask the other.

5th-grade boy

The middle school years are a crucial time for maintaining united parenting. Because adolescents are naturally pushing toward adulthood before they're ready for adult responsibilities, a parent taking a child's side against another parent, teacher, or grandparent is immediately perceived as permission to disrespect the other adult. Note Rimm's Law #1 (from Chapter 12)—*Children are more likely to be achievers if their parents join together to give the same clear and positive message about school effort and expectations*—and its corollary, Rimm's Law #9—*Children become oppositional if one adult allies with them against a parent or a teacher, making them more powerful than an adult.* This becomes even more complex in today's society, when kids may have more than two parents. Sometimes they have one, three, or four parents. Grandparents or aunts and uncles may even help with parenting. According to a Census Bureau report, only half of this country's children live in traditional two-parent families.[1]

It's important that those adults who impact children's lives guide them in a united and reasonably consistent way. Even though the adults may have some differences in their preferred styles of parenting, the view from the children's perspectives should be of fairly similar expectations and limits. If adults are reasonably consistent and work as a team, children will know what's expected of them. They'll also understand that they cannot *avoid* doing what feels a little hard or scary or challenging with the protection or permission of another adult.

Why Do Parents Sabotage Each Other?

You may wonder why it's sometimes so difficult for parents to stay united and so easy to take a child's side against the other parent, thus sabotaging the other parent's power. Parents who love their children and believe they're parenting correctly can easily disagree with their partner if he or she has a different parenting approach. They may even be concerned that the other parent is doing harm to their children. Sometimes parents say things to their kids like, "I understand, Dad is too hard on you," or "I agree, Mom is just too controlling" in an effort to understand and act as a friend to their children. The pressure that parents feel to be a friend and understand can be even worse after a divorce, when parents are afraid of losing their children's favor. Being protective of and a confidant to their kids makes parents feel intimate with them, and in turn, they hope their kids will see them as the good parents.

Their message to their kids, however unintentional, is totally disrespectful of the other parent, thus alienating the second parent or making him or her seem like an ogre or the mean parent. The "mean" or "strict" parent then feels angry, frustrated, and helpless and becomes the victim of the child's disrespect. Once kids are enabled to behave disrespectfully toward one parent, they easily generalize that behavior to other adults.

Parents who sabotage their partners, other adults, or teachers rarely mean harm to their children, although sometimes they feel angry with the other adults. They feel justified because they think they're meeting their kids' needs better than others. The effects of sabotage result in kids' dramatic misbehavior and underachievement. Undermining parents unintentionally teach their kids to find the easy way out of challenge, and as kids avoid challenges in a patterned way, they underachieve, lose confidence, and manipulate adults. Parents' undermining of each other is the most frequent underlying cause of problems I find in families that visit my clinic.

Divorce Can Lead to Manipulation

Even the best divorces can leave open the possibility for kids to manipulate their parents. Parents find it more difficult to say "no" to their children following a divorce because they worry that their kids will prefer their other parent. Parents may unconsciously try to hold on to their children's love by making life easier for them. The "fun" parent who doesn't insist on doing homework or chores, buys too many gifts, or slips them easy money is inviting their kids' manipulation, rebellion, and under-achievement.

Sociologist Chadwick Mennind, PhD, of Ball State University in Muncie, Indiana, conducted a study of 50 teens whose parents were separated or divorced. The teens displayed strategies of manipulation that included:

- Withholding information from a parent to escape punishment or to solidify a relationship with another parent
- Moving from a home with a controlling parent to a home with a more lenient parent
- Alienating one parent entirely from their life

Dr. Mennind notes that these strategies of manipulation are not only used by kids with divorced or separated parents, but they're often used by kids in a single household with two parents.[2] Good parenting involves a team approach, but unfortunately, even in single households with two parents, teamwork may not exist and the very same manipulations found in divorced households may take place. It's absolutely true, however, that divorced families are more vulnerable to these maneuvers by kids. Although this particular study was of teenagers, the manipulations Dr. Mennind documented take place equally for middle schoolers and even younger children.

You're Coaches, Not Judges

I wouldn't listen to my dad because he gets too mad and my mom tells him to calm down.

3rd-grade girl

To avoid the sabotage of another adult, both parents need to be empathic and form alliances with their children in order to reach them effectively.

Coaching parents combine leadership with caring. You'll understand the concept better if you observe a good athletic coach.

Good coaches are enthusiastic, positive, and concerned. They encourage the kids they coach. When you're a coach, you believe your kids will do their best, and they know it. They feel like you're on their side. You can criticize, you can expect a lot, and kids will accept your advice in the spirit of learning. As a coach, you can encourage good results, and your kids will feel you trust and believe in them.

Coaching involves the right tone of alliance as well as the right words. Your job as a parent is difficult, and sometimes even good coaches lose their tempers. Tell yourself, "Remember, I'm on her side, and this is difficult for her," or "I have to reassure him that I believe in him." Calm yourself and try again. Be sure to take some time every day to talk and listen to each of your children separately from their siblings. Furthermore, to maintain a coaching attitude, conversations shouldn't center just on problems. Your more general, loving interest in your kids and their activities and feelings will communicate better that you care and are truly a coach.

In contrast, imagine the judges who are portrayed in courtrooms on TV, who determine whether a person is guilty or innocent and mete out punishments. When you're a judge, you are looking for your child's mistakes and are ready to punish her. When you act as a judge and not a coach, your child will assume you expect her to fail or that she has already failed. She'll feel intimidated or angry and think you're manipulating or threatening her, instead of helping and guiding her. When she works hard or achieves well, she'll expect her judging parents to say, "I told you so," which will make her believe she's lost another argument, robbing her of her sense of accomplishment.

Sometimes your children will still be defensive and resent you for advising them, even if you say the right things as a coach. It's tricky because obviously your kids must learn to accept constructive criticism, direction, and limits. Coaching parents inspire kids, and for that reason, coaches can be powerful leaders. Establishing high expectations is positive and encouraging for children. It's also clear that the very same expectations can cause bitter battles and resentment when they come from parents who act as judges. Being patient while coaching will also help your kids be patient with themselves. Patience is an important characteristic to develop for children's achievement.

How to Have a Whole, Smart Family

Competition between siblings is normal and occurs in all families. This rivalry always exists, even when parents proclaim that their children aren't jealous of each other and are always kind and nice. Sibling rivalry doesn't necessarily mean that children argue or fight with each other, although many siblings do some of that. Sibling rivalry is also expressed through birth order differences, differing personalities (aggressive or submissive, talkative or quiet, disorganized or neat), and unique interests ("I'm the dancer, she plays the flute," "I'm the gymnast, she's the smart one"). There's often a territorial competitiveness that parents perpetuate in the name of individual differences and keeping peace. Unfortunately, it may put each of your children in a restrictive box.

It's hard to discover a way to encourage individual differences without heightening competition between your children. It's important for all your kids to feel intelligent and creative, for all to have reasonable social adjustment, and for all to be physically fit. Your challenge is to help them feel competent in all of these areas without insisting that they be the best in the family. You shouldn't tell your daughter, who says she'll never be as smart as her brother, that she's so much better at gymnastics. Instead, acknowledge that she may not be as intellectually gifted as her brother, but that doesn't mean she isn't highly intelligent. Intelligence is a complex construct, and there are multiple intelligences. She has a great deal of potential for using her good brain for accomplishment. You might also point out that if she lived in another family, she might be considered the smartest child, so feeling like the second, third, or fourth smartest child in your family gives her no disadvantage in school or in the world.

I usually point out to kids who are feeling at a competitive disadvantage in their families that admiring their sister's or brother's intelligence or skill can help them cope with their feelings. If they celebrate their sibling's victories, they, too, will feel supported in their own victories and defeats.

It's important that parents recognize the pressure siblings feel as a result of comparisons to each other. This pressure is exacerbated when parents make actual comparisons, but siblings still compare themselves even if their parents don't.

Dethronement

"Only" children and oldest children are frequently treated like one of the adults in the family. Parents may even treat their kids as consultants and ask questions like, "Where would you like to eat?" or "What would you like to do?" These children may actually make many family decisions early on. Thus, they become accustomed to adult status, and sometimes adult power.

Adultized kids gain the social, intellectual, and apparent emotional sophistication that emerges from a close and enriched experience with their parents. They may appear to have more mature insights into behaviors than their peers. They may also suffer from the feelings of insecurity and powerlessness that emerge with too much adult power. In classroom and peer relationships where they aren't given adult status, they may feel "put down" or disrespected in comparison to the way in which they're regarded at home. They actually feel "disempowered" relative to their feelings of overempowerment at home.[3]

The most difficult problem for adultized children is *dethronement*. When another sibling is born or a parent remarries, the child may feel irrationally and extraordinarily jealous, although he knows he should be happy about the new member of the family.[4] Enthroned children may also be dethroned in a classroom where they must share attention with many other kids. If children have managed to stay very powerful in a small elementary school, their dethronement may first show itself in the middle school years, when it's unlikely they can continue to reign as king or queen. Dethroned children typically exhibit negativity, anger, or sadness. Their personalities may change so dramatically that parents, teachers, and even doctors may assume they're undergoing clinical depression or have Attention Deficit-Hyperactivity Disorder.

I'd like to share an example from my clinical work to emphasize the concept of dethronement. Jonathan, a very bright eighth-grader, had been underachieving in school for years. Despite an IQ score in the superior range, his grades were Cs and Ds. After I met with his parents and set up a study plan, Jonathan's sister, Alison, insisted on talking to me. Alison, an 11th-grader, had a history of excellent grades and wonderful social adjustment. Her parents had assured me that Alison was "practically perfect." Furthermore, she was confident and mature, and her sole perceived problem was that she struggled with math and could manage to get only a B in that subject.

Alison initiated our conversation by explaining that she could help her brother get good grades by working with him every day. She was confident that her plan would be better than any plan to have him work independently. She seemed so earnest and determined to help her brother. I wanted to encourage her support of him, but to give Alison another view on the issue, I posed the situation this way: "Suppose Jonathan turns his underachievement around and begins getting A's on his report card. How would you feel?" Alison said that it would make her happy. Next I asked, "Suppose Jonathan, with his newfound confidence, becomes very good at math and then is allowed to work at an accelerated pace. If he does so well in math that he actually surpasses you not only in his grades, but is also put in a more advanced math class than you, how would you feel?" Intuitively and without thinking, that sophisticated young lady exclaimed, "I'd die, I'd really die!" There was a brief silence, and then Alison said quietly, "I think I understand."

This case is only an example of a common problem for high-achieving, well-adjusted kids when their siblings show productive turnarounds. More often than not, the high achiever will say to the parents, "Why are you making such a fuss about his good grades? I get good grades all the time and no one gets so excited about those." Sometimes the responses are more subtle, like not handing in a few assignments to get some attention from parents. Almost always I'm able to forewarn parents about the problem and prevent it. That perfect child is facing dethronement or not feeling "the best," unless she receives some extra positive feedback and support during her sibling's transition as well as some understanding about the pressures she's feeling.

Acknowledge Competitiveness

The surest way to harm sibling relationships is not to acknowledge that it's normal to feel competitive. When parents add guilt to the situation, kids have nowhere to go to talk about their feelings. Certainly, kids view their parents' treatment of their siblings differently than their parents perceive it. Just as certainly, children will believe you treat their siblings better, even if you don't. It's important to stop and talk about there being more to relationships than competitive performance. You should also remind your children that the race for happiness and success is not within the family, but within the outside world, where the whole family can support each other and be successful. You've probably already told your children that they have the potential for being each other's best friends in life, but if you haven't done that, let me assure you, it's a worthwhile message to give.

Kids Copy Their Older Siblings

Younger children may view their older siblings as role models. Because of the unconscious copying of older siblings by younger children, parents should recognize the importance of giving consistent and fair consequences to older children so their younger siblings can learn what to expect when they reach a similar age. Hopefully, younger kids will then avoid troublesome behaviors. But, if they believe their older siblings are getting away with things and having fun as well, they'll look forward to imitating their bad behaviors.

EPILOGUE

PARENTS CAN FACILITATE
FULFILLING FUTURES

THROUGHOUT THIS BOOK, I've offered you an inside look at the lives of middle schoolers today and how they view their environments, relationships, worries, and pressures. From what you have read in this book and see in your kids, you might assume that your kids are coping with many more pressures than you did at their age. Chances are, your kids think that life is more difficult for them, but they will think this only if you convince them of that fallacy. Kids compare themselves to siblings, peers, and celebrities, and to what their parents tell them about their childhoods. The more you emphasize the differences between your two generations, the greater the gulf will be between you and them. They may assume that you can't comprehend their lives—but only if you say you can't. Kids need desperately to believe that you can understand them. It may be easier for you to relate to your kids and understand them if you compare their experiences to when you were about 2 years older than they are now. By listening to their daily accounts, you can guide your kids with confidence, wisdom, empathy, and optimism based on your recollections of your own adolescence and your good common sense.

Although no two generations face the exact same challenges, growing up continues to mean finding an independent identity, developing age-appropriate skills, coping with sexual maturation and its responsibilities, developing relationships with peers, and discovering adult role models. The greatest advantage you have over your tweens is that you can guide them with a concern for their futures, since most tweens base the majority of their decisions on immediate consequences rather than future outcomes.

Parenting with Foresight

Middle schoolers are self-absorbed with their daily lives and what's happening to them *now*. They rarely think about how their behaviors can affect their futures because the future seems very distant to them. They make decisions based on consequences that will occur in the next hours, days, or sometimes even weeks, but they usually don't consider repercussions that could affect them in upcoming years. Living in a way that enhances their long-term health, their higher education, and the preservation of our society seems irrelevant to most kids.

On the other hand, through their life experiences, parents and educators have the gift of foresight that permits them to guide kids toward positive and healthy futures. Your confidence in your ability to inspire your kids is essential for encouraging them to think intelligently, to believe in themselves, to consider others, and to be inspired to make the world a better place. Your guidance will help keep them from getting sidetracked by negative peers, high-risk behaviors, or the temptation of instant gratification. No matter how they cry out in anger at you, you will at times have to disappoint them for the sake of long-range goals. Despite how much you love them and want them to approve of you, you need to set reasonable limits and actually say "No" to their requests from time to time, even when they accuse you of being a bad parent or claim that you're too strict.

Although the timing of adolescent development appears to have changed, and kids' environments are more perplexing, the basic principles of parenting have remained the same. Allow your kids to experience the joys of childhood by not overempowering them, by not pushing them to adulthood too soon, and by not doing too much for them. You can teach your tweens a work ethic by modeling the satisfaction that comes from your accomplishments. You can help them balance hard work and achievement with fun and laughter. By parenting in a united, moderate, and balanced way, and providing your kids with *both* love and limits, kids will internalize your wise values as they move into their teens and then adulthood. With your guidance, they will be more likely to live fulfilling lives and to make contributions to a safer and more secure future.

NOTES

Chapter 1

1. Kantrowitz, B. and P. Wingert (1999). The truth about tweens. *Newsweek* 134 (16): 62.

2. The Girl Scout Research Institute. September 2000. *Girls Speak Out: Teens Before Their Time.* A special report prepared at the request of Girl Scouts of the USA.

3. Spock, B. (1977). *Baby and Child Care.* New York: Simon and Schuster.

Chapter 2

1. Herman-Giddens, M. E., E. J. Slora, R. C. Wasserman, C. J. Bourdony, M. V. Bhapkar, G. G. Koch, and C. M. Hasemeier (1997). Secondary sexual characteristics and menses in young girls seen in office practice: A study from the pediatric research in office settings network. Pediatrics 99 (4): 505–512.

2. Ibid.

3. Kaplowitz, P. (2004). *Early Puberty in Girls.* New York: Ballantine Books.

4. Herman-Giddens, M. E., E. J. Slora, R. C. Wasserman, C. J. Bourdony, M. V. Bhapkar, G. G. Koch, and C. M. Hasemeier (1997). Secondary sexual characteristics and menses in young girls seen in office practice: A study from the pediatric research in office settings network. *Pediatrics* 99 (4): 505–512.

5. Herman-Giddens, M. E., L. Wang, and G. G. Koch (2001). Secondary sexual characteristics in boys: Estimates from the national health and nutrition examination survey III, 1988–1994. *Archives of Pediatrics and Adolescent Medicine* 155 (9): 1022–1028.

6. Ibid.

7. Ibid; Herman-Giddens, M. E., E. J. Slora, R. C. Wasserman, C. J. Bourdony, M. V. Bhapkar, G. G. Koch, and C. M. Hasemeier (1997). Secondary sexual characteristics and menses in young girls seen in office practice: A study from the pediatric research in office settings network. *Pediatrics* 99 (4): 505–512.

8. Kaplowitz, P. B., S. E. Oberfield, and the Drug and Therapeutics and Executive Committees of the Lawson Wilkins Pediatric Endocrine Society (1999). Reexamination of the age limit for defining when puberty is precocious in girls in the United States: Implications for evaluation and treatment. *Pediatrics* 104 (4): 936–941.

9. Herman-Giddens, M. E., A. D. Sandler, and N. E. Friedman (1988). Sexual precocity in girls: An association with sexual abuse? *American Journal of Diseases of Children* 142 (4): 431–433.

10. The International Breast Cancer Research Foundation. "The Causes of Critical Hormonal Events in Preadolescent Chinese and American Girls." www.ibcrf.org/newcause.html; Herman-Giddens, M. E., L. Wang, and G. G. Koch (2001). Secondary sexual characteristics in boys: Estimates from the national health and nutrition examination survey III, 1988–1994. *Archives of Pediatrics and Adolescent Medicine* 155 (9): 1022–1028.

11. Painter, K. "The Sexual Revolution Hits Junior High." *USA Today,* March 15, 2002, p. A.01.

12. Ibid.

13. Grunbaum, J. A., L. Kann, S. Kinchen, B. Williams, J. G. Ross, R. Lowry, and L. Kolbe (2002). Youth risk behavior surveillance—United States, 2001. *Morbidity and Mortality Weekly Report* 51 (SS-4): 1–64.

14. Howey, N. (2003). Oral report. *Seventeen* 62 (8): 218–221.

15. Rosenthal, S. L., K. M. vonRanson, S. Cotton, F. M. Biro, L. Mills, and P. A. Succop (2001). Sexual initiation: Predictors and developmental trends. *Sexually Transmitted Diseases* 28 (9): 527–532.

16. Jordan, T. R., J. H. Price, S. K. Telljohann, and B. K. Chesney (1998). Junior high school students' perceptions regarding nonconsensual sexual behavior. *Journal of School Health* 68 (7): 289–296.

17. Robinson, K. L., S. K. Telljohann, and J. H. Price (1999). Predictors of sixth-graders engaging in sexual intercourse. *Journal of School Health* 69 (9): 369–375.

18. Valois, R. F., J. E. Oeltmann, J. Waller, and J. R. Hussey (1999). Relationship between number of sexual intercourse partners and selected health risk behaviors among public high school adolescents. *Journal of Adolescent Health* 25 (5): 328–335.

19. Henry J. Kaiser Family Foundation and YM Magazine (1998). "National Survey of Teens: Teens Talk about Dating, Intimacy, and Their Sexual Experiences." Menlo Park, CA: Kaiser Family Foundation.

20. Marin, B. V., K. K. Coyle, C. A. Gomez, S. C. Carvajal, and D. B. Kirby (2000). Older boyfriends and girlfriends increase risk of sexual initiation in young adolescents. *Journal of Adolescent Health* 27 (6): 409–418.

21. Raine, T. R., R. Jenkins, S. J. Aarons, K. Woodward, J. L. Fairfax, M. N. El-Khorazaty, and A. Herman (1999). Sociodemographic correlates of virginity in seventh-grade black and Latino students. *Journal of Adolescent Health* 24 (5): 304–312.

22. Dittus, P. J. and J. Jaccard (2000). Adolescents' perceptions of maternal disapproval of sex: Relationship to sexual outcomes. *Journal of Adolescent Health* 26 (4): 268–278.

23. Ibid.

Chapter 3

1. Wagner, J. D. and S. R. Caudill (June 2003). Women scientists: 9.3 minutes of fame? *Science* [Letters] 300: 1875.

2. Reis, B. and E. Saewyc (May 1999). *Eighty-Three Thousand Youth: Selected Findings of Eight Population-Based Studies.* Safe Schools Coalition of Washington.

3. Human Rights Campaign (1996). "Greenberg Poll Finds Americans Increasingly Support Equal Rights for Gays and Lesbians." Washington, DC: The Campaign.

4. Massachusetts Department of Education (1999). "Massachusetts High School Students and Sexual Orientation: Results of the 1999 Youth Risk Behavior Survey." Boston, MA: The Dept.

5. Garofalo, R., C. Wolf, L. S. Wissow, E. R. Woods, and E. Goodman (1999). Sexual orientation and risk of suicide attempts among a representative sample of youth. *Archives of Pediatrics and Adolescent Medicine* 153 (5): 487–493.

6. Ryan, C. and D. Futterman (1997). Lesbian and gay youth: Care and counseling. *Adolescent Medicine: State of the Art Reviews* 8 (2): 207–374.

7. Sears, J. T. (1991). Helping students understand and accept sexual diversity. *Educational Leadership* 49 (1): 54–56.

8. Ryan, C. and D. Futterman (1997). Lesbian and gay youth: Care and counseling. *Adolescent Medicine: State of the Art Reviews* 8 (2): 207–234.

Chapter 4

1. PRIDE Surveys (October 2, 2003). "2002–03 PRIDE Surveys National Summary for Grades 4 through 6."

2. Ibid.

3. Office of National Drug Control Policy (December 8, 2003). "Teens Need Parents' *Presence* More than *Presents* This Holiday Season." Press Release from the Executive Office of the President, Office of National Drug Control Policy, Washington, DC.

4. The National Center on Addiction and Substance Abuse at Columbia University (August 19, 2003). CASA 2003 Teen Survey: High Stress, Frequent Boredom, Too Much Spending Money: Triple Threat That Hikes Risk of Teen Substance Abuse.

5. The National Youth Anti-Drug Media Campaign. "Teens Need Family *Presence* More Than *Presents:* Involved Parents Remain the Number One Factor in Preventing Teen Drug Use." The Anti-Drug Web site. www.theantidrug.com/advice/giftoftime.html.

6. The National Center on Addiction and Substance Abuse at Columbia University (September 2003). "The Importance of Family Dinners."

7. Cicco, N. "Survey: YMS Drug Use Lower Than Average." *The York Weekly,* February 12, 2003.

8. Ellickson, P. L., D. F. McCaffrey, B. Ghosh-Dastldar, and D. L. Longshore (2003). New inroads in preventing adolescent drug use: Results from a large-scale trial of project ALERT in middle schools. *American Journal of Public Health* 93 (11): 1830–1836.

Chapter 5

1. Rideout, V. G., U. G. Foehr, D. F. Roberts, and M. Brodie (1999). *Kids and Media* Executive Summary. Menlo Park, CA: Kaiser Family Foundation.

2. Education Week. (2004). Technology counts 2004: Global links: Lessons from the world. *Education Week* 23 (35).

3. Hoffman, K. R. (May 2, 2003). Messaging mania. *TIME for Kids.*

4. Ibid.

5. Chung, A. (June 2000). "After-School Programs: Keeping Children Safe and Smart." U.S. Department of Education.

6. Ibid.

7. Centers for Disease Control and Prevention (2003). Physical activity levels among children aged 9–13 years—United States, 2002. *Morbidity and Mortality Weekly Report* 52 (33): 785–787.

8. Slaughter, E. (Spring 2003). Children's Health and Obesity: A National Study of Children Ages 10–17, and Their Parents. *Prevention* magazine and Rodale Inc.

Chapter 6

1. Anderson, C. A. and B. J. Bushman (2001). Effects of violent video games on aggressive behavior, aggressive cognition, aggressive affect, physiological arousal, and prosocial behavior: A meta-analytic review of the scientific literature. *Psychological Science* 12 (5): 353–359; Nielsen Media Research (1998). *Galaxy Explorer.* New York.

2. Anderson, C. A. and B. J. Bushman (2001). Effects of violent video games on aggressive behavior, aggressive cognition, aggressive affect, physiological arousal, and prosocial behavior: A meta-analytic review of the scientific literature. *Psychological Science* 12 (5): 353–359.

3. Crimes against Children Research Center (June 2000). "Online Victimization: A Report on the Nation's Youth." National Center for Missing and Exploited Children.

4. Ibid.

5. Ibid.

6. Ibid.

7. Anderson, C. A., N. L. Carnagey, and J. Eubanks (2003). Exposure to violent media: The effects of songs with violent lyrics on aggressive thoughts and feelings. *Journal of Personality and Social Psychology* 84 (5): 960–971.

8. Eggerton, J. (January 31, 1994). Hundt hits television violence. *Broadcasting and Cable* 124(S): 10–12.

Chapter 8

1. Snyder, H. and M. Sickmund (1999). "Juvenile Offenders and Victims: 1999 National Report." Washington, DC: Office of Juvenile Justice and Delinquency Prevention.

2. PRIDE Surveys (October 2, 2003). "2002–03 PRIDE Surveys National Summary for Grades 4 through 6."

3. PRIDE Surveys (August 29, 2003). "The 2002–03 PRIDE Surveys National Summary/Total."

4. Nansel, T. R., M. Overpeck, R. S. Pilla, W. J. Ruan, B. Simons-Morton, and P. Scheidt (2001). Bullying behaviors among US youth: Prevalence and association with psychosocial adjustment. *Journal of the American Medical Association* 285 (16): 2094–2100.

5. Rivers, I. and P. K. Smith (1994). Types of bullying behavior and their correlates. *Aggressive Behavior* 20: 359–368.

6. Nansel, T. R., M. Overpeck, R. S. Pilla, W. J. Ruan, B. Simons-Morton, and P. Scheidt (2001). Bullying behaviors among US youth: Prevalence and association with psychosocial adjustment. *Journal of the American Medical Association* 285 (16): 2094–2100.

7. Olweus, D. (1993). *Bullying at School: What We Know and What We Can Do.* Cambridge, MA: Blackwell Publishers, Inc.

8. Nansel, T. R., M. Overpeck, R. S. Pilla, W. J. Ruan, B. Simons-Morton, and P. Scheidt (2001). Bullying behaviors among US youth: Prevalence and association with psychosocial adjustment. *Journal of the American Medical Association* 285 (16): 2094–2100.

9. Olweus, D. (1993). *Bullying at School: What We Know and What We Can Do.* Cambridge, MA: Blackwell Publishers, Inc.

10. Olweus, D. (1992). Bullying among schoolchildren: Intervention and prevention. In R. D. Peters, R. J. McMahon, V. L. Quinsey, eds. *Aggression and Violence throughout the Life Span.* London: Sage Publications.

11. Salmon, G., A. James, D. M. Smith (1998). Bullying in schools: Self-reported anxiety, depression, and self-esteem in secondary school children. *British Medical Journal* 317: 924–925.

12. Olweus, D. (1978). *Aggression in the Schools: Bullies and Whipping Boys.* Washington, DC: Hemisphere Publishing Corp.

13. Rigby, K. (2001). Health consequences of bullying and its prevention in schools. In J. Juvonen and S. Graham, eds. *Peer Harassment in School: The Plight of the Vulnerable and Victimized.* New York: Guilford Press.

14. Shakeshaft, Charol (June 2004). "Educator Sexual Misconduct: A Synthesis of Existing Literature." Prepared for the U.S. Department of Education by Policy and Program Studies Service.

15. Peterson, J. and K. Ray. (November 14, 2003). "Bullying and the Gifted: Victims,

Perpetrators, Incidence, and Effects." Presented at the annual meeting of the National Association for Gifted Children, Indianapolis, IN.

16. Olweus, D., S. Limber, and S. Mihalic (1999). *Blueprints for Violence Prevention, Book Nine: Bullying Prevention Program.* Boulder, CO: Center for the Study and Prevention of Violence.

17. Berg-Cross, L. (Fall 2003). Peer supervision: Bullying in childhood. *The Register Report* 29: 28–31.

18. *No Name-Calling Week* Coalition. "No Dissing." www.nonamecallingweek.org.

19. FOX 6 Investigates (November 4, 2003). "Roughed Up at Recess: Undercover Video Shows Big Fights, Little Supervision." FOX 6 WITI Milwaukee.

Chapter 9

1. PRIDE Surveys (August 29, 2003). "The 2002–03 PRIDE Surveys National Summary/Total."

2. Doherty, O. (2003). Violence outside school walls raises concern. *Education Week* 23 (15): 1, 14–15.

3. Ibid.

4. Mulvey, E. P. and E. Cauffman (2001). The inherent limits of predicting school violence. *American Psychologist* 56 (10): 797–802.

5. Edens, J., J. Skeem, R. Cruise, and E. Cauffman (2001). The assessment of juvenile psychopathy and its association with violence: A critical review. *Behavioral Sciences and the Law* 19: 53–80.

6. Zimring, F. (1981). Kids, groups, and crime: Some implications of a well-known secret. *Journal of Criminal Law and Criminology* 72: 867; Zimring, F. (1998). *American Youth Violence.* New York: Oxford University Press; Decker, S. (1996). Reconstructing homicide events: The role of witnesses in fatal encounters. *Journal of Criminal Justice* 23: 439–450; Tedeschi, J. and R. Felson (1994). *Violence, Aggression, and Coercive Actions.* Washington, DC: American Psychological Association.

7. Cairns, R., B. Cairns, H. Neckerman, S. Gest, and J. Gariepy (1988). Social networks and aggressive behavior: Peer support or peer rejection? *Developmental Psychology* 24: 815–823; Cole, J. and K. Dodge (1998). Aggression and antisocial behavior. In W. Damon and N. Elsenberg, eds. *Handbook of Child Psychology.* New York: Wiley.

8. Fagan, J. and D. Wilkinson (1998). Social contexts and functions of adolescent violence. In D. Elliott, B. Hamburg, and K. Williams, eds. *Violence in American Schools.* New York: Cambridge University Press.

Chapter 11

1. Lissau, I., M. D. Overpeck, W. J. Ruan, P. Due, B. E. Holstein, M. L. Hediger, and the Health Behaviour in School-aged Children Obesity Working Group (2004). Body

mass index and overweight in adolescents in 13 European countries, Israel, and the United States. *Archives of Pediatrics and Adolescent Medicine* 158 (1): 27–33.

2. Ogden, C. L., K. M. Flegal, M. D. Carroll, and C. L. Johnson (2002). Prevalence and trends in overweight among US children and adolescents, 1999–2000. *Journal of the American Medical Association* 288 (14): 1728–1732.

Chapter 12

1. Davis, G. A. and S. B. Rimm (1985). *Education of the Gifted and Talented*. Englewood Cliffs, NJ: Prentice Hall; Whitmore, J. R. (1980). *Giftedness, Conflict, and Underachievement*. Boston, MA: Allyn and Bacon; Fine, M. J. and R. Pitts (1980). Intervention with underachieving gifted children: Rationale and strategies. *Gifted Child Quarterly* 24: 51–55.

2. This section includes adapted excerpts from *Guidebook—Underachievement Syndrome: Causes and Cures* by S. B. Rimm, M. Cornale, R. Manos, and J. Behrend (Watertown, WI: Apple Publishing Co., 1989).

Chapter 13

1. Kulik, J. A. (1992). "An Analysis of the Research on Ability Grouping: Historical and Contemporary Perspectives." Storrs, CT: National Research Center on the Gifted and Talented, University of Connecticut.

Chapter 14

1. Usdansky, M. L. "More Kids Live in Changing Families." *USA Today,* August 30, 1994, p. A.01.

2. Menning, C. (November 2003). "Information Games: How Adolescents Exercise Power in Relationships with Non-Resident Parents." Annual meeting of the National Council on Family Relations, Vancouver, BC.

3. Rimm, S. B. (1990). A theory of relativity. *Gifted Child Today* 13 (3): 32–36.

4. Rimm, S. B. and B. Lowe (1988). Family environments of underachieving gifted students. *Gifted Child Quarterly* 32 (4): 353–59.

APPENDIX

Chapter 2: Is Sexual Development Happening Earlier?

BOOKS ON SEXUAL DEVELOPMENT

The Care and Keeping of You: The Body Book for Girls
   by Valorie Lee Schaefer (Pleasant Company Publications)

What's Happening to Me?
   by Peter Mayle (Carol Publishing Group)

What's Happening to My Body? Book for Boys
   by Lynda Madaras (Newmarket Press)

What's Happening to My Body? Book for Girls
   by Lynda Madaras (Newmarket Press)

Where Did I Come From?
   by Peter Mayle (Kensington Publishing Corp.)

Chapter 3: Gender Stereotypes and Sexual Orientation

BOOKS AND NEWSLETTERS ON GENDER ISSUES AND DEVELOPMENT

Always My Child: A Parent's Guide to Understanding Your Gay, Lesbian, Bisexual, Transgendered, or Questioning Son or Daughter
   by Kevin Jennings and Pat Shapiro, M.S.W. (Simon and Schuster)

Boy v. Girl? How Gender Shapes Who We Are, What We Want, and How We Get Along
   by George Abrahams, PhD, and Sheila Ahlbrand (Free Spirit Publishing)

Daughters (The newsletter for parents of girls.)
   34 East Superior Street, Suite 200
   Duluth, MN 55802
   888-849-8476
   www.daughters.com

From Boys to Men: All about Adolescence and You
   by Michael Gurian (Price Stern Sloan)

GLBTQ* The Survival Guide for Queer and Questioning Teens (*Gay, Lesbian, Bisexual, Transgender, Questioning)
   by Kelly Huegel (Free Spirit Publishing)

How Jane Won: 55 Successful Women Share How They Grew from Ordinary Girls to Extraordinary Women
   by Sylvia Rimm, PhD, with Sara Rimm-Kaufman, PhD (Crown Publishing)

Raising Cain: Protecting the Emotional Life of Boys
   by Dan Kindlon, PhD, and Michael Thompson, PhD (Ballantine Books)

Real Boys: Rescuing Our Sons from the Myths of Boyhood
   by William Pollack (Owl Publishing Co.)

See Jane Win®: The Rimm Report on How 1,000 Girls Became Successful Women
   by Sylvia Rimm, PhD, with Sara Rimm-Kaufman, PhD, and Ilonna Rimm, MD, PhD (Crown Publishing)

See Jane Win® for Girls: A Smart Girl's Guide to Success
   by Sylvia Rimm, PhD (Free Spirit Publishing)

Speaking of Boys: Answers to the Most-Asked Questions about Raising Sons
   by Michael Thompson, PhD (Ballantine Books)

Sylvia Rimm on Raising Kids (A newsletter to help parents and teachers.)
   Issues including gender topics: Vol. 9, No. 4; Vol. 11, No. 3; Vol. 13, No. 4; and Vol. 13, No. 3
   W6050 Apple Road
   Watertown, WI 53098
   800-795-7466
   www.sylviarimm.com
   E-mail: srimm@sylviarimm.com

Chapter 4: The Buzz on Drugs

BOOKS TO KEEP KIDS DRUG-FREE

Drugs and Your Kid: How to Tell If Your Child Has a Drug/Alcohol Problem and What to Do about It
   by Peter D. Rogers, PhD, and Lea Goldstein, PhD (New Harbinger Publications)

Taking Charge of My Mind and Body: A Girls' Guide to Outsmarting Alcohol, Drug, Smoking, and Eating Problems
   by Gladys Folkers, MA, and Jeanne Engelmann (Free Spirit Publishing)

Chapter 5: Technology Is Keeping Kids Busy

INTERNET SITES FOR MOVIE REVIEWS AND RATINGS

Hollywood.com
   www.hollywood.com

Movies.com
   www.movies.go.com

ScreenIt.com
   www.screenit.com

Yahoo! Movies
www.movies.yahoo.com

AFTER-SCHOOL RESOURCES

4-H Afterschool
www.4hafterschool.org

Afterschool.gov
www.after-school.gov

U.S. Department of Education
Department of Education Publications

Articles: "Working for Children and Families: Safe and Smart After-School Programs," "Give Us Wings, Let Us Fly," and "Afterschool Action Kit: Get Into Action"
www.ed.gov/pubs/edpubs.html

U.S. Department of Justice
Justice for Kids and Youth Homepage
www.usdoj.gov/kidspage

Chapter 6: Sex and Violence in Music, Movies, and Media

SUGGESTED MAGAZINES FOR MIDDLE SCHOOLERS

American Girl
www.americangirl.com

Boys' Life
www.boyslife.org

Discovery Girls
www.discoverygirls.com

Girls' Life
www.girlslife.com

Junior Scholastic
www.scholastic.com

National Geographic Kids
www.nationalgeographic.com/ngkids/index.html

New Moon
www.newmoon.org

Sports Illustrated for Kids
www.sikids.com

Teen Voices
www.teenvoices.com/tvhome.html

Chapter 8: Bullying in Our Schools

ANTI-BULLYING WEB SITES

Bully Police USA
www.bullypolice.org

Child Abuse Prevention Services: The Child Safety Institute
www.kidsafe-caps.org/bullies.html

KidPower TeenPower FullPower International
www.kidpower.org

Stop Bullying Now
www.stopbullyingnow.com

ANTI-BULLYING RESOURCES

Bullies Are a Pain in the Brain
by Trevor Romain (Free Spirit Publishing)

The Bully Free Classroom: Over 100 Tips and Strategies for Teachers K–8
by Allan L. Beane, PhD (Free Spirit Publishing)

How to Take the Grrrr Out of Anger
by Elizabeth Verdick and Marjorie Lisovskis (Free Spirit Publishing)

Chapter 10: Fitting In with Fashion and Friends

RESOURCES TO HELP KIDS FIT IN

Cliques, Phonies, and Other Baloney
by Trevor Romain (Free Spirit Publishing)

More Than a Label: Why What You Wear or Who You're With Doesn't Define Who You Are
by Aisha Muharrar (Free Spirit Publishing)

Stick Up for Yourself! Every Kid's Guide to Personal Power and Positive Self-Esteem
by Gershen Kaufman, PhD, Lev Raphael, PhD, and Pamela Espeland (Free Spirit Publishing)

Too Old for This, Too Young for That! Your Survival Guide for the Middle-School Years
by Harriet S. Mosatche, PhD, and Karen Unger, MA (Free Spirit Publishing)

Chapter 11: Tween Weight Problems

WEIGHT CONTROL GROUPS THAT INCLUDE CHILDREN

Childobesity.com
www.childobesity.com

Shapedown
www.shapedown.com/page2.htm

Slimkids
www.slimkids.com

The Solution
www.thepathway.org

Weight Watchers
www.weightwatchers.com

RESOURCES FOR NUTRITION

Centers for Disease Control: Overweight Children and Adolescents: Recommendations to Screen, Assess, and Manage (includes weight charts)
www.cdc.gov/nccdphp/dnpa/growthcharts/training/modules/module3/text/page1b.htm

Eat Well and Keep Moving
www.hsph.harvard.edu/nutritionsource/EWKM.html

Get Kids in Action
www.getkidsinaction.org

National Cancer Institute—5 a Day Program
www.5aday.gov

Nutrition.gov
www.nutrition.gov

The Right Moves to Getting Fit and Feeling Great!
by Tina Schwager, PTA, AT,C, and Michele Schuerger (Free Spirit Publishing)

EXERCISE INFORMATION AND/OR WEIGHT CHARTS

Medline Plus—Exercise for Children
www.nlm.nih.gov/medlineplus/exerciseforchildren.html

Shape Up America!
www.shapeup.org

WEIGHT-LOSS CAMPS FOR KIDS

Alpengirl
Camps in Montana, Washington, Scandinavia, Hawaii, and Alaska
www.alpengirl.com

Camp Endeavor
Wisconsin Dells, WI
www.campendeavor.com

Camp Kingsmont
West Stockbridge, MA
www.campkingsmont.com

Camp La Jolla
La Jolla, CA
www.camplajolla.com

Camp Nu Yu
Wildwood, FL
www.campnuyu.com

Camp Shane
Ferndale, NY
www.campshane.com

New Image Camps
Camps in Lake Wales, FL; Pocono, PA; and Ojai, CA
www.newimagecamp.com

BOOKS TO HELP OVERWEIGHT KIDS

Rescuing the Emotional Lives of Overweight Children: What Our Kids Go Through—And How We Can Help
by Sylvia Rimm, PhD, with Eric Rimm, ScD (Rodale)

Chapter 12: Achievement or Underachievement

RESOURCES FOR ACADEMIC ACHIEVEMENT

Family Achievement Clinic, Sylvia Rimm, PhD, Director
Primary Office:
26777 Lorain Road, Suite 410
North Olmsted, OH 44070
216-839-2273 ext.109
Secondary Office:
W6050 Apple Road
Watertown, WI 53098
800-795-7466
www.sylviarimm.com
E-mail: srimm@sylviarimm.com

The Complete Guide to Service Learning: Proven, Practical Ways to Engage Students in Civic Responsibility, Academic Curriculum, and Social Action
by Cathryn Berger Kaye, MA (Free Spirit Publishing)

Learning Leads Q-Cards:
  Parent Pointers
  Student Stepping Stones
  Teacher Tips
by Sylvia Rimm, PhD (Apple Publishing Company)

School Power: Study Skill Strategies for Succeeding in School
by Jeanne Shay Schumm, PhD (Free Spirit Publishing)

Sylvia Rimm on Raising Kids (A newsletter to help parents and teachers.)
W6050 Apple Road
Watertown, WI 53098
800-795-7466
www.sylviarimm.com

Why Bright Kids Get Poor Grades—And What You Can Do about It
by Sylvia Rimm, PhD (Crown Publishing)

Chapter 13: Parenting for Achievement

BOOKS AND COURSE ON PARENTING FOR ACHIEVEMENT

How to Parent So Children Will Learn
by Sylvia Rimm, PhD (Crown Publishing)

Rimm's Parenting for Achievement:
Course Manual for Trainers
Parent Workbook
by Sylvia Rimm, PhD (Apple Publishing Company)

Gifted Modules for Trainer Manual
Gifted Modules for Parent Workbook
by Sylvia Rimm, PhD (Apple Publishing Company)

BOOKLISTS FOR MIDDLE SCHOOLERS

Bank Street College of Education
www.bnkst.edu

The Carnegie Library of Pittsburgh
www.carnegielibrary.org/kids/booknook/gradedbooklists/middleschool.html

Scholastic Inc.
www.scholastic.com/familymatters/read/gr6_8/bl_experts.htm

LEARNING DISABILITIES AND ADHD RESOURCES

2e: Twice-Exceptional Newsletter
985 Clifton Avenue
Glen Ellyn, IL 60137
630-790-2252
www.2enewsletter.com
E-mail: info@GlenEllynMedia.com

Children and Adults with Attention-Deficit/Hyperactivity Disorder(CHADD)
8181 Professional Place, Suite 150
Landover, MD 20785
800-233-4050
www.chadd.org

Council for Exceptional Children (CEC)
1110 North Glebe Road, Suite 300
Arlington, VA 22201
703-620-3660
www.cec.sped.org
E-mail: service@cec.sped.org

Council for Learning Disabilities (CLD)
PO Box 4014
Leesburg, VA 20177
571-258-1010
www.cldinternational.org

International Dyslexia Association
Chester Building, Suite 382
8600 LaSalle Road
Baltimore, MD 21286-2044
(410) 296-0232
www.interdys.org
E-mail: info@interdys.org

LD OnLine
www.ldonline.org
E-mail: LDOnLine@weta.com

LD Resources
www.ldresources.com

Learning Disabilities Association of America (LDA)
4156 Library Road
Pittsburgh, PA 15234-1349
412-341-1515
www.ldanatl.org

National Center for Learning Disabilities (NCLD)
381 Park Avenue South, Suite 1401
New York, NY 10016
888-575-7373
www.ncld.org

Reading Rockets
WETA/Channel 26
2775 South Quincy Street
Arlington, VA 22206
www.readingrockets.org
E-mail: readingrockets@weta.com

The School Survival Guide for Kids with LD* (*Learning Differences): Ways to Make Learning Easier and More Fun
by Rhoda Cummings, EdD, and Gary Fisher, PhD (Free Spirit Publishing)

Schwab Learning
1650 South Amphlett Boulevard, Suite 300
San Mateo, CA 94402
650-655-2410
www.schwablearning.org

The Survival Guide for Kids with LD* (*Learning Differences)
by Gary Fisher, PhD, and Rhoda Cummings, EdD (Free Spirit Publishing)

Teaching Kids with Learning Difficulties in the Regular Classroom: Strategies and Techniques Every Teacher Can Use to Challenge and Motivate Struggling Students
by Susan Winebrenner (Free Spirit Publishing)

RESOURCES FOR GIFTED KIDS

Family Achievement Clinic, Sylvia Rimm, PhD, Director
Primary Office:
26777 Lorain Road, Suite 410
North Olmsted, OH 44070
216-839-2273 ext.109
Secondary Office:
W6050 Apple Road
Watertown, WI 53098
800-795-7466
www.sylviarimm.com, www.seejanewin.com
E-mail: srimm@sylviarimm.com

2e: Twice-Exceptional Newsletter
985 Clifton Avenue
Glen Ellyn, IL 60137
630-790-2252
www.2enewsletter.com
E-mail: info@GlenEllynMedia.com

The Association for the Gifted (TAG)
26 Cedar Hill Place, NE
Albuquerque, NM 87122
505-828-1001
www.cectag.org

Davidson Institute for Talent Development
9665 Gateway Drive, Suite B
Reno, NV 89521
775-852-DITD
www.ditd.org

National Association for Gifted Children (NAGC)
1707 L Street NW, Suite 550
Washington, DC 20036
202-785-4268
www.nagc.org
E-mail: nagc@nagc.org

Supporting Emotional Needs of the Gifted (SENG)
PO Box 6074
Scottsdale, AZ 85261
773-857-6250
www.sengifted.org
E-mail: office@sengifted.org

HOMESCHOOLING RESOURCES

American Homeschool Association
PO Box 3142
Palmer, AK 99645
800-236-3278
www.americanhomeschoolassociation.org

Homeschool.com
www.homeschool.com

Homeschool Central
www.homeschoolcentral.com

Home School Learning Network
PO Box 957
Kihei, HI 96753
877-278-5260
www.homeschoollearning.com

National Home Education Network
PO Box 1652
Hobe Sound, FL 33475-1652
www.nhen.org
E-mail: info@nhen.org

National Home Education Research Institute
PO Box 13939
Salem, OR 97309
503-364-1490
www.nheri.org
E-mail: mail@nheri.org

INDEX

Alcohol use
    increasing likelihood of early
        sex, 30–31
    peer pressure influencing,
        73–74, **73**
    preventing, 74–75
        with parental involvement,
            78–79, 81
        with positive activities,
            76–77
        sample conversation for,
            <u>78–79</u>
        with school programs, 81–82
    punishments for, <u>76</u>
    survey results on, 70, **70**, 71,
        72
Allowances, 257
Alone time. *See* Home-alone time
Appearance issues
    acne, 186–87
    clothing
        importance of brand labels
            in, 182–83
        setting guidelines for,
            181–82, 183
        values communicated by,
            181, 183
    effect of family relationships
        on, 177, **178**
    hairstyles, 174
    increasing with grade level,
        175, 177
    makeup, 184–85
    piercings, 185–86
    shoes, 185

tattoos, 185, 186
weight (*see* Overweight;
    Underweight)
worries about, 172–73, **173**
Asperger's disorder (AD), <u>247</u>
Assessment, for reversing
    underachievement, 224
Attention Deficit-Hyperactivity
    Disorder (ADHD), <u>247</u>, 265

B

Baby and Child Care (Spock),
    adolescence covered in, <u>16</u>
Biographies, role models in, 130–31
Books, for discussing sexuality,
    27–28
Boredom, substance abuse and,
    76–77
Boyfriends and girlfriends. *See
    also* Opposite sex
    of middle schoolers, 8–9
    parental concern about, 9–10
Breast development
    age of onset of, 19, 21
    explaining, to girls, 27
Bullies. *See also* Bullying
    characteristics of, 141–42
    helping, 146–48
Bullying. *See also* Bullies
    author's recollections of, <u>149</u>
    by boys vs. girls, 140
    effects of
        long-term, 142
        social-emotional, 143–44

of homosexuals, 61
leading to violence, 154
onlookers affected by, 141
prevalence of, 140
by school employees, 144
school programs on, 148, 166, 207
types of, 140–41
victims of
characteristics of, 142–43
help for, 148–54, 154, 207
worries about, 145
factors influencing, 145–46, 146, 147

C

Career choices, gender differences in, 54–56, 55
Careers. *See* Work
Celebrity role models, 108–9, 133
Cell phones, 88–89
Chores, 256–57
Cigarettes. *See also* Smoking
ease of access to, 72, 72
Clothing
girls' interest in, 52–53
high heels, 185
importance of brand labels in, 182–83
setting guidelines for, 181–82, 183
values communicated by, 181, 183
Coaching, in parenting, 261–63

Communication
during fearful times, 166–68
with teachers
for building achievement, 224, 232–34
for reversing underachievement, 224
Community help, for weight problems, 206, 207
Community leaders, as role models, 130
Competition
parents teaching about, 237
between siblings, 263–64, 265–66
underachievement and, 222–23, 235–36
Computer use
avoiding, before homework, 243
guidelines for, 118, 119
in schools, 85
Confidence
gender differences in, 48, 48, 49
in parenting, loss of, 18
Conformity, discussing, 35–36, 178, 180
Cooperative activities, encouraging participation in, 237–38
Counseling, for sexual identity concerns, 65
Crushes, 9

limiting technology use, 93, 94
of overweight vs. average-
weight children, 202
parental guidance with, 102–3
preventing substance abuse,
76–77, 83

F

Failure
achievers and, 236–37
parents teaching about, 237
underachievers and, 222–23
Family dinners, for preventing
substance abuse, 81
Family exercise, benefits of, 104
Family members, as role models,
122–23, **122**, 128
Family relationships
good, impact of, 252–53
as influence on
likelihood of early sex, 31
responses to terrorism, 158,
160, **160**
technology use, 94, **95**
time spent alone, 90
worries about appearance
and popularity, 177, **178**
worries about sex, 32
middle schoolers' perceptions
of, 258
play strengthening, 103–4
weight issues and, 202–4, **203**
Family trips, as distraction from
negative peers, 190–91
Fashion. *See* Clothing

Fear(s)
helping children with, 166–68
in school, 139–40
of terrorism, 157–58, **159, 160,**
168
Filtering software, for blocking
pornography, 115, 116
Flexibility, as organizational skill,
242
Flirtatious behavior, learned from
media, 110–11
Friends. *See* Peers
Friendships, negative, preventing,
187–91
Future(s)
of children, parents facilitating,
267–68
optimism about
regarding safety of country,
159–61, **159, 160**
weight affecting, 204
Future plans, gender differences
in, 54–57

G

Game playing, strengthening
family relationships, 103–4
Gays. *See* Homosexuality
Gender differences
in career choices, 54–56, **55**
in choice of school activities,
42–46
in developmental trends,
47–49, **48, 49,** 51–54, **53**
in marriage plans, 56–57

Instant messaging (IM)
coded dialogue for, 86–87, 88
girls' use of, 46
middle schoolers' use of, 85
time spent on, 85
Intelligence
as influence on
participation in school
activities, 42
response to terrorism,
160–61
time spent alone, 90–91
worries about bullying, 145,
147
worries about popularity,
175
parental expectations of, 230
perceptions of
in boys vs. girls, 40–41, 50,
52
influencing technology use,
92–93, 93
in overweight children, 201
self-esteem related to,
211–13
social and emotional
concerns related to,
212–13
reading contributing to, 235
sibling rivalry over, 263–64
work ethic enhancing, 231
worries about, 175, 176
Interest in opposite sex
of middle schoolers, 5–9
parental concern about,
9–10

Interests of child, parents' help in
developing, 234–35
Internet
harmful effects of, 118
middle schoolers' skill with, 114
pornographic Web sites on,
115–16
sexual pop-ups on, 114–15
sexual solicitation on, 116
time spent on, 85
Intimacy
lacking in middle schoolers'
sexual behavior, 28
sex and, 30

J

Jobs. *See also* Work
for building work ethic, 232
Junior high schools, replaced by
middle schools, 4

K

Kindness, gender differences in,
50, 51

L

Laziness, gender differences in, 52
Leadership, gender differences in,
48, 48, 49
Learning
brain growth from, 25
early adolescence affecting, 17
early sex affecting, 32

Puberty
in boys
research on age of, 22–23
underweight delaying, 199
early
hazards of, 26
possible causes of, 23–24
sexual behavior advancing,
24–26
students' perception of, 23,
24, 25
in girls, earlier age of, 20–22
outdated research on, 20
Pubic hair growth
in boys, 22
explaining, 27
in girls, 21
Punishments, for substance abuse,
76

Q

Quietness, gender differences in,
48–49, 48

R

RD (Reading Disorder/Disability),
247
Reading
intelligence linked to, 235
tips for encouraging, 236
Reading Disorder/Disability (RD),
247
Rebelliousness, gender differences
in, 52

Religion, closeness to, after
terrorist attacks, 160, 161,
161
Remembering, as organizational
skill, 241
Responsibility
adult, middle schoolers' desire
for, 14–15
empowerment and, 255
modeling acceptance of, 127
Reviewing, as organizational skill,
241–42
Rimm's Laws on school success,
215, 259
Risk taking, gender differences in,
48–49, 48
Role models
adult, 121–22
celebrity, 108–9, 133
community leaders, 130
family members, 122–23, 122,
128
female, limited view of, 135
from history and biographies,
130–31
negative, protecting children
from, 133–34
nonfamily, 123, 123
parents, 122, 123
how to become, 134–36
positive vs. negative, 124–27
positive peers as, 132–33
for reversing underachievement,
225
siblings, 131–32
stepparents, 127–28

Role models *(cont.)*
    teachers, 128–30
    variables defining, 134–35, 136

S

Safety
    examples of threats to, 156–57
    during school hours, 139
Scheduling, as organizational
        skill, 241
School(s)
    changing, for avoiding negative
        peers, 189–90
    controlling bullying, 148, <u>154</u>
    fear in, 139–40
    influencing worries about sex,
        32
    modeling negative feelings
        about, 125
    programs in (*see* School
        programs)
    safety in, 139
    success in (*see* School success)
    types of, influencing worries
        about bullying, 146
    violence in, 156, 161, **162**,
        163
        predicting, 164–65
        preventing, 165–66
    violence on way to and from,
        163, <u>164</u>
School activities. *See*
        Extracurricular activities
School employees, bullying by,
        144

School programs
    antibullying, 148, 166, 207
    parental support for, 104–5
    sex education, 64
    on substance abuse, 81–82
    for violence prevention, 166
School success
    future benefits of, 210
    grades defining, 210–11
    motivation vs. IQ in, 210
    obstacles to (*see*
        Underachievement)
    parenting for (*see* Achievement,
        parenting actions for)
    peer pressure affecting, 218–19
    relationship between effort and
        outcomes in, 214, **214**,
        216–18
    Rimm's Laws about, <u>215</u>
    signs of, 211
Science
    encouraging girls' interest in, 45
    gender bias in, 44–46
Scout programs, 101–2
Self-confidence
    from achievement, 222
    as influence on
        participation in school
            activities, 42
        time spent alone, 90
        worries about bullying, 145,
            146
        worries about popularity,
            175
    overweight lowering, 200–201
    parents encouraging, 65–66

parents undermining, 234–35
perceptions of, influencing
technology use, 93–94
work ethic enhancing, 231
worries about, 175, **176**
Self-esteem
related to perceptions of
intelligence, 211–13
work ethic enhancing, 231
Sensitivity
activities promoting, 51
gender differences in, 51, 52
Sex. *See also* Sexual intercourse,
early
in media, 26, 27, 109–11,
174–75
among middle schoolers, 31
in movies, 118
in song lyrics, 116–17
talking to children about,
27–28
in television, 118
worries about, 32
Sex education, homosexuality
excluded from, 64
Sexual behavior
portrayed on MTV, 109–10,
111
as possible cause of early
puberty, 24–26
for proving maturity, 33
Sexual development. *See* Puberty
Sexual exploration, confused with
homosexuality, 59–60
Sexual harassment and abuse, by
school employees, 144

Sexual identity
homophobia affecting, 57–58
parental support of, 64–65
Sexual intercourse, early
conditions discouraging, 31
conditions encouraging, 30–31
pitfalls of, 28, 32
statistics on, 29
Sexually transmitted diseases
(STDs), from early sex, 32
Sexual maturity. *See* Puberty
Sexual solicitation, on Internet,
116
Shoes, for girls, 185
Shyness, gender differences in,
48–49, **48**
Siblings
avoiding comparisons with,
232
dethronement of, 264, 265–66
rivalry between, 263–64
acknowledging, 266
as role models, 131–32, 266
Smoking
increasing likelihood of early
sex, 30
preventing
with positive activities,
76–77
sample conversation for, <u>80</u>
punishments for, <u>76</u>
survey results on, 70, **70**, 71–72
Social lives, gender differences in,
51, 53, **53**
Song lyrics, sex and violence in,
116–17